*Ireland in the 1930s: New Perspectives*

# Ireland in the 1930s

*New Perspectives*

Joost Augusteijn

EDITOR

FOUR COURTS PRESS

Set in 10.5 on 12 point Bembo for
FOUR COURTS PRESS LTD
Fumbally Lane, Dublin 8, Ireland
e-mail: info@four-courts-press.ie
*and in North America by*
FOUR COURTS PRESS
c/o ISBS, 5804 N.E. Hassalo Street, Portland, OR 97213.

A catalogue record for this title
is available from the British Library.

ISBN 1–85182–399–9 hbk
ISBN 1–85182–405–7 pbk

Printed in Great Britain
by MPG Books, Bodmin, Cornwall

# Contents

# Abbreviations

| | |
|---|---|
| IRA | Irish Republican Army |
| NA | National Archives, Dublin |
| NCP | National Corporate Party |
| NLI | National Library, Ireland |
| NUI | National University of Ireland |
| MA | Military Archives, Dublin |
| PRO | Public Records Office, London |
| PRONI | Public Records Office, Northern Ireland |
| TCD | Trinity College, Dublin |
| UCD | University College, Dublin |
| UCDA | University College, Dublin Archives Department |
| UCG | University College, Galway |

# Preface

This book of essays fills a void in Irish historical writing. The history of independent Ireland and in particular the somewhat shadowy period of the interwar years has so far mainly been dealt with in a general manner. Much of the existing work has concentrated on political institutions and developments, dominated by the changes and tensions in the constitutional relationship between Ireland and Britain. This volume brings together some of the wealth of exciting research on the 1930s which has been done by postgraduates in recent years. The eight original essays collected herein reflect the changing content of historical study, moving from political to social developments, which often underpinned, affected and contributed to the events in the political arena. This collection does not claim or have the intention of providing a comprehensive picture of Ireland in the 1930s. However, these detailed accounts of a variety of issues, which all relate decisions made on the level of high politics to the experience of ordinary people, reveal many unexpected aspects of Irish life in the period.

It can be rightly asserted that isolating the history of one particular decade is a somewhat artificial exercise, but we feel it is justified in this context as the 1930s effectively constitute the first decade in power of Fianna Fáil, uniquely characterised by the attempts to create an Ireland set apart from its neighbour(s). The essays in this book explore these attempts to develop the Free State into an entity which was not only politically but also socially, culturally and economically independent, and which dealt with its citizens in a purely Irish manner. However, although publicly Ireland and its citizens became increasingly associated with a narrow form of Catholicism and republicanism, these essays show that the population responded to these attempts in a very diverse and often outward looking way, and that at this time the Free State was not just the insular self-obsessed and culturally barren society it has often been portrayed as.

All eight chapters reveal a practical as well as an ideological response to developments in Ireland, both from the Fianna Fáil government and from the population as a whole. Two of the primarily ideologically driven policies, which were implemented against better judgement, are discussed in the chapters on the attempts to make the Irish language the spoken vernacular in the state and on the large-scale building programme of cottages for agricultural labourers. Although it was already clear by 1932 that forcing an unwilling population to speak Irish on a day-to-day basis by teaching them through Irish at school was not working and that agricultural labourers were certainly not the section of society most in need of housing, these policies were pursued because they enabled Ireland to show it was different from Britain. Different because its people spoke another language and because it was hoped that building labourers' cottages would help develop and sustain the kind of rural society de Valera in particular believed was fundamentally Irish. The importance of defining Ireland as different from Britain can also be witnessed during the centenary celebrations for Catholic Emancipation and the Eucharistic Congress. At both events the state sought to establish a close association with Catholicism as distinct from 'British Protestantism'. A more practical approach, even with regard to this catholic self-definition, is revealed in the mere lip service paid by the government to the application of the Pope's somewhat impractical and politically increasingly suspect teaching on vocationalism. A very utilitarian approach was also taken by the government regarding the introduction of a military reserve, initially to facilitate the IRA's acceptance of the state and, when that failed, to undermine its enduring appeal among young men.

The practical response of the population to these initiatives is a recurrent theme in all the contributions, but it constitutes the main thrust of the chapter dealing with the reading habits of the people. This study very clearly reveals that the state has been wrongly described as culturally barren and dreary. The censorship laws, introduced in the late 1920s to placate conservative pressure groups, in particular have been used to nurture this image. Although it is true that many literary works by major writers were banned from Ireland, this chapter shows that the average reader was not particularly interested in them but had nevertheless a ferocious appetite for lighter reading material, much of it written and published by foreigners. The growth of reading as a leisure activity is illustrated by the flourishing of the newsagent cum bookseller in this period. The impact one active person can make on the insularity of a community becomes clear from the essay on the elimination of childhood tuberculosis. In an almost one woman's crusade Dorothy Price forced the medical and ultimately the political community to take medical developments regarding the treatment of TB in countries outside Britain seriously. Lastly a nice combination of government policy, individual action and popular response can be found in the essay dealing with the final years of the career of Eoin O'Duffy and his involvement in the Spanish Civil War.

The initial idea behind this book was to save the work done by former postgraduates, who had since undertaken careers in other fields, from languishing in the archives. By 1996 a large collection of unpublished theses by former MA students had built up in various universities. This book and the conference held under the same title in 1997 were intended to provide these young men and women with an outlet for the valuable work they had done. At the same time a number of postgraduates who were in the process of researching their doctoral dissertations came to participate in this project. Most of them have since obtained their doctorates and some of them are currently pursuing a career in academia. The 1997 conference, which provided the starting point for this book, brought together most of the thirty odd people who had recently done or were then working on a substantial piece of research into aspects of the 1930s in Ireland. Most of the contributors to this volume spoke at the conference while others participated in the discussions, but all benefited from the stimulating atmosphere there. This book now takes in five former MA theses and some of the work done in relation to three doctoral theses.

The conference and therefore ultimately the existence of this book would not have been feasible without the active support of Diarmuid Ferriter and the staff of the Modern Irish History Department in University College, Dublin. Neither would it have been possible without the generous financial assistance of that same department, and of the UCD Presidential Fund, the Royal Irish Academy and the Bank of Ireland. I would like to record our sincerest thanks to these people and institutions. However, my foremost thanks must go to the contributors themselves. Although the life of an editor of a collection of essays by various authors can be frustrating and laborious, particularly when one is forced to pressurise the authors to deliver their contributions before certain deadlines, most of the work is in the end done by the contributors themselves. Without their dedication to this volume, which had to be attended to next to demanding careers in sometimes completely different walks of life, this book would never have seen the light of day. Finally and most importantly, this book would not have been what it is today without the active support and assistance of Professor Mary Daly of UCD, one of the leading experts on the subject and the prime mover in much of the historical research done on the period. Most of the contributors did at least some of their research under her, and without her advice and editorial support the editor himself and most of the contributions would not have made it to the end. Although a large measure of gratitude is therefore correctly bestowed on Mary Daly for her contribution to the quality of this volume, the errors and flaws are entirely the responsibility of the authors and the editor themselves.

Joost Augusteijn
2 April 1999

ELIZABETH RUSSELL

# Holy crosses, guns and roses: themes in popular reading material

Literary critics have long bemoaned the fact that there were no decent book shops in Ireland during the 1920s and '30s. Studies of Irish cultural history frequently declare the state to have been a huge desert when it came to literary endeavours.[1] Lengthy discussions about draconian censorship, inward looking peasants and a dearth of what could be termed better book shops are plentiful. Written from the perspective of elitists who see outside influences as enriching and native Irish ones as insular and backward, they completely neglect the phenomenon of the average Irish reader. Just because popular reading material could be labelled lightweight, it does not mean it was either backward or worth ignoring. Cheap novels, weekly newspapers and periodicals were sold in abundance during these years and they all had seasoned devotees all over the country. Their content was uniform: 'guns and roses'; shoot-outs at corrals and then happy-ever-after tales, and, when home-produced, an extra large smattering of soft nationalism and a nod in the direction of the Vatican were added in for good measure.

While I concur there was a paucity of 'traditional booksellers' in the Free State, there was neither a scarcity of shops which sold books nor was the country comprised of illiterate serfs who never read a page of the printed word. While there were insufficient bookshops, there were alternative stores and libraries where periodicals and cheap novels could be easily acquired. My searches through the business records of the National Archives did not produce numerous 'booksellers-proper' but I discovered a great proliferation of newsagents who were prospering during the early decades of the Free State. Many of them initially incorporated this into their other businesses; for example, Mr Wynne of Castlebar was listed as a 'newsagent and photographer' but even a cursory glance at his accounts shows that his photographic business was soon sidelined in favour of newspapers, magazines, periodicals and books.[2] In 1879 the sum of his photographic endeavours were two photo sessions with

---

1 One such study would be Terence Brown, *A social and cultural history of Ireland, 1922-85* (Glasgow, 1985). 2 Account books of Wynne's Newsagency, Castlebar, 1879-1939, NA, file MAYO 7.

the young daughters of his regular customer Dr Knott. The following year he visited a Mayo prison to photograph the prisoners! From that date onwards, his business constituted of the selling of books, magazines and periodicals. His records continue until 1939 and during the 1930s his business was highly successful: providing the public with the reading material they desired was a lucrative one.

This pattern established itself nation-wide: as Wynne began to specialise in the printed word, shops like McGreevy's, a 'newsagent and grocer' of Bridge Street, Westport followed suit. McGreevy's supplied edibles and other provisions along with newspapers and periodicals.[3] McGreevy's account books from 1927 to 1933 are simply a delight: on 23 December 1930 a Mrs Burns of Temperance Hall, Westport, a regular customer, bought two copies of the *Catholic Fireside* (presumably the bumper Christmas edition, which always sold particularly well throughout the 1930s), a distemper brush, two apples and a bag of sweets. The following April she purchased a cheap, unnamed novel at 2*d*. along with a packet of Rinso and Golden Syrup. On 22 October 1931 she bought another unlisted book costing one shilling.[4]

Mr McGreevy was, no doubt, aware of the importance of impulse buying. He subscribed to *Eason's Monthly Bulletin of Trade News* (a monthly journal published by Charles Eason[5] aimed at booksellers, which chronicled the activities of the book world), and would refer to it regarding new publications or stock for his circulating library. This bulletin, sent directly to Eason's customers (approximately fifteen hundred were printed per month), was very much aimed at the shopkeeper who sold cheap newspapers and books, and was, in effect, a barometer of book sales. In the days before over-the-counter sales were registered and bestseller lists were the norm, *Eason's Monthly* recorded numbers of orders and returns, and predicted future bestsellers. Excellent at deciphering publishers' hype from what customers were actually requesting, the bulletin is a very good indication of what reading material people bought. Newsagents and booksellers reported what was selling well, and reorders, reprints, and republications were all mentioned on its pages. Much more effective than the other book journal the weekly *Bookseller*, which tended to concern itself with lofty ideals and squabbles among doughty publishers, Eason's journal concerned itself solely with the business of book and magazine selling.

Literary yet lively, well written yet extremely informative, it was neither elitist nor obscurantist as the directors of many 'specialist' book shops had been;

3 Business Records of Mr McGreevy, newsagent and grocer, Bridge Street, Westport, NA, file MAYO 16. 4 Account with Mrs W. Burns, Temperance Hall, the Mall, 1927-33, NA, file MAYO 16/1. 5 Charles Eason was the chairman of the Dublin Booksellers' Association, and both a retailer and a wholesaler of books and magazines throughout the Free State. He published occasional works of popular fiction as well as *Eason's Monthly Bulletin of Trade News*. When relaunched after World War Two, the title was shortened to *Eason's Monthly Bulletin* and it began charting sales figures into the shops as well as in-depth interviews and profiles of prominent authors.

if a novel or periodical was likely to sell, Eason's were at the vanguard, inform-
ing their flock. As a result shopkeepers were well aware of what reading material the average Irish person wanted. Eason's bulletin, first published in April
1925, quickly became a bible for newsagents and book sellers. It dispensed
advice on how to display books and magazines, it mentioned forthcoming
books and publication dates. In a very chatty and informal style, it would remind
shopkeepers about price changes while also introducing new writers and genres
of fiction. Consequently, the bulletin became the first modern book trade journal in Ireland.

There were only a few 'pure' booksellers in Ireland, based mostly in urban
areas, who generally believed books were rarefied objects which had to be sold
in a sacrosanct environment. Many of them lacked commercial foresight, and
instead of attempting to make themselves more attractive to the reading public
tended to become involved in protracted battles of words over who had the
right to sell books. Many floundered at this time: where newsagents prospered,
these booksellers failed, deaf to Eason's advice repeated in the bulletin each
month: to provide the public with the books they wanted to encourage them
to buy. In September 1930 Eason's advised their country traders to:

> display the popular weekly papers in a prominent position inside the shop
> as most people are on the look out for light reading material, and *Answers*,
> *Tit-Bits* and *Pearson's Weekly* are all suitable.[6]

A year later, Mr Eason continued to urge retailers to meet the demands of their
customers, asserting that news agents should supply a wider selection of material, he wrote: 'Go for more magazines ... Every customer for a daily or weekly
paper is a potential customer for some one at least of the numerous titles published.'[7] He listed titles appropriate for all interests, from ladies 'concerns' to
amateur photographers, and 'for the religious minded the field is very wide and
here in Ireland we are particularly rich in good class monthlies.'[8]

One such shop which failed at this time, was the Irish Book Shop Limited,
of Dawson Street, Dublin. The directors must not have subscribed to the rum-
bustious prose in Eason's trade bulletin. They may have been savants, yet their
very lofty ideals about how they should stock their shop were not commercially
viable. Abraham Jacob Leventhal, described as a bookseller, and Patrick Sarsfield
O'Hegarty, listed as a civil servant, are registered as having taken over this business as a going concern in November 1923: it had opened for business in 1918.[9]

The Irish Book Shop did not fail simply because it was a bookshop and not
a more accessible newsagent. The document of takeover stated that the new
owners would continue the business as: 'booksellers, newsagents, news ven-
dors, publishers, printers, stationers and fancy good dealers, engravers, enve-

6 *Eason's Monthly Bulletin of Trade News*, September 1930, 6.   7 Ibid., November 1931, 12.
8 Ibid.   9 The Irish Book Shop Limited, NA, Dissolved Companies File, 7218.

lope manufacturers, fancy cards and valentines'. Another clause in the Memorandum of Association stated how the existing reading room and reference library should be maintained 'to furnish the same, respectively, with books, reviews, magazines, newspapers and other publications, including instrumental and vocal music'. At this time, many bookshops contained a library where people could borrow or consult books for a small fee.

The contents of the Irish Book Shop were many, but the owners did themselves a disservice by restricting themselves to Irish material. This was probably an ideological decision. O'Hegarty was a well-known republican who later wrote a biography of Michael Collins. The average household purchased much Irish-produced material, but ironically, during the 1920s and 1930s, there were not enough such titles available to sustain a bookshop. Had they stocked a few shelves of foreign writers such as Charlotte M. Brame, Zane Grey, William le Queux, Edgar Wallace and E.P. Oppenheim, the sale of these popular cheap novels would have helped business. However, nationalists did not wish to be culturally dependent on foreign influences, so these imported money-spinners were excluded from the Irish Book Shop. However, the owners were not supported by the government in their objectives, these novels were considered neither pernicious nor expensive and were certainly not the type waiting to be banned by the Censorship Board. The foreign novels read by the average person were as wholesome and unthreatening as a copy of *Ireland's Own* and the *Catholic Fireside*.

This calamitous business affair could have been different: the Irish Book Shop could have branched into this popular reading material without alienating its devotees. A smattering of Zane Grey and his cowboy chums would have enticed the average reader into the shop; tales of guns and roses may have been anathema to O'Hegarty and Leventhal yet they would have filled a gap. In this way too, the masses could have been introduced to more strident home-produced nationalistic works and also more highbrow literature. The lack of business nous, as displayed by such 'traditional booksellers', enabled newsagents and others to prosper as unorthodox booksellers and librarians.

ROMANCE THRIVES

The 1930s were excellent years for the more commercially minded booksellers. In the June 1930 issue of his bulletin, Eason was both reflective and celebratory. While mentioning the censorship legislation of the previous year and declaring that many erstwhile formidable publications had had their day, he wallowed in the success of a home-produced journal. While dismissing the 'once powerful' *Freeman's Journal* and 'that staid Unionist organ, the *Daily Express*, which had gone into the limbo of forgotten things', he congratulated that most 'up-to-date' journal which 'has kept abreast of the times'.[10]

---

10 *Eason's Monthly Bulletin of Trade News*, June 1930, 4.

Welcoming its delicious recipe of articles commemorating the centenary of Catholic Emancipation (see pp 83-95 below) and the mixture of light, interesting features which made it a regular in the average household, he wished it a happy forty-third year of publication and stated: 'We are glad to learn that the circulation of the *Irish Catholic* has greatly improved during these latter years.'[11]

Eason continued his deification of this Irish weekly – benevolently mentioning its pedigree of having been blessed by a coterie of pontiffs and enjoying the eternal esteem of the hierarchy. Lest we scornfully conclude that greater powers may have caused this glowing description, I should add that this weekly newspaper was one of the soaraway successes of the 1930s. Notwithstanding the fact that at the time religious events such as the aforementioned centenary of Catholic Emancipation and the Eucharistic Congress, which was held in Dublin on 19-26 June 1932, aided sales figures, there was more to the longevity and increasing success of this long-established paper than souvenirs of religious events. The *Irish Catholic* was a microcosm of popular reading habits in Ireland during the decade. It spawned numerous imitators who all wanted the attention of the average reader.

As well as the soft diet of nationalism and Celtic crosses in the home-produced material, there was a great demand for foreign authors, despite forthcoming vicissitudes with protection tax. In the early years of the Free State long depicted as gloomy and unadventurous, readers were sticklers for romance. The 1930s began with a hugely popular Mills and Boon series in great demand. In 1930, one of the most successful titles in shops throughout the Free State was *It wasn't love* by Denise Robins, which was part of a library series. Titles in this series could be bought or borrowed from newsagents nation-wide, as punters could do both in the same establishment. Authors like Charlotte M. Brame and Zane Grey dominated sales during this era. Brame was a most prolific author who specialised in the genre of romance, and her books were snapped up by her numerous escapist Irish fans. *Sweethearts true, The Woolchester scandal, Above suspicion* and *The broken wedding ring* were just some of her bestselling novels during the decade. Grey, meanwhile, was the hero of the Wild West: his tales of daring-do in stagecoaches and adventures on the frontier were devoured. *The light of western stars, The lone star ranger* and *Wildfire* were just three of the titles which were both sold and loaned to readers throughout the Free State. Hearts may have been broken and promises unfulfilled, yet these novels were the perfect fodder for the public at the time. They were wholesome tales in which the villain usually got his comeuppance. There was nothing invidious here with which the watchdogs of culture and decency had to concern themselves.

While elitists may have castigated these magazines and books as simplistic and lowbrow; they were what the ordinary member of the public wanted to read. The tales may appear homespun, yet they cannot be derided or excluded

11 *Eason's Monthly Bulletin of Trade News,* June 1930, 4.

from our cultural history. Discussions regarding censorship have ignored these books, but the fact that they did not worry the board of censors speaks volumes. They did not contain 'loathsome' material and were seen as having no deleterious effects on their readers; therefore they were freely available and, ironically, these were what the average person wanted to read. Most readers wanted Zane Grey and Charlotte M. Brame and their ilk, and a weekly dip into a periodical such as the *Irish Catholic* or *Ireland's Own*. They were unconcerned about the availability of James Joyce's *Ulysses* or Bertrand Russell's *Marriage and morals* which got politicians and groups such as the Catholic Truth Society into fretful arguments about censorship. The Mills and Boon love stories were the very antithesis of the hysteria surrounding vile and unhealthy publications! Polemicists may have mourned the lack of sophistication regarding leisure pursuits, they may have decried the dearth of literary book shops, yet they were members of a derisory minority. Reading fodder for the masses abounded.

The average household read weekly periodicals; they escaped to the wild west with stories of lone star rangers and cheered when a couple lived happily ever after in a state of eternal romance. Cultural sophisticates they were not, and in many ways censorship did not concern them. Nevertheless, in these first years of the Irish Free State, reading as a hobby grew and developed and the influence of these tales of gunslingers and romantic heroes should not be ignored.

## THE POSITION OF THE NEWS AGENCY

During the 1930s the newsagent was becoming more prominent and powerful; stationery representatives (usually employed by Eason's) who travelled the country also supplied books as did Eason's directly in its capacity as wholesaler and distributor. One of the in-store lending libraries which was to prosper during this decade was the Torch library launched in 1929. This supplemented the newsagent's list of books for sale of 'repeaters' were now becoming commonplace in the bestseller world. Well-known authors producing at least one book per year became the norm and they built up an extraordinary following. The works of prolific British authors along with the Americans Zane Grey and E.P. Oppenheim were bought as well as borrowed. Grey was the champion of the western tale, Oppenheim dominated in the area of intrigue and mystery and Charlotte M. Brame was the leader in romantic fiction. A lightweight bunch, their audience consisted largely of those who were not generally buyers of books. The average family purchased some of their favourite author's books and augmented their reading material by borrowing the others from Eason's Torch series. The lists, published in Eason's bulletin throughout the 1930s, illustrate how popular these light romance and adventure genres were: Rosa N. Carey's *Lover or friend* and *Wooed and married* were included as were William le Queux's *Stolen sweets* and *The house of Whisp* and Charlotte M. Brame's easy-to-digest love stories *Her mother's sin* and *Above suspicion* were also very popular. An insert in the bulletin repeatedly alerted all newsagents to these 'world famous authors', creators of 'the most charming love romances', 'the most stirring cowboy thrillers' and 'books of the most popular films'.

The private lending libraries had long been an excellent source of popular reading material; members of the public could pay per book, or per quarter, and the 'books of the most popular films' were very much in demand as audiences began to flock to their local cinema. Free public libraries were still relatively new in rural Ireland; they did not reach all parts of the country until the 1920s, thus allowing the unconventional 'circulating libraries' in newsagents to flourish. In 1915, a report by Professor W.G.S. Adams of Oxford University stated that only 28 per cent of Irish people were served, mostly inadequately, by municipal libraries. This figure compared with 62 per cent of the English population, 46 per cent of people in Wales, and 50 per cent in Scotland.[12]

The rural library system remained piecemeal until 1923 when the Carnegie Trust published a sequel to this report. Established by Andrew Carnegie (1835–1919), a Scottish-born American steel industrialist, the Trust helped found a vast number of libraries in the English-speaking world. However, generally urban centres continued to be better-stocked: the new library which opened in Cork City in 1930 boasted over thirty-six thousand volumes and had four separate sections; adult reading, juvenile material, a reference section and a room for magazines and newspapers. It was well-stocked, up-to-date and clean; other libraries' reference departments were inadequate in comparison. Much depended on the local librarian. Limerick library enjoyed a new lease of life in 1939 when its first trained librarian was appointed; as a result, service and stock were revitalised.[13] Service in rural areas expanded gradually: in 1933 there were three library buildings throughout Co. Wicklow which were located at Bray, Enniskerry and Greystones. Five other urban centres had a library room in a building such as the courthouse and there were smaller centres at thirty-nine rural districts.[14]

As libraries sprung up, they too were sent copies of Eason's bulletin. It informed newsagents and librarians of innovations; it heralded new practices and also told of reading matter which was in a protracted state of decline. One instance of this was the announcement of the end of the Saturday edition of the *Sunday News!* It would now have a proper Sunday edition, which would be 'sent out by us on Monday morning to all newsagents heretofore ordering the Saturday edition. It is also to be permanently enlarged with extra pages and pictures.'[15]

12 W.A. Munford, *A history of the Library Association 1877-1977* (London, 1976), 123.  13 Mary Casteleyn, *A history of literacy and libraries in Ireland* (Aldershot, 1984), 224  14 Ibid. 15 *Eason's Monthly Bulletin of Trade News*, April 1930, 8. Also, note Eason's did not operate on Sundays; therefore rural customers had to wait until Monday morning for this newspaper. City customers began to be served by street sellers during the 1930s.

The hitherto Saturday editions of 'weeklies' had spearheaded a modern mass-market readership during the last two decades of the nineteenth century.[16] A compendium of condensed news from the week plus extra features such as puzzles and cartoons, these weeklies led the way for the explosion of cheap daily newspapers on the market which occurred during the first few years of the twentieth century. Traditionally, the 'weekly' arrived on Saturday evening, and in time they came to be referred to as 'Sundays'. Prior to World War One the only English papers which could be distributed in time for sale in Irish newsagents outside the Dublin area were these weekly editions published on Friday evening or Saturday morning. After 1918 however, the circulation of English Sunday newspapers expanded rapidly in Ireland. National circulation was estimated at 120,000 in 1920 and by 1926 the circulation of the *News of the World* alone was reckoned to be 132,444.[17] During the 1930s however, the *News of the World* endured more mercurial fortunes in the Free State. This very popular newspaper came under scrutiny from the reptilian eye of the Censorship Board. An ideologue of everlasting love in the Mills and Boon vein this newspaper was not for it propagated news of nasty divorce courts. This was really the only time the Censorship Act (1929) impinged on everyday, popular reading habits. Otherwise, the fearful watchdogs fretted over much reading material which was not purchased by the average family. Zane Grey had long since won the battle of the OK Corral over James Joyce.

The *News of the World* had been genuinely popular, however. Temporarily banned in July 1930, it was declared available again from 7 September of that year.[18] This publication then began to produce a special Irish edition, toned down for the readers of the Free State. Indeed, a memo drafted by the Justice minister's office in reply to a suggestion by the Catholic Truth Society to tighten up the Censorship of Publications Act, triumphantly declared how successful the Censorship Act had been in eliminating these malevolent and shocking tales which were being thrashed out across the water in the divorce courts.

> As regards periodicals, in particular English Sunday newspapers, the Act has been, in the Minister's opinion, an unqualified success. Even the most casual observer could not fail to notice the difference between the budgets of divorce and crime ... and the editions now circulating here.[19]

The Minister concluded that there was little interference to business, due to special expurgated Irish editions being on sale in the Free State.

Newsagents also depended on the sale of popular weeklies. One of the most successful of all throughout the 1930s was *Ireland's Own*. Both it and its cross-

16 The growth of weeklies is discussed in L.M. Cullen, *Eason & Son: a history* (Dublin, 1989), 252. 17 Ibid., 261. 18 *Eason's Monthly Bulletin of Trade News*, September 1930, 6. 19 Department of the Taoiseach files: Amendment of Censorship of Publications Act 1929: proposed amendments, 1938-40, NA, S10241. See also, Newspapers and Periodicals: restrictions on importations, 1934-51, NA, S2919A/b.

channel rival *Tit-Bits* were huge sellers throughout this decade. Unlike the *News of the World* they did not contain any current news no matter how condensed. There were no longueurs in these publications – just short, light articles which could be read in a few minutes; a long-running serial, recipes, household hints and the like. The stories may appear simple to modern readers and the recipes far too traditional; but such magazines, and in particular *Ireland's Own*, became one of the most popular and enduring 'reads' of the masses. Just as the newsagent-cum-grocer was one of the most important players in the introduction of mass reading habits to the public, and became, in effect, a focal point in the community; so too did *Ireland's Own* and its genre engender a sense of community and belonging. This weekly helped citizens make their first tentative steps in a newly independent state and brought a sense of pride to its readers.

Articles concerning local towns and villages, features chronicling origins of surnames and the lives of saints hardly transformed its reader into a scholar – but that was never the publisher's intention. The aim was simple – to appeal to as many people as possible, to achieve as many readers as possible. The ploy was to attract a reader's attention and keep it. It may only have been dipped into for a few minutes a week by some; yet, in its own subtle way, it encouraged the reading habit, no matter how simplistic. Recipes for griddle-cakes and the latest detective case solved by Miss Flanagan were hardly deleterious to either body or mind, and genealogical histories were far from sophisticated marketing stratagems, yet they worked. People purchased the magazine, week in, week out.

Its British rival, *Tit-Bits*, was also a long-established favourite in the Free State. Again, this publication had something for every member of the family- puzzles, a serial (usually a love story, or a detective tale), and occasional free gifts. In April 1930, Eason's bulletin announced a new and easy contest in which a lucky player could win £15 per week for life or £4,000 in hard cash. A new serial was to begin – 'The Calendar' by Edgar Wallace. The forthcoming edition was also to include 'a large road map of England and Scotland, given free'.[20] In November 1931, *Tit-Bits* celebrated its jubilee, with more competitions and a subsequent further increase in sales.[21] Its *Yearbook* also recorded huge sales that Christmas. The publication was to be further lauded by Eason's in April 1933 when a Kilkenny competitor, a Mr John Malone, won £1,000 in their 'clue word' puzzle. Eason's effused that this was of particular interest to Irish readers as it proved that 'there is an equal chance open to all competitors, provided skill is used in filling in the coupons'.[22]

CROSSES AND CONGRESSES

Newsagents did not survive on sales of newspapers and popular weeklies alone: another category of bestselling light reading material was the religious period-

**20** *Eason's Monthly Bulletin of Trade News*, April 1930, 8. **21** Ibid., November 1931, 3. **22** Ibid., April 1933, 5.

ical. Just like *Ireland's Own* and *Tit-Bits*, however, these magazines usually included some aspects of moonlight and roses: again harmless fodder which was enjoyed by one and all. Eason's successfully plugged the *Universe* several times during this decade. Billing it, in April 1930, as 'the most popular English Catholic paper', particularly enticing to prospective readers due to a 'tempting money prize' they could win. It was congratulated in September 1931 by the bulletin when a 'gratifying increase in sales' was announced. Mr Eason proudly declared that it had signed up the 'world famous Catholic author of thrillers', Mrs Belloc-Lowndes, to write a wonderful new serial, 'The Wizard's Warning'. The *Universe* continued to serve its readers well: in April 1934 it began a 'home page', which was of special interest to women and children.[23]

Perhaps the most successful year for religious publications during this decade was 1932, when the Eucharistic Congress was held in Dublin. There was a huge interest in this religious occasion, and the 'tie-in' books and magazines witnessed unprecedented sales. Eason's received an almost incessant stream of inquiries regarding commemorative material, and once again they supplied what the local newsagent required. In January of that year, they welcomed a new booklet, which, they quite correctly predicted, would be a bestseller during the months ahead. Retailing at one shilling, it was *The little book of the blessed Eucharist* by Brian O'Higgins. In that same issue, *The treasury of the Sacred Heart* was applauded, in particular the lambskin padded edition, which would make 'a perfect gift' at a cost of five shillings.[24] In February *The life of Matt Talbot* was reprinted. Having been a great success when first published in 1928, it was now reissued at a time when the average reader's thoughts would be turning to religious affairs. Sir Joseph A. Glynn's book was probably the great antidote to all the frivolous tales of cowboy heroes and falling in love with a handsome stranger!

Eason's continued with their religious pilgrimage in subsequent issues: they began taking orders for Congress souvenirs, which were rapidly sold out. The April 1932 edition declared the runaway bestseller to be the aforementioned *Treasury of the Sacred Heart*, described as 'a real devotional souvenir of the Eucharistic Congress.'[25] The following month *The Eucharistic Congress hymn book*, retailing at 2d., was the big seller. 'It has, of course, been issued for some time,' Eason wrote, 'but is still selling freely.'[26] Somewhat lighter religious reading material was included in John Gibbons's *Tramping to Lourdes* which was part of a set costing 3s. 6d. Another elaborate volume was welcomed in the July 1932 bulletin – *The Irish way*; billed as 'fifteen centuries of Irish Catholicism while the eyes of the world are focused on Dublin.'[27] Newsagents also reported that month that they had sold many extra copies of the *Standard*, the *Irish Catholic*, the *Universe*, the *Catholic Times* and *Catholic Herald*, especially during the weeks ending 25 June and 2 July, as they were crammed with articles on

---

23 Ibid., various issues: April 1930, September 1931 and April 1934.   24 Ibid., January 1932.
25 Ibid., April 1932, 12.   26 Ibid., May 1932, 3.   27 Ibid., June–July, 1932, 6.

and reports of the Eucharistic Congress. In August 1932, two books vied for superiority in the shops: the *Souvenir album of the Eucharistic Congress*, described as containing 'eleven interesting photographs of the great event' and *The life of Eamon de Valera* by Matthew Butler, which was 'selling rapidly'. Order forms for extra copies of these two were included in that issue of the bulletin.

Reading material with a religious content continued to do well during the decade. In 1935, the bestselling monthly magazine was *Saint Patrick's missionary bulletin*, which cost 2d.[28] Other religious magazines which sold consistently throughout the 1930s were the *Imeldist* and the *Irish Rosary*. Practically every Catholic household also contained at least some of the Footprints of Irish Saints series, which had been produced in booklet form by the *Irish Messenger* magazine from 1902-27. Over time the ordinary Irish household slowly built quite a collection of this soft nationalist diet chronicling the lives of saints and Catholic heroes.

### THE IMPACT OF CUSTOMS DUTIES

The August 1932 edition also contained words of foreboding for the newsagent: the new customs duties were explained in detail.[29] These duties introduced by the new Fianna Fáil government were to provide not only economic but also cultural protection by discouraging those so-called pernicious foreign magazine publishers from sending their products to Ireland. The sum of 1d. was imposed on novels, but this meant an addition of 1½d. to prices of 2d., 3d. and 6d. novels once trade margins were allowed for. An extra 2d. was added to 1s. novels. Second-hand novels were also liable for tax as were leather-bound books, children's annuals and 'other annuals such as *Punch Almanac* and *Whitaker's Almanac*'. Children's picture books, maps and guide-books, government publications and song books were listed as duty free. Periodicals for trade purposes, craft, religious, scientific and educational ones were also exempt. The same issue included feedback from newsagents regarding the newspaper tax: 'it has caused a falling off in the sales of comics and some of the popular weeklies.' The 1932 budget had introduced an import duty of ¾d. per copy on newspapers with a surface area less than 320 square inches. This was primarily intended to apply to weekly periodicals and Eason's bulletin stated sales of them had decreased by 50 per cent because of it. Tax was extended to daily newspapers the following year; thus protection brought an end to the growth in cross-channel paper sales in the twenty-six counties.

The retailer was in a quandary regarding periodicals, would the customer buy more Irish material if *Tit-Bits* and its ilk were unavailable? After an initial slump in sales, most of the light, and 'acceptable' British periodicals recovered. Magazines which specialised in household hints, long-running serials and com-

28 *Eason's Monthly Bulletin of Trade News*, February 1935, 3.  29 Ibid., August 1932, 8.

petitions with substantial money prizes remained able to tempt Irish readers. If imported daily newspapers did not regain readers, then their loss was mollified by home-produced ones. Sales of the *Irish Independent* rose from 90,000 in 1927 to 110,000 in 1939.[30] In March 1931, Eason's welcomed the earlier deliveries to rural areas of the *Independent* and the *Irish Times*, 'since the new rail and road services organised by Great Southern Railways have come into operation'. They also proclaimed the arrival of the *Irish Press* on 5 September that same year, as 'the biggest event in Irish journalism for a generation'.[31] By 1939 the *Press* had a circulation of 140,000, again proving that news and features with a nationalist hue was a winning formula. The *Press*, however, even went further and pioneered the reporting of Gaelic games, thereby generating a new audience for both Gaelic football and hurling and the paper itself.[32] English Sunday newspapers remained duty-free, but problems concerning their salacious contents frequently dented sales. Their only Irish rival was the *Sunday Independent*, whose net sales had risen to 180,000 by 1939.[33]

Books in the romance and western genres continued to prosper throughout the 1930s, but, due to the anomalies of the protection rules, another area of publishing began to break through. Although fiction accounted for over two-thirds of sales, new practical non-fiction titles appeared on the bookshelves. Dynamic specialist publishers producing craft books, which were exempt from taxes, took advantage of this by advertising how low their prices were. One such example was George Newnes & Company who took a full-page advertisement in Eason's bulletin of August 1932 to promote *Home made sweets*, *Dainty underwear* and *Sportswear for men*, all of which were offered to retailers at a very competitive rate. In October, the bulletin proffered good tidings for Christmas: 'nearly all children's annuals will be supplied to us "free of duty" and the *Film lover's guide* will remain at 2s. 6d.'[34]

Wynne's Newsagents of Castlebar certainly made the most of this: their bestsellers that Christmas were *Teddy Tail's annual* and the Christmas edition of the *Irish Press*.[35] Although annuals were liable to tax, several titles remained exempt as they were classified as 'picture books', and the *Press* was exempt because it was obviously home-produced. Some British publishers decided to have their books printed in Ireland so as to avoid the extra tax. Wright & Brown did just that and they were duly rewarded; two of their bestsellers in the run-up to Christmas were Charlotte M. Brame's *The romance of a black veil* and *The shadow of a sin*. Both were printed in Ireland and remained at 6d. while the 'yellow ninepennies' from Hodder & Stoughton, which were highly regarded, now retailed at 10½d. in the Free State and the 'sixpenny novels'

30 Cullen, *Eason & Son*, 358.   31 *Eason's Monthly Bulletin of Trade News*, March and July 1931, 2.   32 Tim Pat Coogan, *De Valera: Long Fellow, Long Shadow* (London, 1993), 429. 33 Cullen, *Eason & Son*, 358.   34 *Eason's Monthly Bulletin of Trade News*, October 1932, 3. 35 Business records of Wynne's Newsagency, Castlebar. Account books, 1932, NA, file MAYO 7.

were now 7½d.[36] This publisher was also producing two new 2s. 'yellowbacks' per month, aimed at the more discerning, and wealthier customer.

To end the year on a seasonal note: in the world of periodicals, the Christmas edition of the *Irish Catholic* was selling well; the price tag of 6d. was perhaps exorbitant but it included a religious calendar for 1933, and the Christmas editions were frequently 'bumper issues'. *Christmas Chimes* was selling well at 3d., as was the end-of-year edition of the *Christian Herald* which was appropriately named *Holly Bough*.[37] To prove that newsagents did have a varied stock of reading material *The story of Elizabeth* was sent out to them during November 1932. Originally published in 1930, it was reissued for the Christmas market. Retailing at 2s. 6d., it included 'some stories of Princess Margaret which have been added' and this tempted those interested in the lives of the royal family. In April 1935, Eason's customers were selling vast quantities of *The story of the King and Queen* at 6d., a silver jubilee commemoration. This recompensed for the news that same month that the deemed gruesome *True Story* magazine was banned and that *Christian Family* was being discontinued! Hence, an uplifting anniversary of glamorous royals appealed to the Irish public, despite their professed nationalism.

The fascination with royal matters continued unabated during the 1930s: by April 1937 there had been seven hundred and fifty thousand orders for the *Programme of the Coronation* (retailing at 1s. and a de luxe version sold for 2s. 6d.). The following month these books were ready and dispatched to the shops; it is grimly ironic that the other publication in demand that month was the *Irish Independent handbook on emigration to England*, which was 'selling steadily' at 6d.[38]

Notwithstanding the ongoing hardships of life in the Free State, romantic fiction continued to dominate the newsagents, libraries and the average home in the country. Nineteen thirty-three began on an optimistic note with the launch of a new Mills & Boon spring fiction campaign, which proved to be very popular. The top eight titles were listed as *Painted lady*, *Men are only human*, *The miserable sinner*, *Fate knocks at the door*, *So many children*, *Happy heart*, *An exotic young lady* and *Lady gone wild*.[39] That same month saw Eason's updated list of 'popular cheap fiction novels' being sent to newsagents and booksellers all over the country. The same names dominate the fiction scene throughout the 1930s (and indeed, beyond): Charlotte M. Brame, William le Queux, Edgar Wallace, E.W. Savi, A. Fielding and E.P. Oppenheim. In February 1933, Hodder & Stoughton improved the appearance of their books in order to attract more readers. Eason's described it thus: 'the usual yellow jacket picture wrapper is on the back as well as the front – better for display purposes'.[40] 'Yellowbacks' were now within everyone's budget and were much more attractive as well. With the explosion of cheaper novels, even the successful Torch library series was lagging behind and that month's trade news included an

---

**36** *Eason's Monthly Bulletin of Trade News*, November 1932, 3.   **37** Ibid., December 1932, 3.   **38** Ibid., April and May 1937.   **39** Ibid., January 1933, 3.   **40** Ibid., February 1933, 3.

emphatic plea for extra agents. The Collins series of Agatha Christie detective stories were also mentioned as selling well.

## THE SCORCHERS

The 'scorcher' novel was the revelation of 1933: this was a successful series of 'thrilling adventure stories on land, sea and air', and not a list which infuriated the censor. Deeds of macho men suffering madcap mishaps and even trigger-friendly tales of violent frontier men were all allowed to circulate in the Free State. Basically, since there were no references to sex or birth control, this reading material was approved for mass circulation. In the case of popular reading material, censorship was never a big issue; cheap fiction, usually vetted by Eason's, was all very tame, middle-of-the-road, reading. Mills & Boon were never known to ruffle any feathers and, incidentally, their new western series surpassed their trademark romantic tales in sales in Ireland.

The trade bulletin of March 1933 was clearly excited about the prospect of this new series. The first two titles *Outlaw blood* by Eli Colter and *Trouble Ranch* by George M. Johnson retailed at 2s. 6d. A winning formula which flourished during the 1930s and 1940s, this was a light romance set in the ever-popular wild west, a combination of guns and roses in one volume! The only warning about censorship during these years concerning popular reading habits came that same month: a stern message in the bulletin to newsagents and booksellers stated that *Flaming youth* by Warner Fabian had been banned so 'immediately check over your stock of 6d.'[41]

This shows that Eason's, as wholesaler and distributor, weeded out the acceptable books from the pernicious so that neither retailer nor purchaser had to worry about such details. In fact, Eason's frequently published a booklet listing all banned publications which was distributed to all booksellers along with their monthly trade bulletin. *Flaming youth* had temporarily escaped the net, but the observant eye of the wholesaler soon rectified this. In any event, those books and magazines presented to the Irish public for their delectation were not the types of literature censors were concerned about; popular reading habits did not contain any controversial material, as Agatha Christie, Katharine Tynan and Zane Grey provided a staple diet of fiction for the masses. For example, the bestselling novels in February 1935 were the latter's *Robbers' roost* and *The gallows of chance*. Grey was not merely limited to this Irish market, which was frequently scorned as selling only lowbrow, simplistic reading material. He was, in fact, a worldwide phenomenon. Set in exotic deserts or towns in Nevada, his novels had a truly widespread, international appeal. In his home market of the USA alone, Zane Grey sold more than forty million copies of his tales during the first half of the twentieth century.[42] The obsession with flintlocks

---

**41** Ibid., March 1933, 5.  **42** Alice Payne Hackett, *70 years of best-sellers* (New York, 1967), 87.

and sheriffs was not the only popular reading material in Ireland. The ever popular religious tracts and their lighter counterparts such as *Ireland's Own* and *Green and Gold* competed with the imported novels by Charlotte M. Brame and Zane Grey for prominence in the average Irish home.

IRISH COWBOYS FOR CHILDREN

Popular reading material for children and teenagers was of a similar calibre. This mixture of saints and cowboys, chaste kisses in the moonlight plus an element of nationalism all kept the average young Catholic in the twenty-six counties entertained and thus encouraged the reading habit during these years. For those who started reading at a young age, there was also a choice between imported, light reading matter and home-produced material, in which a glorious past was recalled. In Irish books, heroes were given Gaelic names while they fought for good over evil. Perhaps the most famous of this bunch was *Our Boys*, published by the Christian Brothers and available in schools and newsagents all over the country. Founded in 1914, sales reached a zenith in the 1920s due to the growth of street selling. Cowboys were often called Sean and Donall, so the wild west could be transported to towns and villages in the Free State.

Another sentimental publication for the youth was the *Capuchin Annual*; started in 1930 it became a huge success. It was a type of almanac, but with extra features which would appeal to all members of the family. A calendar of events was listed, which was exclusively Catholic, and good works and good deeds permeated the book. Three newsagents whose business records I examined in depth all list sales of the *Capuchin Annual* in their account books.[43] In Mr Wynne's records it is interesting to note that the first recorded sale went to the Reverend Gibbons in 1933 for 2s. 3d. This gentleman's reading was not strictly religious: although he purchased *the Eucharistic Congress record* for 2s. 6d., he also bought *Amateur Photographer*, which cost 3d.

Many readers of the *Capuchin Annual* were children and teenagers, and the stories, although considered lightweight, contained religious overtones and significant morals. Alongside such tales in the 1930 edition as *The Capuchins in Ireland*, *The first Irish missionaries* and *The religious and monastic Wordsworth* was a fable entitled *A Nature lover*, chronicling the fall of a young man named Ciaran into the nasty grip of materialism. There was, however, a happy ending as this 'cultured scholar, the doyen of the smart set, the scoffer at the simple faith of others' repented at his mother's deathbed.

To be fair, many of the stories were neither as morbid nor as dreary, and a good indication of its rising sales is to consider the numerous companies and

---

**43** Business records of Burke, newsagent, Cashel, 1932-57, NA, file TIP 23; McGreevy, newsagent and grocer, Westport, 1927-33, NA, file MAYO 16 and Wynne's Newsagency, Castlebar, 1879-1939, NA, file MAYO 7.

organisations who booked either a half or full-page advertisement in the annual.
Various booksellers, publishers and printers were all included as well as a prominent advert for the *Imeldist* – recommended for children to 'build up for them
a background of right-thinking and right ideals'. For the devout and disciplined
young boy, there was also *The Catholic Scout*, hailed by Eason's in 1932 as being
a very interesting new magazine 'for all boys from age 7 to 70'. For those
youngsters interested in novels, Eason's were also selling a new series of 2*d*.
boy's novels entitled *Wild West yarns*.[44] Four new titles would be published
each month and provided to newsagents nation-wide for sale or stock for their
libraries. *The Stage Coach annual* sold consistently well each Christmas; this
retailed at one shilling and included 'five complete western stories.'[45] *Boy's Own*
and *Boy's Favourite* were for broader tastes while female readers could enjoy
*Miss Modern*. This monthly magazine was launched in a blaze of publicity in
September 1930. Along with the first issue came a free 'Mickey the Mouse
mascot pin'.[46] The following January it had an exclusive interview with Maurice
Chevalier, 'the popular film star'. Would-be readers were also enticed with the
fact that 'in the film supplement is included a photograph of Maurice Chevalier
ready for framing'.[47] By mid-decade it had begun to include sewing and knit-
ting patterns and a romantic serial, one of which was 'Let's ask a lot from
Love'.[48]

For the pre-teens there was the Christmas favourite, *The Shirley Temple
annual*, retailing at 2*s*. 6*d*. and which promised many 'anecdotes about her
charming little self'. *Bobby Bear's annual* and *Teddy Tail's annual* were also peren-
nial bestsellers, the latter having been a long-running cartoon in the *Daily Mail*.
For those favouring a home-produced magazine, *Our Girls* was launched in
September 1930. The stories herein, although romantic and moralistic, also
delved into the lives of saints and Irish scholars. Eason's recounted how the
special St Patrick's Day edition in 1931 was completely sold out within a fort-
night.

Thus Irish publications were snapped up by young and old, but not enough
were being produced to satisfy readers' demands. These easy-to-digest weekly
magazines, newspapers and cheap novels made establishments such as Wynne's
of Castlebar a huge success. Sentimental they may seem, but shortly after the
foundation of the state this barely-formed society was not interested in highbrow literature or in those weeklies condemned by county councils throughout the decade as 'vile and unhealthy'. Irish readers, *en masse*, were interested
in sanitised magazines, wild west heroes, easy-to-complete puzzles and love
everlasting. It is a pity that Irish publishers were not more adventurous at this
time: the political climate may have been conservative and life gloomy with
many hardships, but home-grown publishers should have tapped into this potential. The soft diet of nationalist publications boomed, but because there was not

---

**44** *Eason's Monthly Bulletin of Trade News*, March 1932, 8.   **45** Ibid., various issues.   **46** Ibid.,
September 1930, 10.   **47** Ibid., January 1931, 11.   **48** Ibid., May 1934, 5.

enough of it in 'novel' form, foreigners like Charlotte M. Brame and Zane Grey were tops. Just as in *Our Boys*, where cowboys suddenly fought in corrals in rural Wicklow, more romance with an Irish setting would have been very welcome. The only two such Irish authors who were promoted tirelessly by their publishers at this time were Annie M.P. Smithson and Maurice Walsh. They had the winning formula: in Smithson's case one of her most famous novels, *Her Irish heritage*, was a tale set amid the grim aftermath of the 1916 Rising, while Maurice Walsh's *The small dark man* was the most eagerly-awaited fiction title during the summer of 1932 by a public hungry for light Irish fiction.[49]

Probably the most successful and prolific publishing house to pursue the growth of a mass market in Irish fiction was Talbot Press, which had numerous bestsellers in the thirties. Books in the style of Charlotte M. Brame, with an Irish setting, were the most popular. Irish readers wanted to escape to romantic settings in Dublin and Galway as well as the usual, more exotic locations. During the 1930s Annie M.P. Smithson remained their number one fiction author. Talbot Press also developed a winning formula with their non-fiction titles. Aware of what the market was like and what the average person read, they launched their Irish Lives series in May 1935. Three titles were initially available, all retailing at 2s. 6d. each: *Thomas Davis* by J.M. Hone, *W.B. Yeats* by J.H. Pollock and *Rebel Irishwomen* by R.M. Fox. They scored a huge non-fiction success with Dan Breen. Eason's bulletin reminded its readers that Breen's *My fight for Irish freedom* had been turned down by several publishers and only the Talbot Press had been willing to accept it. This investment had been wise as the book, first published in 1924, 'turned out to be the bestseller of the year in Ireland' in 1931 and paid dividends to all involved in the book trade.[50] The bulletin went on to lament the dearth of books published in Ireland: this was pitiful they concluded since we had such a glorious past which could, and should, be written about. Local and national events could all be commemorated in fiction and non-fiction and it was shameful these were not being exploited.


CONCLUSION


Eason's knew what the Irish public wanted to read, and they continually endeavoured to get home-based publishers to realise this. They were not interested in supplying books that their customers, the newsagents, would be unable to sell. Crosses, guns and roses were the key elements – religion with a little adventure and escapism; all the more welcome when the setting was Irish. Indeed, Charles Eason junior replied curtly when asked by writer George Russell to stock books of a more literary merit: 'As to James Joyce, I need not tell you we have not got his *Ulysses*, nor have we got any other work of his.'[51]

---

**49** Ibid., July 1932, 11.  **50** Ibid., November 1931, 14.  **51** Correspondence of 1929, Letter

Eason may have been on a moral crusade by dismissing Liam O'Flaherty's books as 'coarse' and stating that 'there are far more novels of a suitable character', but judging by requests and subsequent sales, the 'suitable' books were what the punters wanted.

One of the few people who would have purchased *Ulysses* was a wine merchant and book collector, a Mr Thomas Doolan from Waterford City. His business records reveal that he acquired a vast collection of books during the 1920s and 1930s, at a time when most of his compatriots were reading Agatha Christie and the *Catholic Fireside*. He subscribed to booksellers in London, Glasgow, Birmingham and Cambridge and was always searching for rare first editions. He corresponded with the Library Association of Great Britain from whom he bought miscellaneous reference books in March 1930. Booksellers throughout Britain were frequently sent lists of books which he required. W.G. Neale, a new and second-hand bookseller based in Eastbourne, wrote occasionally to let this collector know of his stock. W.G. Neale's letterhead stated: 'late of Dublin'; presumably he was another failed bookseller whose market had been far too specialist for the Irish trade.[52] Doolan's collection, however, would have been far removed from the cheap novels, halfpenny newspapers, penny periodicals and sixpenny magazines which were standard fare in most other homes.

Crosses, guns and roses were the ingredients of the mass-market reading material during the 1930s in Ireland. Eason's monthly trade journal contained an element of populism in order to woo the rural newsagent. And woo him it did: sales of cheap, lightweight reading material constituted the bulk of publications which were bought throughout the Free State. The hitherto gentlemanly occupation of bookselling may have been invaded by common shopkeepers, but the latter knew what potential customers were willing to buy. George Russell noted ruefully: 'I doubt whether a single literary man in Ireland could make the income of an agricultural labourer by royalties on sales of his books.'[53] Russell and other literary men were engaged in clamorous battles of words with politicians over the right to have certain books available for readers. Irish readers however were not listening: they had escaped to a saloon bar in the wild west (decorated with religious icons), for action and romance.

from Charles Eason to George Russell, dated 20 September 1929, Eason Archives, Dublin.
52 Business records of T. & H. Doolan, wine merchants, Waterford. Thomas Doolan's correspondence with booksellers are in, NA, file WAT 24/B/44, entitled Library, 1890-1945.
53 *Irish Statesman*, 12 January 1924.

ADRIAN KELLY

# Cultural imperatives: the Irish language revival and the educational system[*]

The establishment of the Irish Free State in 1922 meant that the revival of the Irish language was taken from the sole care of cultural pressure groups and placed firmly on the agenda of the independent Irish government. Government policy emphasised the need to preserve and expand the existing Irish-speaking areas – mainly scattered rural communities on the seaboard – and restore the language in the rest of the country through the education system, particularly the primary schools. While Gaeltacht policies have received much attention and were a central part of the revival effort, the subjection of the education system to the dictates of the language revival has been widely ignored while it affected a far greater number of people, who were English- rather than Irish-speaking. Also, while inhabitants of Gaeltacht areas were often actively demanding state intervention to preserve the economic, social and linguistic fabric of their communities, the revival policies concentrating on the education system were often imposed on pupils, teachers and parents who were neither prepared for nor necessarily accepting of the extent to which the schools were being Gaelicised.

The curriculum of the schools, principally the primary or 'national' schools but also the secondary schools, was redefined to include the bringing about of what, it was hoped, would be a linguistic revolution, i.e. the displacement of English by Irish as the spoken language of the majority population. The attainment of this linguistic shift was established as a cultural imperative following independence. As the revived interest in the language prior to independence was regarded as a necessary ingredient in the gaining of independence, so too was the revival of Irish as the spoken language after independence associated by many leading cultural thinkers and politicians with the survival of the nation. However, such a revival required nothing short of a cultural revolution, and it was thought that the schools were the most appropriate institution to achieve this as they were held responsible for replacing Irish with English in the nineteenth century.

There were also attempts to Gaelicise other aspects of life. From the establishment of the Free State, Irish became compulsory for entry to the civil service. To assist civil servants in retaining, improving and cultivating their lan-

* The author wishes to acknowledge the assistance of Professor R.V. Comerford who supervised his MA thesis upon which this chapter is partially based.

guage skills Cumann Gaodhalach na Stát Sheirbhíse was established in 1926. Irish also became necessary for many local authority positions.¹ In 1937 Irish was made a compulsory subject in the entrance examination for the Garda Síochána, many local garda officers taking voluntary steps to provide language classes for force members.² The national radio station, Radio Éireann, broadcasted up to 172 programmes in Irish per year by the late 1930s, averaging fifteen minutes each, although the effectiveness of this Irish language content was occasionally called into question.³ There were other official and voluntary initiatives but none comparable in scope, intensity or intent to the policies focused on the education system. Indeed, many of the initiatives outside the schools were introduced in order to provide a *raison d'être* for the schools-based revival programme.

By the early 1930s primary and secondary schools had already become the chief vehicles of the Irish language revival in English-speaking areas. The Fianna Fáil government, which came to power in 1932, displayed a renewed vigour in its attempts to Gaelicise the education system. These attempts and the ramifications they had for both the education system and the status of the language are the subject of this chapter. Particular attention is paid to the reasons why the education system became the focus of the language revival; the changes made in the curriculum and elsewhere to implement the policy; the competence with which the school-based language revival was approached; and its level of success. A further issue is the extent to which children's education was adversely affected by the revival effort. That the focus on the language revival had negative consequences for the quality of education received by schoolchildren was acknowledged politically but was seen as a necessary and acceptable price to pay. The fact that children's education suffered due to the emphasis on the language revival was partly responsible for the fact that the initial enthusiasm for the language among the wider public turned into apathy, or even antagonism. Perhaps the extensive system of grants and bonuses made available to pupils and teachers and the additional examination marks for answering state examinations through Irish was an official recognition of this lack of enthusiasm.

This chapter argues that the school-based revival policy became more finely tuned in the 1930s, with attention being paid to practical issues, but that although many people obtained a certain fluency in Irish, the aim of displacing English with Irish was not brought any closer. While it would have been politically difficult to change the policy given the political identification of the Irish language with independence, the more vigorous pursuance of the school-based revival policy in the 1930s had negative consequences for education standards and popular perceptions of the language.

1 Mary E. Daly, *The buffer state: the historical roots of the Department of the Environment* (Dublin, 1997), 167–71. 2 Liam McNiffe, *A history of the Garda Síochána* (Dublin, 1997). 3 Conradh na Gaeilge, *An Gaedheal agus an radio* (Dublin, 1936).

EDUCATION AND THE IRISH LANGUAGE PRIOR TO THE 1930S

Under pressure from language enthusiasts the British Government had facilitated the teaching of Irish long before the granting of independence. From
1879 the teaching of Irish outside ordinary school hours was permitted in
national schools, while the new school programme of 1900 allowed the teaching of Irish as an optional subject during ordinary school hours. The position
of Irish was further strengthened in 1904 when the Commissioners of National
Education announced their approval of a bilingual programme during ordinary
school hours in Irish speaking districts with effect from the school year 1906-
7. In the intermediate – or secondary – system, Irish had had a foothold from
the inauguration of the system in 1878; while the introduction of compulsory
Irish for matriculation within the National University of Ireland (NUI) in 1913
substantially increased the number of second-level students taking Irish.[4]

Following independence the status of Irish changed from being a near minor
or fringe subject to becoming the core subject of the curriculum while it was
also strongly promoted as the first language of instruction. The importance of
the language revival to nationalists became immediately evident. While discussions on the Treaty were taking place in the Dáil, the Minister for Education,
Michael Hayes, stated that every primary school was at liberty to implement
the – as of then unfinalised – report of the First National Programme
Conference of Primary Instruction which emphasised the Gaelic element in
the curriculum.[5] One of the first acts of the newly appointed Provisional
Government was to issue 'Public Notice Number 4' in February 1922. It stip-
ulated that Irish be taught or used as a medium of instruction for not less than
one hour each day and that schools were to make whatever arrangements necessary to ensure this.[6] This was to take effect from St Patrick's Day of that year.

The second national programme conference on primary instruction, established in November 1924, placed an even greater emphasis on Irish, insisting
in particular on the use of Irish as a medium of instruction in infant classes
where the teacher was sufficiently qualified, with the progressive use of Irish
as a medium of instruction in other grades. Every aspect of class work was to
go into 'training the children to understand Irish and to speak it distinctly and
correctly as their natural language'.[7] In March 1926 the Second National
Programme was accepted as the official programme of the primary schools.

In parallel with the developments in the primary sector, a commission on
secondary education was established in September 1921, its recommendations,
which again emphasised the Gaelic core of the curriculum, were adopted

---

**4** *Comisiún um athbheochan na Gaeilge: Summary in English of Final Report* (1963), 10.   **5**
National Programme Conference, *National programme of primary instruction* (Dublin, 1922).
Copy of statement in *Irish Schools Weekly*, 21 March 1922.   **6** D/T, Irish language: devel-
opment in the schools, NA, S7801c.   **7** Second National Programme Conference, *Report*
(Dublin, 1926), 22.

through the Secondary School Programme. From the school year 1927–8 Irish became a subject necessary for the award of the intermediate certificate,[8] replacing the previous regulations which required the teaching of Irish or English.[9]

FOCUSING ON THE EDUCATION SYSTEM

It is easy enough to understand why it was felt necessary to restore Irish as the national language. The three most widely used arguments were based on the historical significance of Irish and the idea that its extinction would constitute a betrayal of previous generations of Irish people; its significance as a cultural badge marking the Irish out from all other cultures, particularly the Anglo-Saxon; and the idea that the Irish nation would not survive or prosper without its own language. From time to time other arguments were put forward, such as the promotion of the 'high spirituality' of the Gaelic language.[10] While the principal reasons for the displacement of Irish with English in the century prior to independence were social and economic,[11] the reasons now being put forward to encourage people to part take in the revival of Irish were entirely cultural. If the revival of the language was a social or economic necessity, then it was never portrayed as such, while the abstract arguments based on cultural significance were less than convincing when left unqualified and ignored, for example, the fact that Irish authors writing in English were receiving international acclaim for their work at this time. However, it were these reasons which were put before teachers in an effort to galvanise them into activity. The *Notes for teachers, primary school: Irish* (1933) in particular hyped the significance of the language in ensuring the political and cultural survival of the nation: 'That Gaelic attitude ... gives us our individuality as a nation, without it we become an amorphous or a hybrid people.'[12]

Regardless of the strength or otherwise of the general arguments put forward for the restoration of the language, what is significant here is why the emphasis came to be placed on the education system and why it was decided to subjugate the system to the revival of the language. The idea that 'the effort to revive Irish as a spoken language undoubtedly rests very largely with our schools'[13] was based on the already noted and unquestioned nationalist assump-

8 Department of Education, *Regulations regarding curricula, certificates, examinations and scholarships with programme for the year 1927-28*, 10.  9 Ibid., 7.  10 Department of Education, *Notes for teachers, primary school: Irish* (Dublin, 1933), 55.  11 See for example Caoimhín Ó Donachair, 'The Irish language in Co. Clare in the nineteenth century', *North Munster Antiquarian Journal*, xiii (1970), which underpins the extent to which the Irish were surrounded by a world whose business was carried on through the medium of English and which was seen as economically more prosperous than Gaelic speaking Ireland, Irish often being associated with poverty.  12 Department of Education, *Notes for teachers, primary school: Irish* (Dublin, 1933), 54.  13 Tomás Ó Deirg, DD, vol. 51, 21 March 1934, col. 1603.

tion that the education system of the nineteenth century had caused the spread of English and was the major factor in the decline of Irish. Now the work of the schools would cause, it was hoped, the reverse to happen, making natural and fluent Irish speakers of all pupils. The department's *Notes for teachers: Irish* (1933) makes this expectation clear to teachers, stating that all the teacher's efforts were to go into the achievement of this goal.

Much was expected from using Irish as a medium of instruction. The Gaelic League cultivated the idea that Irish in particular when studied or used as a medium of instruction provided a unique intellectual training which went far beyond the possibilities of modern languages,[14] an idea supported by the Department of Education.[15] Seán T. Ó Ceallaigh, actively involved at various levels in the Gaelic League and President of Ireland from 1949 to 1959, cited the better examination results obtained by those pupils who received their education through the medium of Irish.[16] Shán Ó Cuív, journalist and author of many Irish language textbooks, claimed that Irish as a medium 'tends to clarify the meaning and give the children a better grasp of the subject', although only when 'the language is taught properly and the children know it'.[17]

## SHORTCOMINGS

To make the school-based language revival a success a number of huge practical difficulties needed urgent attention right from the outset in 1922. However, teachers were offered little support or advice on bilingual education. At no stage was the revival either at policy or curriculum level based on practical considerations, but rather on the idealism of a perceived cultural imperative, which for various reasons became a political imperative. Such practical issues as teacher qualifications and the provision of textbooks were addressed in a haphazard manner if at all.

Perhaps the most significant practical problem was the lack of qualifications in Irish among teachers, the majority of whom had little knowledge of the language. In 1922, out of 12,000 lay teachers, only 1,107 had the bilingual certificate (which qualified teachers to use Irish as a medium of instruction) while 2,845 had the ordinary certificate (which qualified them to teach Irish as a subject).[18] Until 1929 the Department of Education provided annual summer courses in the Gaeltacht for teachers,[19] but it felt that by then serving teachers had been given ample opportunity to learn the language and with the coming

**14** Report of the opening of the Gaelic League in Derry by Rev. M. Bradley, vice-president, St Columba's College, in *Irish Schools Weekly*, 6 Oct. 1928. **15** See for example *Notes for teachers: Irish*, 54 and *Report of the Department of Education, 1930-31*, 18. **16** DD, vol. 38, 22 May 1931, col. 1823-4. **17** Shán Ó Cuív, *The problem of Irish in the schools* (Dublin, 1936), 12. **18** *Report of the Department of Education, 1940-41*, 16. **19** *Report of the Department of Education, 1928-29*, 18.

on stream of newly qualified teachers competent in Irish it was deemed unnecessary to provide such courses that year. However, by 1931, 38 per cent of
teachers still had no formal qualification in Irish while only 30 per cent were
qualified to use Irish as a medium of instruction.[20] Therefore, ten years after
the introduction of the new government's language policy it was still, in the
words of Ernest Blythe,

> undoubtedly a fact that a great many – perhaps the majority – of our
> teachers are not able to give instruction through Irish. We have to do the
> best that can be done with them, but a great many of them are hardly
> competent even to teach Irish satisfactorily.[21]

The Department of Education recognised the problem, but lay the blame
squarely with the teachers themselves:

> There had been … a number of those [i.e. teachers] well within the age
> when reasonable fluency in Irish might be attained, who have failed to
> respond, whether through mere lethargy or indifference to the demands
> of patriotism, to the appeal which was made to them.[22]

Having the appropriate fluency was not always an advantage either. Indeed
those who did qualify with the Ard-Teastas, the highest qualification in Irish,
often complained of being disadvantaged in so far as inspectors expected more
exacting work from them.

Not only did the department fail to deal with the lack of competence in
Irish among teachers but it failed to pay any practical attention to what is possibly the most important consideration when teaching a language, namely, the
balance between oral and written exercises. Since the idea of teaching Irish was
to make it a vibrant and living language, it might have been expected that the
emphasis in class work would be on spoken Irish; that, as *Notes for teachers: Irish*
pointed out, 'continuous speech must be practised'.[23] It might also have been
expected that examinations in student proficiency would have included a strong
oral element. However, despite the repeatedly stated aim of reviving the language as a spoken tongue or a second vernacular, the emphasis in the schools,
the primary instrument of the revival campaign in English-speaking areas, was
on the written word. It was one of the many paradoxes underlying the revival
policy and contributed greatly to its failure.[24]

The provision of Irish language textbooks was another serious problem. An
Gúm, the publication arm of the Department of Education responsible for producing such books, was still unable to provide for the needs of primary schools

**20** Francis Fahy, DD, vol. 38, 21 May 1931, col. 1714-15.  **21** DD, vol. 44, 28 Oct. 1932,
col. 750.  **22** *Report of the Department of Education, 1931-32*, 20.  **23** Department of Education,
*Notes for teachers: Irish*, 42.  **24** Ó Cuív, *The problem of Irish in the schools*, 16.

by the end of the 1920s. As a result the Department of Education had to suggest to teachers that they carry out their work without recourse to textbooks, especially in junior standards of the primary school:

> Smaoineadh nua a bheadh é na naoidheanáin a mhúineadh gan an leabhar. Tá an iomad muinghine ag ár múinteoirí go léir as na leabhar – agus as leabhair shuaracha leis – agus is deacair leo oibriú gan an leabhar.[25]

A significant obstacle to the production of sufficient Irish language textbooks was the lack of a standardised or indeed any terminology. The latter was a particular problem in the teaching of science and technical subjects. To overcome it, a Coiste Téarmaíochta was established under the Department of Education which by the school year 1928-9 had published two books of terms, one relevant to the teaching of history and geography and the other relevant to the teaching of grammar and literature. A more serious problem, which could not be easily resolved, concerned the lack of a standardised spelling and grammar. While linguists could argue about the merits of dialectical diversity and richness as opposed to standardised forms and grammar, the lack of standardisation was hampering government initiatives.

NEW INITIATIVES

By the 1930s, therefore, there were a number of evident and acknowledged weaknesses in the school-based revival campaign, progress falling far short of contemporary expectations. Despite eight years of policies and enthusiasm, the teaching force remained largely unqualified; there was a shortage amounting to a near absence of Irish language textbooks; while the emphasis on Irish in the classroom was on written rather than oral work. It is important to note that these shortcomings were obvious and acknowledged at the time. Given such contemporary recognition of the difficulties it was clear, or at least should have been, that a radical rethinking of the policy was necessary. In this context the 1930s is a pivotal period. Faced with the obvious lack of progress – indeed the negative indications of the policy thus far – it could have been decided to reassess both the language revival policy itself and the central role played in it by the schools. However, such a reassessment would have been politically difficult, carrying with it an admission that one of the first major enterprises of the Free State government was a failure. The fact that the enterprise had been so closely associated with the concept of nationalism made it almost impossible to admit failure. Instead, it was decided to pursue a patently unsuccessful

---

**25** *Report of the Department of Education, 1929-30*, 31 (trs: A new concept would be the teaching of infants without recourse to books. Teachers have too much faith in books, many of which are of questionable value, and find it difficult to work without them).

policy with increased vigour in the hope that the added momentum would change its fortunes. It was this increased momentum, fuelled by the coming to power of Fianna Fáil, that characterised the revival policy in the 1930s. The extent to which the education system in the 1930s was actually subjugated to, and the education of children superseded by the dictates of the language revival, without any attempt at scientific or pedagogic evaluation, is remarkable.

In July 1931, shortly before leaving office, the Cumann na nGaedheal government issued a circular to managers, teachers and inspectors of primary schools reiterating the intention of the school programme and calling upon them to play their part in reviving the language as a spoken tongue by giving pupils a mastery of it.[26] This was preceded in June by a circular stating that in future the rating of teachers as 'efficient' or 'highly efficient' would be equated with the level of Irish used.

A few weeks after taking office it became clear that there would be no rethinking of the school-based revival policy by the new Fianna Fáil government. The Taoiseach, Eamon de Valera, an avid supporter of the language movement, took the opportunity of a radio broadcast on St Patrick's Day 1932 to let it be known that the policy of the new government would be to progressively develop the use of Irish in the schools.[27] The responsibility for its implementation lay with Tomás Ó Deirg, the Minister for Education for all but nine months between 1932 and 1948. By 1933 he had circulated *Rules and regulations for national schools*, which stressed the importance of extending the use of Irish, especially in infant classes,[28] and *Notes for teachers: Irish* which called on teachers to direct their efforts towards ensuring that students from English-speaking areas on leaving primary school were capable of conversing freely in Irish.[29]

A circular of 1936 reminded inspectors and school managers: 'the main purpose of the teaching [of Irish], particularly in the lower standards, is to ensure that pupils *speak* the language freely and fluently'.[30] Despite this guideline, however, there was a continuing failure to focus practical attention on the teaching of oral Irish. This situation was mirrored in the secondary schools where the insufficient emphasis on spoken Irish with no oral examination was described by Daniel O'Rourke, a government deputy and former primary teacher, as 'a grave injustice to the Irish language'.[31]

The availability of textbooks had deteriorated by 1931, the production of material for primary school children being almost non-existent. Recognising this fact the Department of Education reached agreement with the Department

**26** Department of Education, Circular 11/31 to managers, teachers and inspectors on teaching through Irish, D/T, Irish language: development in the schools, NA, S7801. **27** Maurice Moynihan (ed.), *Speeches and statements by Eamon de Valera* (Dublin, 1980), 195. **28** Department of Education, *Rules and regulations for national schools under the Department of Education* (Dublin, 1932), 44. **29** Department of Education, *Notes for teachers*, 2. **30** Department of Education, Circular to inspectors, 4/36. With original emphasis. **31** DD, vol. 83, 27 May 1941, col. 1060.

of Finance to offer special bonuses to authors and translators producing reading material for the seven to eleven years age group in an attempt to encourage a greater volume of publication.[32] Such schemes were relatively successful: the remainder of the 1930s saw a total of between twenty-seven and seventy-five books being published annually by An Gúm, compared with figures as low as twenty-one in 1929 and nineteen in 1930.[33] However, much of what was being produced was judged by contemporaries to be suspect in terms of standard and topic. In 1939 the *Leader*, itself a deeply nationalist newspaper, pointed out that young people were being turned off reading Irish because too many texts discussed the Irish language itself and the saving of it.[34]

One significant problem, that of terminology, had been comprehensively addressed by 1939, with books of terms being available for history, geography, science, music, business and games. However, the more serious problem of standardising Irish was not addressed until the 1940s. In 1943 Dr Johanna Pollak, a Czechoslovakian educationalist,[35] was asked by the government to assess the situation. She incorporated her views on the issue in an unpublished report, *On teaching Irish*, dated May 1943. In her opinion: 'If an agreement could be attained regarding a standard Irish, a great amount of difficulties would probably be overcome.'[36]

An INTO report of the previous year had urged that a body be established to look objectively at the standardisation of spelling and the simplification and standardisation of Irish grammatical forms, implementation of which would significantly benefit both the student and teacher. Examples of the lack of standardisation in school editions of prose texts sanctioned by the Department of Education were given in the INTO report to illustrate the extent of the problem:

1. Varieties of spellings:
   *Gaodhluinn, Gaoluinn.*
   *Gaedhilg, Gaedhilige.*
   *Amárach, amáireach.*
   *imbárach, imbáirerach.*

2. Irregular verbs:
   *níor chuaidh, ní dheachaidh.*
   *Chuala, chualaidh.*

3. Other verb forms:
   *ag fágáil, ag fágaint.*
   *le cloisint, le cluinstin.*

**32** D/Fin., Publication of books in Irish: production of short stories suitable for children, NA, S18/4/31. **33** D/T, Publications in Irish: An Gúm, NA, S9538. **34** *Leader*, Nov. 1939. Quoted in, Bernard Shane, *The emergency: neutral Ireland 1939-45* (Dublin, 1987), 107. **35** Parallels were drawn between linguistic patterns in Ireland and Czechoslovakia, *Irish Press*, 3 Nov. 1944. **36** Dr Johanna Pollak, 'On teaching Irish', 26 May 1943, D/T, Irish language: development in schools, NA, S7801.

4. Rules governing aspirations and eclipses:
   *ar an gcapall, ar an chapall.*
   *Gan chuardach, gan cuardach.*[37]

The lack of qualifications in Irish among primary and secondary teachers was finally addressed successfully. Despite a decision in 1929 to discontinue the annual summer programme for primary school teachers, courses were run intermittently after that date while teachers wishing to engage in private study in Gaeltacht areas were facilitated.[38] In any year between twenty and fifty days could be spent learning Irish, with a concomitant reduction in the number of school days to a minimum of two hundred.[39] To encourage teachers, financial pressure was placed on them to become familiar with the language. It was decided that from June 1932 salary increments would not be paid to teachers who did not possess a certificate of competency in Irish and from June 1935 to those who did not possess a certificate of competency in bilingual instruction. Although this regulation was found to be unlawful by the Supreme Court in 1940 and the government was forced to rescind its decision and provide back pay to those affected, it did influence the actions of teachers before that date.[40]

To enhance the competence of teachers the training colleges were thoroughly Gaelicised. In St Patrick's Training College, Drumcondra, all subjects were taught through Irish, while its student teachers were sent for practice to schools where all standards were taught through the medium of Irish. A similar trend emerged in the other teacher training colleges. The majority of work in the de la Salle Training College in Waterford was carried out through Irish while the Department of Education described the atmosphere of Mary Immaculate Training College in Limerick as 'thoroughly Gaelic'. Progress in the use of Irish at Our Lady of Mercy Training College, Carysfort, was also said to be 'highly satisfactory'. The Department of Education acknowledged this 'marked progress and marked appreciation for the Gaelic tongue, which stands out in bold contrast to the difficulties in this connection which were met with in the past'.[41] This comment referred specifically to Carysfort but could fairly be applied to teacher training in general. However, it would appear that such linguistic diligence was without significant conviction. In a further comment on Carysfort with wider resonance the department stated that:

> The lessons, in their selection and preparation failed to reveal any new inspiration, or any high ideal on the part primary schools could and should play in the Ireland of the future … Even when the language is efficaciously taught, it is somewhat like an electric wire with the current off.[42]

37 INTO, *Inquiry into use of Irish as a medium of instruction* (Dublin, 1942), 63-4.  38 Department of Education, Circular regarding extra personal vacation for teachers attending special summer courses of instruction or study, 9/36.  39 Ibid.  40 T.J. O'Connell, *A history of the INTO: 100 years of progress* (Dublin, 1968), 383-4.  41 Irish and teaching of Irish in training colleges, Department of Education Library, file no. 38290.  42 Ibid.

There was also a move to introduce compulsory Irish language courses and examinations for all students in NUI colleges, irrespective of the subject they were studying. This was particularly successful in University College, Galway (UCG), where from 1930 all students had to show that they were competent in Irish, no student being permitted to sit a university examination without having attended an Irish conversation class for one hour per week during the preceding session. Before a degree could be awarded students also had to pass an oral examination.[43] The University College, Galway, Act, 1929 legislated for the increased use of Irish as a medium of instruction and the provision of favourable entry conditions for Gaeltacht students in return for increased government funding. The UCG (Increase of Grant) Order of 1932 provided for an extra £750 to be granted for the year commencing on 1 April 1931, and an additional £1,500 to be paid in each subsequent year.[44] Among other initiatives, this allowed UCG to establish a demonstration school in Irish as part of the Higher Diploma in Education course.

In University College, Dublin (UCD) a new scheme was initiated in 1932 and the college authorities agreed with the government to provide that no student, irrespective of faculty, should be permitted to present for any degree examination unless they had previously passed an oral examination in Irish. A small group was exempted, including foreign students. Students were also required to attend Irish conversation classes during their first and second years of study. This was given effect by the University College, Dublin, Act, 1934 which, in recognition of UCD's efforts regarding the language, provided £3,000 per year 'for the purposes of the Department of Modern Irish Language and Literature'.[45] Similarly, by the academic year 1940-1 all first year students of University College, Cork, not taking Irish as a subject had to attend an oral Irish class and subsequently pass an oral Irish examination before graduating.

This focus on Irish in the universities had a bearing on Irish in the secondary schools, especially in its use as a medium of instruction. By 1934, 19 per cent of the 314 secondary schools were using Irish as a sole medium of instruction ('A' schools), while 55 per cent were offering bilingual instruction.[46] From 1932 the Department of Education refused to give secondary schools grants for students on their rolls who were not learning Irish, while from 1934 Irish became an obligatory subject for the award of the leaving certificate. Beginning in the school year 1934-5, secondary schools were expected to examine entrants in Irish by means of a written examination. From the school year 1937-8, this was for the first time combined with an oral examination.

A significant and enduring extra-curricular initiative of the 1930s was the organisation of Irish courses for young people in the Gaeltacht. The first official scheme, Sgéim na Roinne, established in 1932, provided an opportunity for children between the ages of eight and twelve years who could speak Irish

**43** NUI, *The National University handbook 1908-32* (Dublin, 1932), 135-38. **44** UCG (Increase of Grant) Order, 1932. **45** UCD Act, 1934. **46** DD, vol. 51, 21 March 1934, col. 1348.

reasonably well and who had the capacity to gain fluency in it, to spend a period of time in the fíor-Ghaeltacht.[47] Two years later, in 1934, the first organised voluntary effort to send children to the Gaeltacht was set up by Coiste na bPáistí. Established in Dublin its aim was to bring English-speaking pupils between the ages of eleven and fourteen years whose parents had insufficient means to the Gaeltacht for a period of at least four weeks during the summer. In the first year eighty children were sent to Irish-speaking areas, increasing to 644 children by 1937.[48] By this time there were branches in Dun Laoghaire, Navan, Tipperary, Limerick and Dundalk.[49]

Coiste na bPáistí received funding from the Department of Education in recognition of the fact that there was 'nothing more beneficial for the revival of Irish than the opportunity for children from the Galltacht to spend some time in areas where Irish is spoken as the ordinary language of the people'.[50] Although the department at first suggested a grant of £3 per student (half the entire cost), it was finally agreed, after objections voiced by the Department of Finance, that for every pound collected by Coiste na bPáistí, the department would contribute another, up to a limit of £1,000 per year, a sum which the Department of Education still felt was too small in the context of the 'work of national significance' being carried out by the coistí.[51]

Other groups, such as Clann na h-Éireann which was formed by a group of Dublin parents anxious that their children should be given every opportunity to learn Irish, also organised courses in the Gaeltacht for schoolchildren, initially bringing a group of pupils to Na Forbacha, Co. Galway, in 1935. By 1939 the Clann had, with the help of a government loan, built Brú na Midhe at Gibstown in Co. Meath, which was officially opened by Eamon de Valera. The Brú was geared towards the ten to sixteen years age group and had accommodation for one hundred children. Each course at the Brú lasted two weeks, attendance at which during school term was considered by the Department of Education as school attendance.

The Gaeltacht schemes reinforced the school-based measures aimed at improving the teaching of Irish and ensuring the revival of the language. However, despite the more practical approach to the revival policy in comparison to what went before, there is no evidence to suggest the policies of the 1930s were more successful in achieving the aim of an Irish-speaking Ireland. At the same time, the greater emphasis on Irish was bound to have a concomitant effect on the education system in general. Contemporaries felt that in particular the use of Irish as a medium of instruction in English-speaking areas was having a negative effect on the standard of education.

47 Páistí sgoile a chur go dtí an Ghaeltacht: sgéimeanna le n-aghaidh seo, 22 June 1936, R/Gael., Grants for children: scholarships to the Gaeltacht, NA, F 7/7/36.  48 D/T, Irish language: summer courses for children, NA, S9280.  49 Ibid.  50 Letter from Department of Education to Department of Finance, 13 Dec. 1937, D/T, Irish language: summer courses for children, NA, S9280.  51 Ibid.

EDUCATIONAL DISADVANTAGE AND THE IRISH LANGUAGE

While some concerns were voiced about the emphasis on Irish in the schools during the late 1920s, it was only from 1930 on that they began to be raised on a consistent basis. In that year *Irish Schools Weekly*, an INTO publication, discussed the issue of disadvantage in relation to the use of Irish as a medium of instruction in schools in English-speaking districts. Mentioning the fact that: 'some people hold that there is a retardation in progress', it stated it was inevitable that pupils' educational achievement would be considerably hampered by the use of a non-vernacular as a teaching medium.[52] John O'Sullivan, the Cumann na nGaedheal Minister for Education, acknowledged that damage could be done to both the education of the child and the language revival movement if Irish was used as a medium of instruction where 'conditions were not present that could ensure success'. He referred in particular to the use of Irish as a medium of instruction in standards higher than infants. In infant classes, however, he was satisfied that the instructions of the National Programme Conference on Primary Instruction ensured educational achievement would not be hindered.[53] However, such an acknowledgement stopped well short of dealing with the issues alluded to in *Irish Schools Weekly*.

Deputy James Dillon, one of the most out-spoken critics of the school-based language policy, warned in the Dáil in 1932 of the growing public opposition to compulsory Irish outside the Gaeltacht. He called on the new minister, Tomás Ó Deirg, to 'get it into his head that [if he thinks] he can dragoon this country into the learning of the Irish language before public opinion is ready for it, he will kill the Irish language absolutely, finally and irrevocably'.[54] In 1934 Dillon, then vice-president of the new Fine Gael party, used terms like 'crime' and 'victimised' to describe the pupil and teacher whom he felt were being coerced into receiving or giving instruction in subjects other than Irish through the medium of Irish:[55]

> You must make it possible to teach Irish and provide education at the same time. It is an intolerable proposition that this whole generation of our people should be denied education in order that they should be used for the purpose of handing on Irish to the generation to come. The thing is grotesque.[56]

It would be easy enough to dismiss Dillon's comments as hyperbole given his at times maverick nature, were it not for the support he received among politicians and academics. Right across the political divide, deputies warned that the compulsory approach to Irish was causing a general resentment among the

---

**52** *Irish Schools Weekly*, 19 April 1930, 488.   **53** DD, vol. 38, 21 May 1931, col. 1685-86. **54** DD, vol. 44, 28 Oct. 1932, col. 746.   **55** DD, vol. 51, 21 March 1934, col. 1577-78.   **56** DD, vol. 61, 24 March 1936, col. 115.

people. There was a feeling developing that children were being sacrificed on the altar of the Irish language to the detriment of their education,[57] and that the policy being sustained by the Department of Education under Fianna Fáil was resulting in people being 'illiterate in two languages'.[58] Indeed the schools based revival policy was being increasingly associated with Fianna Fáil. Two years into office Ó Deirg expressed disappointment at the level of achievement under Cumann na nGaedheal,[59] while in 1936 James Dillon said of Fianna Fáil deputies: 'the more precarious their seats become ... the more daring they are on the subject of compulsory Irish'.[60]

The INTO became increasingly concerned that both pupils and teachers were suffering adversely because of the use of Irish as a medium of instruction. At its annual congress in 1930 the INTO passed a resolution stating that 'the time is now ripe for an educational assessment of the use of Irish as a teaching medium in schools in English-speaking districts'.[61] In 1934 the INTO met with officials of the Department of Education to express its concern. The response of the department was not to review the Irish policy but rather to lighten the teaching load in other subjects, an avenue previously pursued by the department.[62] A circular issued by the department in February 1934 assured teachers that if they failed to cover the entire syllabus in history and geography due to their efforts in Irish, their marks in efficiency would not be affected. This was followed in September 1934 by a *Revised programme of primary instruction* which considerably lightened the curriculum with the explicit aim of promoting Irish. Rural science was omitted as a compulsory subject. In mathematics, algebra and geometry were made optional in one- and two-teacher schools, three teacher mixed schools and 'in all classes taught by women', a provision it was not thought necessary to explain.[63] As a result algebra and geometry were now only taught in 'large boys schools'.[64]

Equally alarmingly, English was no longer compulsory for first standard in primary schools, while it was 'permitted' in infant classes for half an hour each day. At all levels the new programme in English was described as 'less ambitious in scope than that hitherto in operation'.[65] In effect this 'simplification' meant a lowering of standards with books previously used in fourth class now being recommended for sixth class.[66]

It was expected that the revised programme, which remained largely unchanged until 1971,[67] would 'make for more rapid progress and more effec-

57 Shán Ó Cuív, speaking at the annual convention of the A.S.T.(I.); reported in the *Irish Times*, 5 April 1956. 58 Frank MacDermot, DD, vol. 65, 17 Feb. 1937, col. 434. 59 DD, vol. 51, 21 March 1934, col. 1346. 60 DD, vol. 61, 24 March 1936, col. 119. 61 INTO, *Inquiry*, 12. 62 See document dated 20 Nollaig 1948, D/T, Irish language: development in schools, NA, S7801. 63 Department of Education, *Revised programme of primary instruction* (Sept. 1934), 3. 64 *Report of the Department of Education, 1934-35*, 27. 65 Department of Education, *Revised programme of primary instruction*, 3. 66 *Report of the Department of Education, 1934-35*, 21. 67 Áine Hyland and Kenneth Milne, *Irish educational documents* (Naas, 1992), vol. II, 113.

tive work in the teaching of Irish and in the development of teaching through Irish'.[68] It was now clear that the standard of education was being sacrificed and that the concerns expressed by the INTO to the Second National Programme Conference in 1926 that the teaching of history, geography and mathematics would come second in importance to the teaching of Irish, were justified.[69] The situation, described two years earlier in the Dáil by Eamon O'Neill, a Cumann na nGaedheal deputy and a prominent member of the Gaelic League in the early days, now became even more pertinent:

> Is éagcóir ar na leanbhaí sa Ghalltacht gan aon Bhéarla do labhairt leo i scoileanna na naoidheanán, ná aon Bhéarla do mhúineadh dhóibh agus gan aca féin ach Béarla, agus gan ach Béarla á labhairt agus á chlos aca lasmuigh de'n scoil. An fhaid atá an sgéal mar sin sa Ghalltacht, tá na múinteoirí sa Ghaeltacht ag briseadh a gcríodhe ad' iarraidh Béarla do mhúineadh do leanbhaí na Gaeltachta![70]

However, even supporters of the policy who recognised the detrimental effect it was having on the education system simply excused it in terms of a necessary sacrifice.[71]

The report of the Department of Education for the school year 1934-35 expressed satisfaction with the new *Revised programme of primary instruction* (1934), and described it as a 'positive, progressive step'.[72] Inspectors, nevertheless, remained unhappy with the teaching of Irish in infant classes. The problem was that use of Irish was almost entirely restricted to the formal class atmosphere, while children once outside the classroom invariably reverted to English.[73] Two years after the introduction of the new programme Tomás Ó Deirg expressed satisfaction that in places where English and Irish were heard previously, Irish was now the common tongue, while in areas where Irish was seldom heard except among older people, it 'is now being used as the ordinary language of conversation in many homes'.[74] However, the cost of achieving this, even if we accept the accuracy of Ó Deirg's statement, was seen as unnecessarily and unacceptably high by, among others, John O'Sullivan the former Minister for Education.[75]

In 1936 Shán Ó Cuív spoke about the 'repressive' atmosphere of the Irish medium class leading to a slowing of the mental development of pupils and an

---

**68** Department of Education, *Revised programme of primary instruction*, 3. **69** The submission is outlined in INTO, *Report of commission of inquiry into use of Irish as a teaching medium to children whose home language is English* (Dublin, 1942), 10. **70** DD, vol. 44, 28 Oct. 1932, col. 766 (trs: It is unjust not to speak English to infants from English speaking districts, or not to teach them English, when English is the only language they speak and hear outside the schools. While this pertains in the English speaking areas, teachers are breaking their hearts trying to teach English to children from the Gaeltacht). **71** For example, James Hughes, DD, vol. 83, 26 May 1941, col. 1181. **72** *Report of the Department of Education, 1934-35*, 24. **73** Ibid., 25. **74** DD, vol. 61, 24 March 1936, col. 92. **75** DD, vol. 90, 12 May 1943, col. 108.

impaired power to express themselves or to learn.[76] In particular, there was growing concern over evidence suggesting pupils' grasp of numeracy was adversely effected. Thomas O'Connell, leader of the Labour Party 1927-32 and general secretary of the INTO 1916-48, although expressing satisfaction in general with the National Programme Conference, warned as early as 1924 of the dangers to children who had a poor grasp of Irish being taught arithmetic through the medium of Irish. A further problem was the alternating use of Irish and English within the primary sector and between the primary and secondary sectors. For example, a child might start learning arithmetic through Irish in the junior standards of the national school but in the senior standards be taught through English. If the child then proceeded to secondary education it was possible that skills in numeracy would be taught and learned again through Irish. It was hardly unreasonable to claim this resulted in quite an amount of confusion.[77]

Perhaps as a reaction to this growing debate on the policy, the Department of Education issued a circular in March 1936 to school inspectors and managers referring back to circular 11/31 and reiterating: 'the warning it contains against using Irish as a teaching medium in schools or classes where the conditions set out in the circular as necessary for the success of such teaching are not present.'[78] However, calls for an investigation into the effect the policy was having on the attainment of children, the quality of education being received and the position and status of the language were ignored. Such calls were partly deflected through efforts to discredit critics of the policy. The 1934 report of the Department of Education claimed that most critics failed to understand what they were talking about and were unfamiliar with the work of the schools.[79] The *Irish Press* also came to the defence of government policy, claiming that criticism came mostly from 'people who, for one reason or another, have no language but English'.[80] Such statements did a disservice to the critics and ultimately to the language, leading to an increasingly widespread opinion that not only was the policy of instruction in a non-vernacular unsound from an educational point of view, but that it was detrimental to the revival of Irish.[81]

CONCLUSION

It can be safely argued that qualified practical measures were taken in the 1930s to redress the glaring shortfalls of the school-based revival policy evident from the 1920s. The measures taken were qualified in the sense that the wisdom of

**76** Shán Ó Cuív, *The problem of Irish in the schools*, 17.   **77** Charles Fagan (Fine Gael), DD, vol. 74, 23 March 1935, col. 2391. See also INTO, *Inquiry*, 36.   **78** Department of Education, Circular 4/36 to inspectors.   **79** *Report of the Department of Education, 1934-35*, 25.   **80** *Irish Press*, 22 Nov. 1944.   **81** Michael Tierney, DD, vol. 34, 21 May 1930, col. 2181-82; J.A. Costello, DD, vol. 55, 4 April 1935, col. 1979; James Dillon, DD, vol. 66, 31 March 1937, col. 154.

the school-based revival effort in English-speaking areas itself was never questioned, but measures were taken to ensure the education system was better able to cope with the linguistic demands placed upon it. These measures included an emphasis on teacher qualifications, but excluded the introduction of oral Irish examinations. The failure to carry out any scientific analysis into the level of success of the policy, or the effect it was having on the curriculum and the standard of education, despite contemporary calls to do so, perhaps betrayed an unease that such an investigation would have resulted in a largely negative evaluation, as did the INTO investigation of the 1940s. As already noted such a negative evaluation may have been perceived as too high a price given the assumed links between the revival of the language and the survival of the nation.

For similar reasons, criticisms of the school-based revival policy were ignored as were criticisms of other aspects of the revival policy. For example, the government simply disregarded the observation of the Commission of Inquiry into the Civil Service in 1935 that the emphasis on ability in Irish in recruiting staff: 'militated against obtaining an adequate supply of good candidates.'[82]

The schools-based revival policy in the 1930s had a number of clearly negative consequences. It resulted in a narrowing of the curriculum to facilitate the teaching of Irish, while the use of Irish as a medium of instruction in English-speaking areas had the potential to adversely affect both the standard of teaching and the standard of education received by pupils. In particular, it compounded the educational disadvantage of those with high rates of absenteeism or who left school early – two other contemporary influences on educational attainment – and in this context in particular contemporary criticism of the policy as retarding educational development was justified. On the other hand the policy, while failing to achieve its aim of Gaelicising English-speaking areas, did have some success. The numbers capable of understanding written Irish were certainly increased as a result of the policy. It is also clear that despite the absence of oral examinations, pupils were capable of conversing in Irish at some level. Partial proof of this may be taken from the fact that in the period 1924-34 lack of proficiency in oral Irish was cited in only three of the 29 cases where civil servants failed to become established.[83]

However, whatever the written or oral ability in Irish on leaving school, it was soon lost because of the lack of opportunity outside the schools to use Irish. While some initiatives were taken, the failure to promote Irish outside the schools to anything like the extent to which it was promoted within them, placed the schools in the position of being a unique Gaelic and Gaelicising institution within an overwhelmingly English-speaking society. This was not so much proof that the cultural imperative of revival was not shared by the wider society, but rather underpinned the extent to which it was felt that the

**82** *Commission of inquiry into the civil service, 1932-35: interim and final report* (Dublin, n.d.), 104.
**83** Ibid., 170.

schools *alone* could revive the language, an attitude based on the incorrect premise that the schools alone had been responsible for displacing Irish with English in the nineteenth century.

Already during the 1930s, but more so thereafter, it became obvious that the schools were working in isolation; that there were only limited opportunities to use Irish outside of them; and that there was an unfair burden being placed on pupils and teachers in the national effort to revive the language. There is evidence from subsequent decades to suggest that the revival of the language lost its status as a cultural imperative in the minds of the majority of the population, who nevertheless wished to ensure its survival as a peripheral and ceremonial language. It was the 1960s, however, before government policy began to reflect this shift from revival to survival.

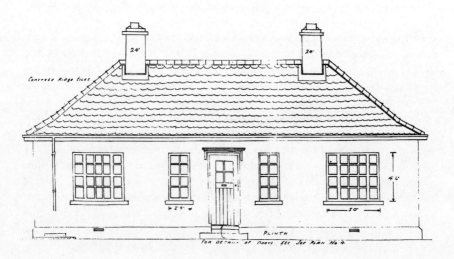

Cottages for labourers: building schemes and the initiation of the purchase scheme in the 1930s

ANNE-MARIE WALSH

# Root them in the land:
# cottage schemes for agricultural labourers

Thousands of sturdy cottages dotted the rural landscape as Eamon de Valera travelled to Dublin, and his seat in government in 1932. Some showed signs of decay, gaps on the roof where slates once lay, and doors eaten by woodworm leading into damp interiors. Nevertheless, most of them were a welcome sight for the agricultural labourer who wandered home after work.

Most of these cottages had been built for the rural labouring classes by successive British governments since 1883. Although they were originally constructed as a form of compensation for the labourer's exclusion from land legislation in the 1880s, many of them had already slipped from his possession. By the time Fianna Fáil entered government some of the cottages were inhabited by gardaí and shopkeepers, a situation which decades of local government control by nationalists had failed to prevent.

This was partly due to a change in the complexion of the rural workforce by 1932. Few labourers were bound to single farming employers, and even fewer to the land. Every year, thousands of rural workers migrated to work on British farms at harvest time. Many others were part-time labourers and were employed in local towns or worked for the county council.

Urban employment disqualified most of these employees from becoming tenants of state-built cottages. In the early 1930s the legislative definition of an agricultural labourer excluded anyone who was not working full-time as a labourer or in a trade or handicraft in a rural area, as well as anyone in possession of more than a quarter acre of land. However, it was very difficult for local government officials to turn away non-labouring families who lived in rundown shacks as cottage applicants when acceptable candidates were often happy with little more than hay in a shed. Few local government board members wanted to associate themselves with the eviction of families who were unlawful tenants of the state-built cottages. Their tendency to turn a blind eye to the varied occupations of cottage tenants went practically unnoticed because it was not a widespread cause of concern among agricultural labourers.

Despite the changing social composition of rural Ireland, Fianna Fáil pressed ahead with a large-scale housing programme in the 1930s which was specifically targeted at agricultural labourers. Although over forty thousand labourers' cottages had been built by 1932, de Valera felt the housing issue had been overlooked and the agricultural labourer should be the main beneficiary of a new building drive. His comrade in government, the Minister for Local Government and Public Health, and Tanaiste, Sean T O'Kelly, agreed with the Taoiseach. 'These abominable housing conditions', said O'Kelly, 'arose because of British administration and from hereditary and economic causes arising out of foreign domination.'[1] However, abominable housing conditions in the 1930s existed mainly in urban centres, while in rural Ireland small farmers often suffered from housing conditions which were far more desperate than those experienced by agricultural labourers.

Fianna Fáil had yet to prove its administration of cottage building schemes could be more successful than the British government had managed. Distaste for foreign domination did not prevent the party's reliance on a body of housing legislation passed at Westminster before independence, which laid out the regulations for cottage building. Although the provisions for the building of labourers' cottages had originally been conceived as a temporary measure, by 1932 this legislation constituted over twenty acts and amendments, and had become known as the labourers' code. However, the existing code did not always ensure that the needs of the rural labourer were met. In 1903 the labourers' acts were described at Westminster as 'a farce and a scandal'. It was said that farmers behaved publicly as sincere friends of the labourer, but were 'privately his sincere good enemies, pulling the ropes the other way and working the oracle against him'.[2] After the introduction of the Local Government Act of 1898 which for the first time gave labourers the vote, they 'became a very worthy class, indeed, to be courted and flattered at election times and wheedled with all sorts of fair promises'.[3] However, most elected representatives on the cottage-building local authorities were farmers who paid the rates which were used to financing these schemes. Therefore, progress was slow.

Hostility towards labourers in local communities was heightened because most labouring families failed to establish strong roots in them due to the uncertainty of work and migration, and they were often seen as an unwelcome minority. Opposition by local farmers to the implementation of the first labourers' act in 1883 had led to some violent clashes. In Kilmallock, Co. Limerick, in May 1887 labourers armed with sticks entered the courthouse during a public inquiry and attacked farmers who refused to give up their land. Two farmers were badly beaten.[4] The compulsory purchase orders on farm land for cottage building irritated land owners and may indeed have encouraged the image of the labourer as an unnecessary imposition on the land.

The labourers' code laid out the regulations for cottage building even if local politics interfered with the due process of the law. Normally, a committee was appointed to examine the need for new cottages in a locality. It checked

1 DD, vol. 43, 8 July 1932, col. 513.   2 *Hansard's Parliamentary Debates*, vol. 126, 3 August 1906, col. 1212-3.   3 Daniel Desmond, Sheehan, *Ireland since Parnell* (1921), 176.   4 *Cork Examiner*, 4 May 1887.

out possible sites in the area and formed a list of potential candidates for cottages. After this, a public inquiry was held where labourers made known their interest in a new cottage and were questioned by a housing inspector from the Department of Local Government and Public Health, who decided if they were suitable tenants. Landholders, who objected to cottage sites, which were selected on their land, were also represented at the inquiry. Following this, the inspector who held the inquiry drew up the final scheme. The scheme was then confirmed by the Minister for Local Government and Public Health and the cottages advertised in the local newspaper.

In response to criticisms levied at the labourers' acts since 1903, the state decide in 1906 to pay for 36 per cent of the cost of building a cottage but the remainder was still to be met by a charge on the local rates. In this way it was thought local resistance against building cottages could be reduced, and labourers' agitation could be dealt with 'in a final and complete manner'.[5] By 1920, the British government had spent over £9m building 47,966 labourers' cottages. Forty per cent of the cottages were situated in Munster, 36 per cent in Leinster, 19 per cent in Ulster, and five per cent in Connacht. The same year, the Local Government Board in its annual report said it was satisfied that the needs of the agricultural districts had been 'met to a considerable extent'. It recommended that further operations of the labourers' acts should be confined to semi-urban areas.[6]

The building scheme had been so successful that by the 1920s labourers were often better housed than small farmers. The exact state of affairs was revealed by an analysis of the 1926 census figures conducted by the Cumann na nGaedheal government in 1929. This analysis, which compared the housing conditions of labourers and small farmers, suggested that the labourers' acts had made a significant difference in the standard of housing for married agricultural labourers. Almost half of married farmers with one to five acres of land lived in dwellings with one to two rooms compared with just over one fourth of married agricultural labourers. Twenty-two per cent of small farmers of up to ten acres lived in overcrowded conditions compared with just 14 per cent of agricultural labourers.[7] Overcrowding was particularly bad for small farmers in the west of the country. In Mayo, 43.7 per cent of labourers lived in houses of one to two rooms, compared with 63.8 per cent of farmers, with one to five acres and 50.3 per cent of farmers of five to ten acres.[8]

Although the Cumann na nGaedheal government was encumbered by high construction costs during its term in office, there was a considerable amount of building undertaken around the country during the 1920s. Approximately fourteen thousand houses were built for small holders in the congested districts and for urban artisans with the help of government subsidy between 1922 and

**5** *Hansard*, op. cit., 28 May 1906, vol. 158, col. 107. **6** *Report of the Local Government Board, 1919-20*, lxxvii-lxxix. **7** *Preliminary Analysis*, 1926 Census, vol. 4, Statistics Branch, Department of Industry and Commerce, August 1929, 23. **8** Ibid., 24.

1929.[9] Following the analysis of the census in 1929, Cumann na nGaedheal made a number of significant improvements to the labourers' code before leaving office to facilitate an enhanced building programme.


FIANNA FÁIL'S BUILDING PROGRAMME

Despite the efforts of Cumann na nGaedheal, housing was an issue which de Valera used to increase his party's electoral appeal, particularly to those groups who would traditionally vote Labour. If Fianna Fáil was to succeed with its programme of constitutional change, which was one of the main reasons for the party's decision to enter the Free State Dáil in 1927, it could not allow the Labour Party to become a significant opposition party.

De Valera's anxiety regarding Labour's potential during this time was evident in a letter to an Irish-American confidante:

> [It is] vital that the Free State be shaken at the next election, for if an opportunity be given it to consolidate itself further as an institution, if the present Free State members are replaced by farmers and labourers to other class interests, the national interest as a whole will be submerged in the clashing of the rival economic groups. It seems to be a case of now or never – at least in our time.

Housing would be used as a safeguard to keep rural class agitation from the political arena.[10]

However, Fianna Fáil's commitment to cottage building and purchase schemes cannot be wholly explained as political expediency. For de Valera, the labourer epitomised the cultural and economic values of a rural idyll. But the idyll was tarnished by poverty, poor health and housing conditions. The resulting high levels of emigration caused uneasiness in government circles. It was felt that a cottage and small plot at a low rent would provide the labourer with a mainstay at all times and root him in Ireland. It was not envisioned that this would lead to a luxurious live-style. De Valera recommended that the Irishman

> give up the idea of having around him the cushions and all the rest that a servant in the mansion might have, and the various things that might come from the table of the lord – If a man makes up his mind to go out into a cottage – he had to make up his mind to put up with the frugal fare of that cottage.[11]

---

**9** *Statistical Abstract*, 1931, t. 87, p. 94 quoted in, J.J. Lee, *Ireland 1912-1985, Politics and society* (Cambridge, 1989), 125. **10** Cronin, Sean, *The McGarrity papers* (Tralee, 1972), 141. **11** 29 April 1932, Maurice Moynihan (ed.), *Speeches and statements by Eamon de Valera* (Dublin, 1980), 154-5 and 227.

When Fianna Fáil came to power in 1932 it increased the government subsidy for cottage building considerably from 36 to 60 per cent of the authorities' loan repayments, under the Housing (Financial and Miscellaneous Provisions) Act. The Department of Local Government and Public Health, which was responsible for cottage building, maintained that new sanitary housing would also provide protection from the scourge of tuberculosis (see pp. 67-82 below) and promote healthy living conditions. This would cause a reduction in the need for sanatoria, public hospitals and mental homes. Tuberculosis sufferers together with families living in one-roomed dwellings and those living in houses declared to be unfit for human habitation were given preference when cottages were distributed under the same act of 1932. At the Fianna Fáil Ard-Fheis in November 1932 de Valera promised forty thousand new houses, which would 'supply the housing needs of the people' within five to six years.[12]

De Valera's empathy with the smallholder, and an economic philosophy which discredited British market values had been evident before this. Together with Sean Lemass he was a signatory to a minority report of the Committee on Wheat Growing in 1928, which argued that external competition had not been beneficial to the country. Ireland, they claimed, had suffered from a population decline that had been more rapid than that witnessed in any other country in the past eighty years; labour-intensive tillage, according to them, would improve agriculture and 'employ more fully the persons at present engaged in the industry, and help to retain them on the land'.[13] They did accept, however, that this would not necessarily result in an increase in the number of people employed in agriculture.

Fianna Fáil's attempt to use housing as a device to detract potential emigrants from leaving the grassy shore was not matched by a significant increase in the traditional mainstay of agricultural labour – tillage farming. The government did introduce a number of schemes to promote tillage which indeed increased the acreage under tillage by 11 per cent between 1930 and 1936, but this fell again to 102 per cent of the 1930 level in 1939.[14] At the same time, there were indications that tillage was no longer the main supplier of agricultural employment. In the 1930s agricultural employment fell fastest in Leinster, where there was the greatest national increase in tillage, and slowest in Connacht, where the tillage acreage fell.[15] Nevertheless, the main thrust of Fianna Fáil's rural housing drive continued to aim at the traditional tillage employee, the agricultural labourer. The analysis of the 1926 census had shown that there were 9,307 married agricultural labourers whose families lived in houses of one to two rooms; however, in the same year there were 20,812 married farmers who lived in similar overcrowded conditions.[16]

12 Moynihan, (ed.), *Speeches and Statements*, op. cit., 229. 13 *Reports of the Economic Committee on Wheat Growing and the Question of a Tariff on Flour*, 41. 14 Agricultural Statistics 1927-33 and 1934-56 in, Raymond, Crotty, *Irish agricultural production. Its volume and structure* (Cork, 1966), 9. 15 J.J. Lee, *Ireland 1912-1985*. op. cit., 185-6. 16 *Census 1926*, vol. iv, Housing,

Some boards of health and public assistance acknowledged the poor housing conditions of Irish farmers and a commission of inquiry into the sale of labourers' cottages in 1933 also made reference to the small farmer's disadvantaged position. On 2 May 1936, the chairman of the Meath board expressed 'satisfaction and hope' that the plight of the small farmer would be recognised, and he described the small farmer as 'the salt of the earth'.[17] This did not fall on deaf ears, and subsequently the housing needs of the small farmer did receive some attention from the Fianna Fáil government. Grants for building new cottages covering up to 90 per cent of the mortgage in particularly necessitous cases were made to individuals and public utility societies. As a result, over ten thousand cottages were built by small farmers during the decade using government grants. The 1936 Labourers' Act, which allowed for the sale of cottages to labourers, eased the plight of the small farmer somewhat by extending the definition of an agricultural labourer to include all rural persons working for hire at the time they became tenants even if they currently worked in the local post office, garda station or had other urban employment. A substantial number of small farmers who had been labourers when they first became cottage tenants were now also possible candidates for buying their cottages.

Fianna Fáil's housing scheme was targeted at married labourers and rural workers in permanent employment. For migratory single workers the advantages of a cottage may not have been as obvious as the necessity of employment. For married labourers, however, a cottage was a sheet-anchor when employment was difficult to find. Cottage rents were usually low, between 1s. and 2s. per week, inclusive of rates, and came with a plot of land, between half and one acre, which enabled subsistence in times of economic difficulty.[18]

There is little evidence of a comprehensive national plan for the implementation of the labourers' acts by Fianna Fáil. Building schemes were generally undertaken when local boards of health and public assistance, composed of ten members of each county council, decided there was a housing need in the locality, which could be sustained financially by the rates. The involvement of the local boards had obvious advantages for cottage building. They existed in every Irish county and local officials were often familiar with applicants for cottages and had a good knowledge of the land in their vicinity. However, there were also clear drawbacks. Local government in Ireland has been criticised for 'amateurishness, incompetence, venality and political favouritism'.[19] The fact that local authorities represented the interests of ratepayers, to a large extent consisting of middle to large farmers, meant a lot of potential resistance to building schemes. However, de Valera dealt rigorously with local government when it tried to obstruct schemes. He directed his TDs to 'move after' the local authorities to make them work faster. He also took a strong line with

table 23A, 152.   **17** *Drogheda Independent*, 3 October 1936.   **18** *Annual Report of the Department of Local Government and Public Health, 1933-4*, 129.   **19** Eunan O'Halpin, *City and county management, 1929-1990 – A Retrospective*, 2.

the Department of Local Government and Public Health and criticised departmental 'red tape' which had bound many schemes in the past.[20]

Cottier tenant associations which had sprung up around the country in the early 1930s, local Fianna Fáil cumainn and the party's Labour-partners in government also helped spur the progress of the building programme by pressuring the government into action. With a precarious balance of power on the county councils after the 1934 local elections, when Fianna Fáil and Cumann na nGaedheal achieved an almost even balance of power, it appeared that the implementation of government-sponsored programmes might be difficult However, few opposition party officials were likely to ignore the appeal of cottage schemes at election time.

To speed things up the Department of Local Government and Public Health, based at the Custom House in Dublin, tried to centralise building operations, but the finer detail of the schemes remained heavily influenced by local authorities. The department's greatest asset was its housing inspectors, who travelled around the country to chair public housing inquiries. Petty power struggles, which in some cases may simply have amounted to bureaucratic confusion, led to a developing conflict between local and central authority. Members of the Limerick Board of Health and Public Assistance were made look absolute fools at a housing inquiry, according to its chairman. He complained that the board had not been invited to the local housing inquiry by the department. As a result, the public were not made aware that the board had money to build fifty cottages, which were urgently needed.[21]

The Minister for Local Government and Public Health, Sean T. O'Kelly, who had the power to approve or reject a housing scheme, often took an ambiguous approach to de Valera's hard-line attitude to local officialdom. He may not have wished to impinge too much on the powers of the local authorities lest cottage schemes were delayed unnecessarily. In response to a request by the Labour Party leader to expedite a building scheme in Clare, O'Kelly said that the local board was an elected, democratic body with its own rights and powers. He said he liked to give as little direction as possible and objected to being asked to use 'a sort of dictatorial powers'.[22] In other instances, however, when housing was not at issue, O'Kelly was prepared to use his ministerial power. Before the local elections in 1934, he suspended four councils with Fine Gael majorities: South Tipperary, Laois, Kilkenny, and Waterford.

The land chosen to site cottages was a particularly contentious issue during building schemes. Final decisions on the situation of cottages and their tenants were made by the department but the local boards maintained considerable control. Cottage sites were selected by sites committees set up by the local board which often favoured the interest of larger landowners. The lack of local knowledge by the department inspectors meant that very often they relied on

**20** Moynihan, *Speeches and statements*, op. cit., 229. **21** *Limerick Leader*, 30 July 1938. **22** DD, vol. 65, 3 March 1937, col. 1125-6.

the local board for information relating to cottage sites and applicants for housing on them. As a result, the efforts of central government were often retarded by slow and inadequate responses by the local authorities.

In Carlow, it was alleged that the sites committee did not visit sites selected for cottages before a public inquiry,[23] and in Limerick in 1939 it seemed that housing needs had not been investigated at all. One official had not attended a local housing inquiry because of heat oppression and another was on holiday. His colleague, who was working there for six months, said he was not yet familiar with the district. Another official felt he had not been given enough time to investigate and another admitted he had never done a complete housing inspection.[24]

A large number of sites were rejected because the stipulations for good cottage land drawn up by some of the boards were often exceptionally high. In Kilkenny these requirements included good land, easy access, good drainage, good aspect, convenient supply of water, economy of fencing, and finally, minimum damage or inconvenience to the occupier and owner.[25] This led to a considerable amount of irritation among landowners who were unwilling to give up their best land for labourers they did not employ. Their objections led to the greatest delays in cottage building. When a compulsory purchase order was made in Tipperary South Riding in May 1935, alternative sites were chosen in 93 per cent of cases by the inspector. Therefore, a second inquiry was held by Mr Frank Murphy, solicitor to the board of health, an appointment which was just one example of a weakened centralised power. Nevertheless not all landholders were successful. Some corresponded with the department for decades before their objection was examined.[26]

Sometimes, the sites selected left the landowner with very little land for his own use. An inordinate amount of cottage sites were selected on the land of small farmers whose housing conditions were, ironically, often worse than those of agricultural labourers. This was possibly due to an overrepresentation of larger farmers on the committees selecting sites. A small farmer, Benjamin Ryan from Newport in Co. Limerick, said that the local sites committee passed over six nearby farms of between thirty-five and eighty-seven acres which had no cottages. He claimed that a man had been situated on his farm who allowed goats to eat his vegetables, owned a ten-acre wood, and had been offered another house. 'God knows', he said, 'it is extremely hard on me to live and keep equal, and I need looking after and giving me a fair do.'[27] A holding of ten acres was selected to site three cottages in one instance.[28]

Some small farmers believed that political influence was used by big farmers so that cottage sites were not taken on their land. In August 1933, Eugene

23 NA, DLGPH, op. cit., Co. Carlow, box 33, 16 September 1936.  24 Ibid., Co. Limerick, box 370, 20 June 1939.  25 Ibid., Co. Kilkenny, box 470.  26 Ibid., Co. Tipperary, box 736.  27 Ibid., Co. Limerick, box 540, 13 May 1937.  28 Ibid., Co. Tipperary, box 737, 6 July 1934.

O'Doherty told the department that ill feeling against two small farmers by the promoter of a scheme was the reason sites were selected on their land. According to O'Doherty, one of the men, Mr Boyle, who was over seventy years of age, made his livelihood selling milk from cattle who grazed on a field he rented from the county council. His own pasturage was said to be less than three acres.[29]

A widow, Eibhlis Bean Ui Shioda from Kilmallock, Co. Limerick, complained that a very large landowner in her village who had a handsome salary and lived several miles from his land used his influence to prevent the acquisition of cottage sites on his acreage. Ui Shioda, who had four children and twenty acres of land, claimed the site selected on her land was the only field suitable for meadowing. Because she was a teacher with a salary she felt she was not listened to at the public inquiry. She said: 'We unfortunate people who have no friends in high quarters cannot work any influence and must submit without any hope of pity to wrongful decisions of the board of health.'[30]

Seamus O'Murchadhta, a department inspector, showed some compassion to complaints like Ui Shioda's and refused to confirm cottage sites on farms under thirty acres. He advocated this as a more admirable approach in a report to the department. O'Murchadhta hinted that the popularity of sites on small farms was not just the result of political manoeuvring. He said that applicants often chose small farms for their cottages because they were nearer the town: 'There is good cause for the attitude when the labourer works in the town.'[31] John O'Donnell a rent collector from Bruree, Co. Limerick, shared O'Murchadhta's insight into the changing social scene in rural Ireland, and asserted that it had become increasingly difficult to get work as a full-time agricultural labourer.[32]

No matter how much they might complain about political corruption, both labourers and farmers used Fianna Fáil's social ideology to get the politicians on their side. By playing the green card, showing loyalty to Fianna Fáil and the Irish language, de Valera's idealism was used for capital gain.[33] The rural workforce mobilised through the cumainn, Fianna Fáil's local associations, which were situated in almost every parish in the republic.

The Tim Hennessy Cumann of Ballysimon in Co. Limerick conducted a vociferous correspondence with the department for at least six years in relation to cottages in his area. Some of the sites already built on, according to J.J. Nolan, the chairman, were 'not worth two pence – any old hole or swamp seems good enough'. He demanded that the Minister intervene and said there was 'regret and dismay at our last meeting and was characterised as mere defence of officialdom, and a direct contradiction of the pledge given at the general election and a complete reversal of your policy on housing'. Nolan enlisted the help of TDs Robert Ryan and Donnacha O'Briain and the Fianna Fáil party

**29** Ibid., Co. Donegal, box 327, 5 August 1933. **30** Ibid., Co. Limerick, box 526, 24 May 1939. **31** Ibid., Co. Tipperary, box 737, 29 April 1934. **32** Ibid., Co. Limerick, box 526, 21 March 1938. **33** Ronan, Fanning, *Independent Ireland* (Dublin, 1983), 106.

headquarters in Dublin to ensure his organisation was not overlooked. The department sent him diplomatic replies to placate him. In 1938, the department said the board had left it to a later date than usual to ascertain whether there were tenants in need of the cottages in his vicinity. In response Nolan threatened to dissolve the cumann if the cottage plots were not handed over for tillage. He complained that the cottage scheme had been undertaken almost two years ago and no building had taken place to date.[34]

In 1938, John O'Donoghue, a cottage applicant from Limerick, wrote to the department stating that he had been living in a condemned house with his wife and eight children for twelve years. He said it was an old mud cabin covered with sheet iron, containing a small room and kitchen, and that he had been looking for a new cottage for twenty-seven years. The Catholic curate had intervened on his behalf with the local board but there was no outcome. O'Donoghue stated that the old Sinn Féin Kilmallock rural district council had done all it could for him, and was in 'no doubt but that only for its abolition before a suitable house in the locality became vacant, or before it could carry out any new housing scheme, I would not be in the position in which I find myself today and would not be troubling you with my complaints'. He added that he had been a member of the Committee of Kilfinane Fianna Fáil Cumann since its inception, and that a great number of his family he 'might mention incidentally' were Gaelic speakers. Another two, he said, were members of An Fainne.[35]

Peadar O'Doinnall, also a Limerick resident, wrote a letter of objection to a site on his land to Donnacha O'Briain, TD. He said he'd been promised land for his services with the IRA West Limerick Brigade, but had never received any so he had purchased his farm. He congratulated O'Briain on his election in 1937, and added somewhat menacingly that he had been 'very lucky'. The department replied that his complaint had been noted. It seems that O'Briain's site was excluded when the other sites in the scheme were confirmed.[36]

Controversy over site selection was not the only issue which delayed building schemes. The amount of compensation to the farmers for cottage sites, which varied considerably throughout the country, was another thorny issue. In 1930, up to £128 was paid per acre in north Co. Dublin while in Wexford, eight years later, an acre could be had at £15.[37] The high transport costs for cottage building, caused by the arbitrary location of selected sites in the countryside, made it more difficult for local boards to estimate the initial cost of building programmes and plan ahead.

It was natural that farmers would be reluctant to give up their land even if adequately compensated, but some landowners' objections seemed contrived. Digby Hussey de Burgh of Dromkeen North, Co. Limerick complained that

34 Op. cit., NA, DLGPH, Co. Limerick, box 526, 11 April 1934 to 9 February 1939. 35 Ibid., box 540, 5 March 1938. 36 Ibid., August 1937. 37 *Annual Report of the DLGPH, 1930-1*, 120 and *Annual Report of the DLGPH, 1938-9*, 62.

a cottage site would interfere with his tennis court.[38] A parish priest complained that a cottage would interfere with the view from his hall door and expressed surprise that anyone would apply to situate a site on ecclesiastical property.[39] In Tipperary someone built imposing piers on the land of an adjoining site 'presumably to block a cottage'.[40]

Despite these difficulties 16,526 cottages were built between 31 March 1932 and 31 March 1940, and one-thousand cottage schemes were completed in some areas.[41] It was difficult to maintain a low-cost programme when the cottage sites selected were often situated on land of the highest quality. In 1938, the average cost per cottage exceeded the £300 government subsidy limit in eight counties.[42] The Department of Finance, under Sean MacEntee, was strongly opposed to the expense incurred by government building, as evident in a cabinet memo of November 1937. It stated there was no parallel in any other country to the assistance afforded by the government of the Saorstat for housing and the time had arrived when the burden on the exchequer should be eased.[43]

In spite of their high cost, most of the cottages built were simple in design. They were generally warm and made good use of space although sanitary conditions were poor. In 1946, more than half of farm dwellings valued under £10 did not have an indoor lavatory. For valuations of under £2, which would include the majority of labourers, just 7.4 per cent had an indoor lavatory. Only 3 per cent of farm dwellings with a valuation under £10 had a fixed bath, while for dwellings valued under £4, the figure was just 0.4 per cent.[44] Despite the good intentions of Fianna Fáil, a man who lived in a labourer's cottage all his life said they were generally TB-ridden. He had meat once a week and a dry toilet with no running water, straw beds, and no fuel for fires. His family also suffered from lice, fleas and cockroaches.[45]

Although a lot of time was taken to find good quality sites for cottages there were many complaints about construction details. 'These cottages were designed to a price rather than an ideal', wrote the consultant engineer for Kildare board of health and public assistance, Mr O'Dwyer, to the secretary of the Department of Local Government and Public Health in 1943. In 1940 the secretary of the Limerick Cottage Tenants' Association and Land Settlement Committee, J. Tierney, draw the attention of Sean T. O'Kelly to 'the deplorable jerry building employed at present in the vicinity of Knocklong'. He said that cottage foundations had been badly laid and consisted of 'boulders and stones of large dimensions, with a few cwts weights of concrete scattered through'. He suspected high-handed business by some member of the board because previously

**38** NA, DLGPH, Co. Limerick, box 540, 11 May 1937. **39** Cahir inquiry, 13-14; ibid., Co. Tipperary, box 737, 6 February 1934. **40** Ibid., 29 July 1934. **41** *Annual Report of the DLGPH, 1932-3,* 119 and *Annual Report of the DLGPH, 1939-40,* 64. **42** *Annual Report of the DLGPH, 1938-9,* 63. **43** Op. cit., Department of the Taoiseach, NA, S10341, 9 November 1937. **44** *1946 Census, General Report,* 197 and 199. **45** Letter to the author from Joseph O'Neill, Ivy Cottage, Co. Laois, 4 November 1994.

suspended supervisors and a clerk of works had been reemployed to 'carry out the same old gamble'.[46]

A Fine Gael TD, and medical officer, Dr T.F. O'Higgins, maintained that the building schemes had done more harm than good. His comments, published in the *Drogheda Independent*, concerned the arbitrary nature of building schemes, which led to abuse of the system.[47] He said that during his fifteen years experience in housing he had learned that a large building scheme without a building plan did nearly as much harm as good. He rejected the concept of unlimited housing schemes in which all the cottages built were advertised for together. This created a situation where many applicants would abandon their cottages, or move into shacks to be considered for the new cottages, he claimed. He suggested that housing plans should be drawn up each year based on the reports of housing officials. Then, cottages should be advertised one by one as they became available. In this way, applicants who were best qualified for the cottages would be catered for. He also advocated the repair of cottages above the building of new houses.

In spite of such criticisms, housing conditions improved by over one third in all provinces in the intercensal period 1926 to 1936. The average number of persons per room in rural areas declined from 1.19 in 1926 and 1.08 in 1936 to one person per room in 1946.[48] Traditional variations in housing standards were reversed in the provinces. By 1946 overcrowding was greatest in Ulster and lowest in Munster where most labourers lived. However, the overall rate of improvement in housing conditions between 1936 and 1946 was greatest in Connacht and Ulster although the number of cottages built in these provinces was lower than in the other two.[49] It can be inferred that the market economy, the availability of employment and migration had a larger impact on overcrowding than cottage building. This was acknowledged by the census commissioners in the general report on the 1946 census.

Bad planning by the Fianna Fáil government was clearly revealed by the census figures. There seemed to be very little correlation between local demand for cottages and the numbers built. In counties like Wicklow where the number of labourers actually dropped between 1926 and 1936 some 541 cottages were built between 1932 and 1936. In counties Cavan and Clare, where the number of labourers increased, significantly smaller numbers were build with schemes of ninety and ninety-four cottages respectively in the same years.

THE COTTAGE PURCHASE SCHEME

Rural cottage building did not have a detectable impact on labourer demography despite the wishful thinking of Dáil deputies. Neither did the decision

---

**46** O'Dwyer to DLGPH, NA, DLGPH, Co. Kildare, box 435, 19 Nov. 1943; op. cit., NA, DLGPH, Co. Limerick, box 535, 1 May 1940.   **47** Annual Report of Dr T.F. O'Higgins, Co. Meath, Medical Officer of Health, *Drogheda Independent*, 24 November 1945.   **48** *1946 Census, General Report*, Table 165, 179.   **49** Ibid., Table 169, 182. Overcrowded is defined

taken in 1936 to sell cottages to their tenants further the attempt to keep labourers on the land. Cottage purchase was an idea which had the backing of many Dáil members well into the following decade. In a Dáil speech in 1944, Mr Davin, a Labour party TD, said:

> everybody realises that in the long run the home is the sheet-anchor on which economic defence in adversity rests. If you can ensure tenants of labourers' cottages an interest in their homesteads, you root them in the land; not only do you root them in the land but you give them a source of permanence there. You give them a defence against the temporary economic blizzards which unfortunately blow across their abodes from time to time.[50]

It was an optimistic assessment. Most labourers were hesitant to avail of cottage purchase due to the potential costs involved. They were particularly reluctant to take responsibility for the upkeep of the cottages. During the hard times caused by the economic war with Britain, they preferred to wait for the most favourable terms even though it was in lieu of rent. It was suggested that labourers wanted the same conditions as existed in land purchase schemes since the 1890s whereby farmers' annuities had not exceeded their rent. No doubt, during the depressed conditions of the economic war, many labourers may have found their rent alone was a considerable burden.

Purchase legislation was first advocated to defray labourer demands for land legislation in the 1880s when a rural agitator, Fr Matt Ryan from Tipperary, asked for tenant purchase for labourers after ten years' tenancy.[51] Labourers from Limerick were also favourable towards purchase legislation, according to the Committee on Agricultural Labourers in 1884. At this stage, however, no cottages had been built under the first labourers' act of 1883. The demand for purchase legislation were not taken seriously until the possibility was investigated by Cumann na nGaedheal over forty years later.

There were mixed feelings among the local authorities about such a scheme, and a number of problems were anticipated. As the terms would have to be attractive to labourers this could place an enormous burden on local government finance. Deciding who would shoulder the responsibility for cottage repairs was a major stumbling block. It was also feared that labourers' cottages would pass from the hands of bona fide labourers as a result of a tenant's death, change of occupation, or sale offers by farmers. In 1934 the Department of Local Government and Public Health expressed its dissatisfaction that a purchase scheme might result in the permanent misappropriation of cottages. This

as having more than two people per room. **50** Op. cit., DD, vol. 94, 29 September 1944, col. 2432-4. **51** J. O'Shea, *Priest, politics and society in post-Famine Ireland. A study of Co. Tipperary, 1850-91* (Dublin, 1983), 128.

fear was reiterated by a local rent collector in Limerick: 'When these cottages were given away originally' he said; 'none but genuine labourers were appointed tenants, but their descendants had, owing to change of circumstances to pursue other walks of life to make a living.'[52] The occupations of 610 cottage tenants in south Cork in the early 1930s showed that full-time agricultural labourers were in short supply among the tenants: 109 of the tenants were tradesmen, 171 road workers, 2 teachers, 11 farmers, 18 postmen, and another 128 did not work on the land.[53]

The department had come to realise that the expression 'agricultural labourer' had developed a broad application. It recognised that tenants who did not come within the definition had been for a 'considerable period' in occupation of labourers' cottage. Because this occupancy was at the expense of the state and local authority, the department felt it:

> aggravated the seriousness of the tenant's imposition on the community rather than enhanced his claim for consideration as a prospective purchaser of a labourer's cottage … The incidence of cases of this kind really is the greatest objection to a scheme of sale as it prevents the cottages which have been provided at great expense to both central and local funds being held available for a particular uneconomic class.[54]

It was ironic that 'misappropriation' of the cottages was already possible under a loophole in the 1883 Labourers' Act. Following the death of a labourer, his cottage was to be offered to his successor in title. However, if there was no successor, the cottage could be sold to the landowner on whose land the cottage was sited. If the landowner declined to purchase the cottage, it was deemed to have 'ceased to be required for the purpose of those [Labourers'] Acts' and could pass to any willing tenant. Death, therefore, ensured that cottages would eventually pass from the hands of cottage owners without successors. Resale at the death of the tenant to an agricultural labourer would have prevented this possibility.

The impetus behind the formulation of a purchase scheme came from the local authorities. The general council of county councils passed a resolution in favour of a scheme of sale in 1927. Their action was influenced by dissatisfaction with growing repair bills, and the burden on the rates left over from previous building schemes. Contemporary housing maintenance figures showed that the local authorities were left with a 40.8 per cent loss on the rates after they had received a 21.3 per cent government subsidy and 37.4 per cent from rent receipts.[55]

52 NA, DLGPH, Co. Limerick, box 526, 21 March 1938.   53 Minority Report of John Collins, *Report of the Commission of Inquiry into the Sale of Labourers' Cottages*, 24-25.   54 Memorandum on Proposed Bill for the Sale of Labourers' Cottages and Plots, Department of Local Government and Public Health to the Executive Council, 24 September 1934, Department of the Taoiseach, NA, S8218.   55 *Annual Report of the DLGPH, 1927-8*, ap.

A deputation from the general council visited the minister, and a draft purchase scheme, known as the Kildare draft scheme, was forwarded to the Department of Local Government and Public Health. The scheme was calculated to reduce the local board's expenditure to less than a fourth of its current level. It was determined that the tenants would be liable for the burden of repairs and that purchase annuities would be calculated at 75 per cent of the rent. These provisions were considered very harsh by labour organisations around the country.

Cottier tenant associations organised meetings and angry speeches were made by Labour party members and agricultural labourers in opposition to the Kildare scheme. It was felt that the authorities had used the purchase issue for their own financial advantage. At a cottier tenants meeting in Limerick the Kildare draft scheme was described as a: 'departmental red herring drawn across the path of purchase.' Patrick Clancy, a Labour TD, attending a conference at Pallas Green organised by the Cottage Tenants' Association in Co. Limerick, told the labourers to use their votes to show the government their attitude 'to the terrible attempts they were making to keep the cottage tenants in slavery and to prevent them from becoming the owners of their homes.' Edward Mansfield, chairman of the association, complained that the burden of repairs was a 'liability growing with the age of the cottages,' and pointed out that the agricultural grant had been increased recently to the benefit of the ratepayer. He said that a commission of inquiry representing the interests of cottage tenants should be established to give the cottage purchase issue the attention it deserved.[56]

The tone of other demonstrations was similar. Labourers were told that the government had done little to elevate them from slavery, cottier tenancy or an untenable position as caretakers of their homes for the board of health.[57] Labourers used these meetings as a forum for wider demands and attacks on the farming community. A letter from an agricultural labourer in the *Drogheda Independent* on behalf of his labourer friends, complained about the benefits farmers had received in land legislation over the years, and asked for a couple of acres of land for labourers in return. He said that only then would labourers have 'consideration by men of Christian principles actuated by a desire to deal honestly by their less fortunate fellow countrymen'.[58]

Although they initiated the Kildare draft scheme, the local authorities had mixed feelings about the sale of cottages and were slow to commit themselves to a general purchase scheme. The department sent out a reminder to the secretaries of the boards to respond to a circular which asked for their opinions on the scheme but by January 1930 just six boards in Monaghan, Cavan, Westmeath, Wicklow, Wexford, and Kildare had adopted draft purchase

xxix, 193. **56** Taken from an undated newspaper clipping headed: 'Conference in Pallasgreen in response to the Department's recent circular', found in NA, DLGPH, Co. Limerick. **57** *Drogheda Independent*, 9 February 1929. **58** Op. cit., *Drogheda Independent*, 17 November 1928.

schemes for their county health areas.[59] It seemed likely that some form of nego-
tiation between the interested parties was necessary to formulate a workable
scheme. The demand for purchase did exist among labourers, but on more
favourable terms than the Kildare scheme offered. L. Walsh, a rent collector in
Thomastown, Co. Kilkenny, received numerous representations from tenants
who wanted to purchase.[60] On 2 January 1931, Mr P. Bradley from Cork
County Council noted that labourers in his county had decided not to vote
for any candidate who did not support purchase legislation in the national elections.[61]

Fianna Fáil took up the purchase issue in 1932. A commission of inquiry
into the sale of cottages and plots provided under the labourers' acts was set up
on 20 September that year. In an apparent attempt to influence the labourers'
vote the report of the commission was published prematurely in the *Irish Press*
just before a snap general election in 1933. In the Dáil, General Richard
Mulcahy, TD, referred to this development as a 'great Fianna Fáil swindle'.[62]

The commission went into immense detail on the financing of building
schemes and how a purchase scheme would affect the losses already incurred
by the local authorities, concluding that purchase legislation was feasible. Some
disagreement about the justification for a general scheme existed, but four of
the seven commissioners agreed that the terms farmers had received under land
legislation warranted a purchase scheme that was favourable to labourers. These
commissioners stated that because substantial reductions of at least 50 per cent
were being made in all annuities payable by tenant farmers and others after
Fianna Fáil had stopped passing these payments on to the British Government,
favourable consideration should also be given to the position of existing cottage tenants. They emphasised the fact that the labourers deserved some consideration because their rents had, like the farmers' annuities, been part of the
payments made to the British national debt commissioners by an Saorstat.[63]

Despite this recommendation, the commission did not substantially alter
the terms for cottage tenants from those granted to labourers by the Kildare
scheme. The burden of repairs would still fall on the cottage tenant. Labourers'
annuities would be calculated as 75 per cent of their current rent. Because the
commissioners admitted that the cost of repairs 'will most probably increase
considerably', it was likely that the labourers' actual costs would exceed the
current rent charge. They nevertheless reiterated popular ideas promoted by
local authority officials and members of government, that cottage purchase
would improve the living standards of agricultural labourers and encourage tenants to upgrade and beautify their homes.

John Collins from the Department of Local Government and Public Health
put together a minority report which demonstrated an understanding of the

59 Op. cit., NA, Co. Kilkenny, box 460. 60 Ibid., box, 2 March 1929. 61 Ibid., Co.
Cork, box 531, 2 January 1932. 62 Op. cit., DD, vol. 59, 20 November 1935, 1170. 63
*Commission of Inquiry into the Sale of Cottages and Plots Provided under the Labourers' Acts*, 19.

complexities of the labourer's position regarding purchase legislation. He did not believe that purchase legislation would radically change the standard of living of the agricultural labourer due to wage decreases during the economic war. He doubted there was a widespread demand for purchase among labourers. Where it did exist, he felt, it was made by the wealthiest tenants. He felt that labourers would not be favourable to the liability for repairs without a 50 per cent reduction in the purchase annuity.

A similar line of debate was used by Labour and Fine Gael TDs in the Dáil, who argued that labourers suffered as badly, if not more than farmers, because of the economic war. Opposition to the Kildare purchase scheme by cottier tenant organisations throughout the country five years earlier suggested that labourers would probably not be happy with the purchase provisions envisaged by the commission. Wage levels in the 1930s were not far above the average wage for labourers at the end of the nineteenth century. Wages were as low as 5s. per week in some counties, while the average was not more than 17s. rising to about 20s. in the mid 1930s. In comparison the average council worker was paid over 30s., while dole entitlements of over 15s. for men and 12s. for women were available under certain conditions in the same period. However, poverty among agricultural labourers was alleviated to some extent by the establishment of an Agricultural Wages Board in 1936, which set a minimum average wage of 24s. in 1937. But average food costs of 10s. a week and the adverse impact of the economic war on labourers' income at least partly explain the increase in rent arrears from £34,440 in 1932 to £51,303 in 1937 and a general reluctance to avail of the purchase scheme in the 20 years after the Labourers' Act of 1936.[64]

However, when the Labourers' Act was introduced in 1936 it followed the recommendations of the 1933 commission. The purchase annuity was calculated at 75 per cent of rent, but this could vary with local conditions, such as excessive rent. The minister did not wish to increase the financial burden on the ratepayer because he felt this might inhibit further cottage building.[65] As a concession to the labourer, O'Kelly decided that cottages would be put into tenantable order before they were vested in tenants. The labourer would assume responsibility for repairs thereafter. The purchase provisions were also made available to tenants who were no longer labourers, but had been when they first became tenants of their cottage. O'Kelly further agreed to consider a funding proposition put forward by Mr Murphy TD which asked for a remission in rent for particularly necessitous tenants. This would mean writing off arrears where they were thirty times the weekly rent. Without this provision, Murphy felt purchase schemes would be: 'just as bad as the old Land Acts.'[66]

Despite some opposition from Fianna Fáil TDs, which was effectively dealt with by their chief whip, the Labourers' Act passed into law on 19 June 1936.

**64** *Annual Report of the DLGPH, 1931-2,* 120 and *Annual Report of the DLGPH, 1936-7,* ap. xlix, 352b. **65** Op. cit., DD, vol., 30 November 1938, col. 1259. **66** Op. cit., DD, vol. 62, 12 May 1936, col. 210-22.

Purchase annuities would be paid to the Land Commission by tenants who were not in arrears of rent and it was compulsory for each Board of Health to put all cottages built to date in tenantable order within six months of 31 March 1937. On 19 March 1937 regulations governing procedure, publication and advertisement of purchase schemes, together with a memorandum explaining the act were sent to every board. The boards were responsible for initiating the scheme of sale for their area, which the labourer could avail of voluntarily. The minister's decision was needed to approve or modify a scheme. If put to the Dáil, a resolution could be made to annul a purchase order. Three weeks were given for objections to an order, after which the minister could decide to amend the order. After the general election of July 1937, Fianna Fáil were again reliant on Labour Party support, which they had dispensed with in 1933. Following that, improvements to the 1936 act were introduced. In the Housing and Labourers' Act, 1937 a funded annuity scheme was made available to tenants who had been in arrears as long as they paid their arrears or one-quarter of their rent.

Overall, the take up of the scheme was rather slow, indicating that labourers were less than satisfied with its terms. By the end of September 1943, just 14.5 per cent of 62,592 cottages were vested in their tenants. There were also large differences between the regions where vesting had taken place. In that same year, 918 of the 1,248 cottages built in Cavan had been vested. South Cork, in comparison, had vested just 197 of its 4,535 cottages, and Kildare, 139 of its 3,003 cottages. In Laois, which had an active cottier tenants' association, the purchase provisions had not been used at all by that date, indicating large-scale resistance among tenants.[67] Sales grew slowly thereafter and, by the end of March 1954, 20 per cent of all cottages had been vested. (However, another 32.5 per cent of cottage residents had made applications for vesting.)[68] This slow uptake was probably due to a campaign calling for a reduction of the purchase annuities to 50 per cent of the existing rent. Among the other reasons given for a lack of enthusiasm for the purchase provisions among tenants were: a disinclination to take on the liability for repairs, objection to the period of the purchase annuity, discouraging effect of delay due to title difficulties, and absence of provision to enable tenants to acquire their cottages by payment of lump sums.[69]

Contrary to the hesitance of the labourers, the local authorities demonstrated a general desire to exercise the provisions of the act of 1936 to the fullest possible extent.[70] Sometimes they resorted to scare mongering tenants to participate in purchase schemes. It was reported that a commissioner in Co. Westmeath, Mr P.J. Bartley, had said that a revision of rents would take place if tenants did not purchase their cottages and plots.[71] The desire of ratepayers and the local authorities to rid themselves of their financial burdens was also

67 Op. cit., DD, vol. 94, 29 September 1944, col. 2358-464.  68 *Annual Report of the Department of Local Government, 1953-4.*  69 P.J. Meghen, *Housing in Ireland. Guide to the public services: 1* (Institute of Public Administration, Dublin, 1963), 53.  70 Ibid.  71 Op. cit., DD, vol. 76, 7 June 1939, col. 677.

evident in numerous motions made by the farmers' party, Clann na Talmhan, against rates on roads, mental hospitals, and houses.

After the 1930s attempts to make the purchase of cottages more attractive continued. Near the end of the Second World War, the Labour party introduced two amendments to the 1936 Labourers' Act, with this intent. The amendments proposed to lower the purchase annuity payments from 75 to 50 per cent, introduce a loan repayment period more favourable to tenants, and fix a more favourable interest rate, which was normally 4.75 per cent. It was also proposed that the heir to a cottage need not be resident there at the time of death of the original tenant in order for him to inherit. However, Sean MacEntee, O'Kelly's successor as Minister for Local Government and Public Health, was fanatical about the evils of the expropriation of cottages and both amendments were defeated. William Norton, the Labour leader, once responded to his uncooperative attitude by suggesting that MacEntee 'be locked up and chained'.[72]

The Labour Party had more success in the first inter-party government and a number of concessions were made to the labourer. In March 1951, a departmental circular to the boards announced that 50 per cent purchase annuities were now deemed acceptable, and on 4 June the same year, it was agreed that the period of annuity repayment would be limited to between twenty and thirty years. The 1951 Housing (Amendment) Act gave priority to cottage applications from families in need of accommodation for medical or compassionate reasons.

A change in the government's attitude to the agricultural labourer became apparent from a clause in the 1956 Housing Act which made all members of the working class acceptable applicants for cottages. The dream of tying agricultural labourers to the land had now clearly been abandoned in favour of a social housing policy. When it was drawn to the attention of the Minister for Local Government, M.J. Keyes, who took over from T.J. Murphy in 1949, that members of the defence forces were being provided with cottages, he said it was 'one of the existing anomalies that I hope to have amended'.[73] The changed government attitude was summed up by, Jim Corr, a housing official in South Cork Corporation after the War: 'the definition of who was an agricultural labourer became wider and wider so that the definition eventually became anyone who was in need of housing and could not provide a house from their own resources'.[74]

This change in government policy was a result of the unstoppable decline of the agricultural labouring class, which was chiefly due to the increasing number of tractors. The number of labourers diminished by approximately 70 per cent between 1946 and 1971.[75] One labourer remembers how 'the hard

---

**72** Op. cit., DD, vol. 94, 29 September 1944, col. 2470.   **73** Op. cit., DD, vol. 11, col. 161.
**74** Interview with Jim Corr by the author, November 1994.   **75** P.G. Cox, 'Labour on Irish farms – trends, problems and policies', in Economics and Rural Welfare Research Centre, *The land question; utilisation, acquisition and price: proceedings of conference* (Dublin, 1980), 19.

work had gone out of it at that time. I spent eight years in Birmingham. In the 1940s and 1950s, farm labourers moved about a lot, but most ended up in England, plenty of work building what Hitler had blown down.'[76] A white paper on housing published in January 1948 estimated that 42,781 houses were needed in urban areas, compared with only 18,067 in rural areas.[77] The number of cottages built by 1961 in rural areas exceeded the number of labourers by over one third. The number of cottages vested almost equalled the number of agricultural labourers, although not all of the tenants belonged to the labouring class. A final change in the labourers' code came in the 1966 Housing Act which allowed for the inclusion of newly-built cottages in purchase schemes. All these measures put together clearly attracted tenants, whether labourers or not, to purchase their cottages so that by 31 March 1970, 76,238 cottages had been vested.[78] However, it was clear that at this stage that labourers' housing was no longer an important political issue.

De Valera's Ireland never became the home of people who valued material wealth only as the basis of 'right living'; who were satisfied with frugal comfort and devoted their leisure time to things of the spirit. However, Fianna Fáil's revival of the labourers' code meant that the cosy homesteads of de Valera's Ireland were not entirely wishful thinking.[79]

The success of the large-scale building programme facilitated by the resurrection of this body of legislation is most obvious in the short term. The main achievement of Fianna Fáil's building programme was a considerable improvement in living conditions for agricultural labourers. Cottage schemes did provide a sheet-anchor in economic adversity, but they did not root the labourer in Irish ground. The rapid depletion of the labouring class after the 1930s showed that cottages alone could not withstand the forces of emigration, mechanisation and urbanisation. They had little effect on the agricultural system in Ireland, apart from providing a ready supply of labour for farmers at harvest times. Nevertheless, the agricultural labouring classes may have diminished more rapidly if almost eighty thousand state-subsidised cottages had not been built by 1964.

Although providing labourers with decent housing and temporarily stemming the decline in their numbers, cottage schemes were a cause of irritation to landowners and local authorities, and may have contributed to a hostile attitude towards agricultural labour. However, class relations in the Irish countryside remained relatively peaceful. As a labourer working in the 1940s put it: 'the farmers in my area were not too bad, but the big farmer was inclined to look down on us. Anyway, it never worried us because we knew that we would finish up with as much land as them, in the cemetery.'[80]

**76** Pat O'Sullivan, Cork labourer, letter to the author, November 1994. **77** Meghen, *Housing in Ireland*, op. cit., 63. **78** *Annual Report of the Department of Local Government, 1967-71*, 48. **79** *Irish Press*, 18 March 1943. **80** Letter from Pat O'Sullivan to the author, November 1994.

# Dr Dorothy Price and the elimination of childhood tuberculosis[1]

> It is probably inevitable that a small nation which has just achieved self-government should be preoccupied with its own affairs to the almost total exclusion of what is happening in the rest of the world.[2]

This view of 1930s Ireland has pervaded and it is presumed that few international influences impinged on Irish life. However, public health and, more particularly, the fight against childhood tuberculosis, benefited greatly from research conducted during the 1930s by one of the lesser-known Irish doctors. Much of the credit for the elimination of Tuberculosis (TB) in Ireland has gone to Dr Noel Browne, Minister for Health between 1948 and 1951.[3] Yet, there has been a tendency to exaggerate his role. The groundbreaking efforts to prevent TB in children prior to his term in office have been largely neglected. This required a vaccination known as BCG (Bacillus Calmette-Guerin, named after the two French scientists who discovered its properties). It was already being used on the Continent in the 1920s, and although its introduction to Ireland in the 1930s encountered much opposition, the fact that it predates its introduction in the UK illustrates an openness not generally perceived as characteristic of the period.

This lack of awareness of the outside influences on medical practice in Ireland can be explained by the limited attention public health has received from historians until recently. With the exception of brief biographies by Coakley and Lyons[4] we know very little about public health professionals in

---

1 My thanks to the following for their help in the preparation of this paper: Dr Joost Augusteijn, Dr John Cowell, Dr H.E. Counihan, Professor Mary E. Daly, Dr Pearl Dunleavy, Professor J.B. Lyons, Robert Mills (librarian, Royal College of Physicians), Mary O'Doherty (archivist, Royal College of Surgeons) and Dr Barbara Stokes. 2 F.S.L. Lyons, *Ireland since the famine* (London, 1973), 550. 3 Dr Noel Browne's controversial time in office and his efforts to combat tuberculosis in Ireland in the face of resistance and apathy are recounted in his autobiography *Against the tide* (Dublin, 1987). His description of events has been criticised since; cf. James Deeny, 'Towards balancing a distorted view', *Irish Medical Journal*, vol. 80, viii (August 1987). 4 Davis Coakley, *Irish masters of medicine* (Dublin, 1992); J.B. Lyons, *Brief lives of Irish doctors* (Dublin, 1978).

the twentieth century. Even less is written about the treatment of TB before the tenure of Noel Browne. The autobiography of Dr James Deeny, who was very interested in tuberculosis and published widely on the subject, fails to mention the introduction of BCG in the 1930s. Instead he concentrates on his activities as Chief Medical Officer in the newly formed Department of Health in the 1940s and 1950s.[5] This paper will try to address this gap by analysing the impact of the BCG vaccination campaign of Dr Dorothy Stopford Price.

### CAREER OF DR DOROTHY STOPFORD-PRICE

Born in 1890, Dorothy Stopford was the third child of Constance and Jemmett Stopford, a Dublin accountant. Her maternal grandfather, Evory Kennedy, was master of the Rotunda Lying-in Hospital.[6] Her aunt was the famous historian Alice Stopford-Green. Stopford's early upbringing in Ireland was comfortable with a governess brought over from Britain to educate the young Stopfords. However, when her father died from typhoid fever in 1902 the family moved to London to live with relatives. As a foundation scholarship student at the newly established St Paul's Girls' School in London, Dorothy Stopford bene-fited from the progressive atmosphere there. Dr Barbara Stokes, later a col-league of hers at St Ultan's Hospital for Infants and at the Royal City of Dublin Hospital, Baggot St, Dublin, was also a student at St Paul's. She recalled that the students were not encouraged to think about whether they would have a job or not but 'what kind' of a job they would seek.[7] At school Stopford's 'steady enthusiasm for social work' was noted.[8] After school Stopford worked

5 James, Deeny, *To cure and to care* (Dublin, 1994). See also James Deeny, *The end of an epi-demic. Essays in Irish public health 1935-65* (Dublin, 1995). 6 Material on Dr Price (1890-1954) is available in the following: Liam Price (ed.), *Dr Dorothy Price. An account of twenty years' fight against tuberculosis in Ireland* (Oxford University Press, for private circulation only, 1957); my thanks to Pauric Dempsey for locating this book for me in the Royal Irish Aca-demy; Dorothy Price Papers, NLI, ms. 15,343; Correspondence of the Crowley family of Kilbrittain, Co. Cork, NLI, Accession 4767; St Ultan's Papers in St Ultan's Archives, Royal College of Physicians Archives; Sarah, Prichard, 'Dorothy Stopford Price and the Control of Tuberculosis in Dublin' in Alexandra College Archives (I am grateful to the author for permission to cite this excellent essay and Anne O'Connor for alerting me to it); T.G.M., 'In Memoriam. Dorothy Price M.D.', *Irish Journal of Medical Science* (March 1954), 95 (cour-tesy of Royal College Surgeons Archives); H.E., Counihan, 'In Memoriam for Dr Price', *Journal of the Irish Medical Association* (March 1954), 72, 84; *British Medical Journal* 6 (March 1954); *Lancet*, 13 (March 1954); Kirkpatrick Biographical Archive, Royal College of Phy-sicians Archives; *Irish Times*, 8 Jan. 1925, 5 Oct. 1951; J.B. Lyons, *Brief lives of Irish doctors* (Dublin 1978), 160-1; Leon Ó Broin, *Protestant Nationalists in revolutionary Ireland. The Stopford connection* (Dublin, 1985); Davis Coakley, *Baggot Street. A short history of the Royal City of Dublin Hospital* (Dublin, 1995). 7 Interview with Dr Barbara Stokes, Nov. 1995. 8 Test-imonial of Dorothy Stopford by Frances Gray, St Paul's, 25 Apr. 1911, NLI, ms. 15,343(1).

with the Charitable Organization Society, which provided social services in London and she hoped to become an almoner (social worker). Although passing the entrance exam for Regent St Polytechnic, she returned to Dublin to begin her medical studies in TCD in 1916. At twenty-five years of age she entered Trinity with 'flying colours in oral Euclid – [and] a squeak in Algebra'.[9]

At Trinity she encountered the discriminatory attitude towards women which permeated the profession at the time. The Dublin University Biological Association for instance refused her membership because they did not admit women. Considering the content of the papers delivered to the society it is not surprising that the Biological Association was unwilling to allow females to become members. In 1912 Mr J. N. Armstrong, in a paper on 'Women's Work and its Relation to the Race', suggested that the

> sudden and dominant importance of the brain in guiding both natural & sexual selection probably marked the advent of men … True women [he continued] display their sex in two long recognised varieties – the Mother, the wealth of the nation, and the Courtesan, the latter varying in her pose according to the taste of the age.

Women who worked were acting contrary to the interests of the race because they bore no children, were willing to take lower wages and therefore deprived mothers of the 'necessities of life'.[10] This superficially economic argument was, in fact, based on views of what was appropriate for females. It was a familiar one at the time and was often used to deprive women of employment.

Dorothy Stopford was particularly keen to get involved in the scientific side of the association. There is an envelope addressed to the secretary of the Women Medical Students' Committee in the Price papers so it is probable that Stopford had assumed this position. Dr Euphran Maxwell, a sister of the historian Constantia who began lecturing in ophthalmology at TCD in 1915, is also mentioned so perhaps the female medical students sought her support in gaining admittance to the Biological Association.[11] Her efforts were to no avail. In 1930 the association decided that women should be excluded from its annual dinner altogether. The association eventually accepted women as full members in 1941.[12] Despite these restrictions she was to get plenty of clinical experience

**9** Dorothy Stopford Letters 1916, NLI, ms. 21,205(4).   **10** General Meeting 15 Feb. 1912, minutes of the Dublin University Biological Association, Mun. Soc. Biol. 1909-55, TCD, Manuscripts Dept.   **11** Dr Euphran Maxwell worked in the Royal Victoria Eye and Ear and Adelaide Hospitals and she was the first opthamologist, male or female, to be appointed to the Meath Hospital in 1918, Peter Gatenby, *Dublin's Meath Hospital* (Dublin, 1996), 94. In 1915 TCD appointed her to the 'recently established Montgomery lectureship in ophthalmology', Kirkpatrick Biographical Archive, Royal College of Physicians, *Lancet*, 12 (June 1915); *British Medical Journal*, 12 (June 1915).   **12** Dorothy Price Papers, NLI, ms. 15,343(1); John Fleetwood, *The history of medicine in Ireland* (Dublin, 1983), 290.

as a student in Trinity during the 1918-19 influenza epidemic. Professor William Boxwell was particularly important in her professional development. Stopford was his clinical clerk for six months in the early 1920s, when he described her as taking 'life seriously' and having a 'shy personality'.[13] His emphasis on the importance of post mortem examinations, later proved useful in her work on TB for which it was vital to ascertain the exact cause of death.[14]

In 1921 after 'trying without success for various posts in Dublin and being quite penniless by this time, ... [she] decided to apply really for the Kilbrittain dispensary, in west Cork'.[15] During her appointment at Kilbrittain dispensary Dr Stopford met Dr Alice Barry[16] who had also worked there and whom she described as 'great on babies'.[17] The local government files reveal that Dr Stopford was very concerned about sanitation in Kilbrittain village. Poor hygiene had led to an outbreak of diphtheria in the village. She argued that with some 'simple reforms' the conditions could be improved.[18]

While working in Kilbrittain she met her first case of TB. Her comments regarding the patient reflect the backward nature of Irish medical research at that time something she later tried to rectify through research and publication:

> [A] woman was dying of pulmonary tuberculosis, and alongside of her in the cottage her nine months old baby was fading away; repeated physical examination revealed no signs in the lungs, and when he died, in puzzled ignorance I certified the death as 'Tuberculosis Diathesis'. [Diathesis is a pathological tendency to get certain diseases.] Quite incorrectly, there is no such thing; but in 1921 we in Ireland were not taught that infants died of miliary tuberculosis, and I for one had not heard of the tuberculin test, although it was discovered in 1907 by von Pirquet.[19]

The latter had published widely on childhood tuberculosis in the 1910s and 1920s and miliary tuberculosis derives its name from the 'little white spots that are found in the human organs attacked by tuberculosis which are very like

---

13 Dr Boxwell 27 March about 1921, Dorothy Price Papers, NLI, ms. 15,343(1). 14 When Dr Price used the BCG vaccine initially on two infants at St Ultan's Hospital one of them died. After a post mortem examination it was revealed that the infant died from a stomach infection, which was unrelated to the vaccine. 15 Quoted in Ó Broin, *Stopford connection*, 173. 16 Dr Alice Barry qualified in 1904 and was closely associated with the Babies' Clubs in Dublin which were organised by the Women's National Health Association (WNHA). William Lawson, 'Infant mortality and the Notification of Births Acts, 1907, 1915', *Journal of the Statistical and Social Inquiry Society of Ireland*, vol. xii, part xcvii, (Oct. 1919) 479-97. Between 1912 and 1929 Dr Barry was in charge of the nine Dublin Babies' Clubs and she became Resident Medical Officer at Peamount which had been established by the WNHA to cater for TB patients, *1929-30 Peamount Sanatorium Annual Report*, 5. Peamount Archives. I am grateful to Frances Carruthers for introducing me to the extensive Peamount Hospital archives. 17 Quoted in Ó Broin, *Stopford connection*, 141. 18 Dorothy Stopford to Bandon Rural District Council 28 Nov. 1921, NA, DELG 6/2. 19 L. Price, *Dr D. Price*, 13.

millet seeds'.[20] During the 1930s Dr Stopford and Dr Barry were to administer the tuberculin test in St Ultan's Hospital in order to ascertain the presence of tuberculosis.

Dr Stopford's nationalist outlook led to her appointment as medical officer to a Cork brigade of the IRA. She mentions that she had instructions from the headquarters of Cumann na mBan to lecture on first aid to the Kilbrittain branch which: 'was closely caught up in the activities of the West Cork Brigade of the IRA and its Flying Column'.[21] A student at Alexandra College, where Dr Price subsequently was appointed as the school doctor, remembered her wearing a man's gold watch given to her by the IRA.[22] She resigned from the Kilbrittain Dispensary in 1923 but over twenty years later she still remembered the 'warm west Cork feeling' and the 'warm hearted spot'.[23] Dr Price's subsequent career was spent primarily in St Ultan's Hospital for infants and Royal City of Dublin Hospital (known as Baggot Street), where in the 1930s she made use of the radiological facilities to survey children who were susceptible to TB. In 1925 Dr Stopford married Liam Price, a barrister and district justice in Co. Wicklow, who published widely on the local history of his native county.[24] In a reflection on the relative status of either profession he would have earned £1,200 a year, while dispensary doctors (who admittedly could also have a private practice) earned £300 a year in the late 1920s.[25] Liam Price wrote that it was 'only after several years' experience in dealing with diseases of infants in St Ultan's that Dorothy commenced to take a special interest in tuberculosis.'[26]

In one of her letters to the Crowley family from Kilbrittain, with whom she had kept contact, she asked if Kilbrittain had seen any more 'Doctoresses, [they are now] as common as pebbles on a beach'.[27] However, this was quite an exaggeration: while the number of female doctors in the Free State doubled from 208 to 430 between 1926 and 1946, they still constituted less than 10 per cent of all medical practitioners.[28] Women physicians were particularly attracted to paediatrics and public health, and both specialities were combined at St Ultan's Hospital. Female doctors capitalised on the increasing interest in public welfare, and were active in Babies' Clubs, which were established in order to cater for the health of children, and to instruct mothers in childcare.[29] By the 1930s, this innovative hospital for infants, which had been established by Dr Kathleen Lynn and Madeline Ffrench-Mullen in 1919, provided female doctors with an institution which encouraged research in the hope of reduc-

**20** George Bancroft, *The conquest of tuberculosis* (London, 1946), 120. **21** Quoted in Ó Broin, *Stopford connection*, 169. **22** *Alexandra College Magazine* (hereafter ACM), June 1926, 53. **23** Dorothy Price to Bridie and Cissie Crowley, 27 Dec. no year, NLI, Accession 4767. **24** I am grateful to Andrew O'Brien for a copy of his unpublished bibliography of Liam Price's articles. **25** J.P. Shanley, 'The state and medicine', *Irish Journal of Medical Science* (May 1929), 191-6. **26** Price, *Dr D. Price*, v. **27** Dorothy Price to Bridie and Cissie Crowley, 27 Dec. no year, NLI, Accession 4767. **28** Free State Census 1926 and 1946. **29** See for example Lawson, 'Infant mortality and the Notification of Births Acts, 1907, 1915'.

ing infant mortality.[30] St Ultan's actively sought to improve the daily lives of children in the newly independent state, and was very open to outside influences. As early as 1922 the hospital's bacteriologist, Miss Jones, visited Berlin to carry out research, establishing a tradition in the hospital of continental research.[31] Dr Price was to enhance that tradition through her tuberculosis and BCG research in Germany and Sweden.

### THE INTRODUCTION OF BCG

The advantages of the BCG vaccine were not universally accepted from the outset, and as a result its introduction was controversial worldwide. Although the vaccine was given successfully to infants in Paris as early as 1923 and Dr Price noted that Professor Wallgren had achieved good results with BCG in a children's hospital in Gothenburg, Sweden in the 1920s,[32] it was not until the 1950s that it was generally accepted by the medical profession. In Northern Ireland BCG vaccination only began in 1949. By the end of 1953 just twenty-two thousand vaccinations had been given, while another twenty-four thousand were administered in 1954. This suggests that Dr Price's use of the vaccine in 1937 was all the more radical.[33]

Why did it take so long for the vaccine to achieve acceptance? Medical historian F.B. Smith has suggested that its acceptance was delayed by 'insularity, ignorance and innuendo.' He reports that the French had adopted the vaccine in 1924, but that 'British doctors dismissed the information and blocked lay attempts to act on it'.[34] British doctors were engaged in a mini Anglo-French war and were instrumental in discouraging New Zealand and Australia from introducing the 'French' vaccine in the 1930s. This resistance within the medical profession was exacerbated by the 'impenetrable' figures and 'gimcrack statistics' presented by Calmette, one of the vaccine's discoverers, to prove its

---

30 Dr Kathleen Lynn had graduated from the Cecilia St Medical School in 1899. After working in Sir Patrick Dun's, the Rotunda, Coombe and Royal Victoria Eye and Ear Hospitals she devoted the rest of her career to St Ultan's and her private practice at Belgrave Road, Rathmines. During the 1916 Rising she was a captain in the Irish Citizen Army (ICA). See Smyth, Hazel, 'Kathleen Lynn M.D., F.R.C.S.I. (1874-1955)', *Dublin Historical Record*, vol. xx, no. 2 (March 1977), 51-7; St Ultan's papers and Kathleen Lynn Diaries in Royal College of Physicians Archives. Madeline Ffrench-Mullen shared the political outlook of Dr Lynn and was a sergeant in the ICA. She acted as the administrator of St Ultan's. R.M. Fox, *The history of the Irish Citizen Army* (Dublin, 1944), 231.   31 Official Minute Book of St Ultan's Hospital 17 Aug. 1922, St Ultan's Archive, Royal College of Physicians.   32 Price, *Dr D. Price*, 3.   33 Emmett Gill, 'Tuberculosis and the Northern Ireland Tuberculosis Authority' (The Queen's University of Belfast MA thesis, 1999). See also, H.G. Calwell, and D.H. Craig, *The white plague in Ulster. A short history of tuberculosis in Northern Ireland* (Belfast 1989), 44.   34 F.B. Smith, *The retreat of tuberculosis 1850-1950* (London, New York and Sydney, 1988), 194-5.

effectiveness. Some of the early sample groups of infants 'disappeared', so it was difficult to calculate mortality rates accurately.[35]

Given the strong connections between British and Irish doctors the determination of the British to dismiss French science delayed Dr Price's work. She believed that tuberculosis was a 'closed book' in Ireland due to 'the fact that doctors in Ireland did not read or visit German-speaking centres, and took everything via England'.[36] For example, in 1933 (when Dr Price was attending post-graduate courses in Germany on childhood TB) Professor William Mervyn Crofton of University College, Dublin declared that BCG was 'beset with dangers' and furthermore, he maintained that it led to mortality. However, he did not provide any evidence for his assertions.[37]

Dr Price studied under Dr Wassen, who had introduced BCG in Sweden, with great success, and was so impressed with his work that she determinedly told him she would 'brandish' his 'decreased mortality figures in the faces of the authorities'.[38] They were worth brandishing. In Gothenburg the death rate for infants declined from 3.4 per thousand between 1921 and 1926 to 0.3 per thousand in 1933.[39] In the same year, the infant mortality figures in Ireland were frightening: the national rate in 1933 was 6.5 per thousand but 12.6 and 8.3 per thousand respectively for Limerick and Dublin County Boroughs. Figures for England and Wales were not much better with an infant mortality rate of 6.4 per thousand.[40] If one compares the proportion of deaths among Scottish males under one year of age caused by TB (55.92 per cent) with their Swedish counterparts (14.78 per cent), then the effect of BCG is clear. The figures for children between the ages of one and four are even more striking with 53.68 per cent for Scotland and 10.61 per cent for Sweden.[41]

Yet as late as 1953 there were still those who doubted the value of BCG. The authors of a new book, *The white plague. Tuberculosis, man and society*, which Dr Price was asked to review, rejected the role of BCG in reducing mortality rates. She felt the book failed to 'make a good case against' the vaccine, while the statistics cited on page 165 actually made its effectiveness quite clear. When BCG was introduced 'tuberculosis mortality in Japan fell from two hundred and eighty per thousand in 1945 to 181 in 1948'.[42] Yet the authors declared: 'this does not prove that BCG played any significant part in the control of the disease for expertise has repeatedly shown that tuberculosis increases during wars and revolutions and recedes rapidly when social conditions return to normal'. Furthermore they argued, in a passage which was highlighted, probably by Dr Price, that 'tuberculosis will recede as it has always done sponta-

---

**35** Smith, *Retreat of TB*, 194, 195, 198, and 209 (note 151).  **36** Price, *Dr D. Price*, 3.  **37** Smith, *Retreat of TB*, 200.  **38** Price, *Dr D. Price*, xi, 6, 26.  **39** Ibid., 15.  **40** *Annual Report of the Dept. of Local Government and Public Health 1933-34*, 67.  **41** J.B. McDougall, 'The incidence of tuberculosis in different countries', Deeny papers, Tuberculosis box, Royal College of Surgeons, Archives.  **42** Jean and Rene Dubos, *The white plague*. op. cit., 165. Dr Price's notes are in the Royal College of Surgeons' (RCSI) copy of the book.

neously when life has become easier and happier'.[43] These social explanations, while partially accurate, provided yet another barrier to the introduction of BCG.

BCG IN IRELAND

The medical care of infants was not given a high priority in Ireland in the first half of this century. The scientific approach in medicine was relatively new and there was still much research to be done particularly in paediatric medicine. Dr Price's investigations into childhood tuberculosis became her 'life work'. Not one to depend on tradition or old wives' tales 'she tested everything out for herself in a thoroughly critical scientific spirit'. The resistance that the application of new knowledge encountered led her at one stage to declare: 'the blood stream does not obey nuns' rules' when trying to explain how children infected each other in hospital.[44] At this time it was not uncommon for healthy children to walk through tuberculosis wards in Irish hospitals despite the risk of infection.[45]

Dr Price's approach to TB was influenced by a number of other Irish doctors. Dr Katherine Maguire's work at St Ultan's[46] had a powerful effect. It 'was from Dr Katherine Maguire that I learnt to take an interest in clinical observations; or rather renewed an interest inculcated in my student days by Professor William Boxwell.' In a wonderful vignette she described learning from Dr Maguire:

> For about nine years I had imbibed wisdom from her in St Ultan's Hospital, making a point of doing her round with her, and she would pause at the last cot, with the baby clutching her fingers whilst she drifted off into a very interesting discourse, drawing on her great experience and her wealth of reading. She was a very clever woman and Sister Mulligan and I enjoyed these bedside talks, when she would range far and wide … Dr Maguire encouraged any never-so-feeble evidences of an enquiring

43 Dubos, *The white plague*, RCSI copy, 165 and 167.   44 Price, *Dr D. Price*, v-vi, 3.   45 Information courtesy of Professor J.B. Lyons.   46 Dr Katherine Maguire graduated in first place in her final medical examinations at the Royal University of Ireland in 1891 and was one of the first female students admitted to the Adelaide. She had a private practice in Mount St and later in Merrion Square in Dublin. Noted for her involvement in social work; her paper in 1898 to the Alexandra College Guild on 'Social Conditions of the Dublin Poor' motivated the guild to establish model tenement houses, Kirkpatrick Biographical Archive in Royal College of Physicians Archives; *British Medical Journal* 22 (Aug. 1931); *Irish Times*, 3 Dec. 1931; ACM June 1898 258-61; Maryann Gianella Valiulis, 'Toward the moral and material improvement of the working classes. The founding of the Alexandra College Guild Tenement Company, Dublin, 1898', *Journal of Urban History*, vol. xxiii, no. 3 (Mar. 1997), 295-314.

mind, and urged one to take trouble to find things out and to read and publish. During her last illness in 1930-1 I carried on her extensive practice for her which indeed she left in my hands in the end. She wrote me frequent and almost indecipherable letters about her patients up to the end. She was very indignant when I said some lady was suffering from Anno Domini.[47]

It is clear from Dr Price's later career that she heeded Dr Maguire's advice to read and publish. As a lecturer on hygiene at Alexandra College since 1893, Dr Maguire was described as an 'exceptionally gifted teacher'.[48] However, she was reticent to promote her work to her fellow professionals. Although a member of the Academy of Medicine, her 'self-effacing disposition did not permit her to speak or to show cases'.[49] Dr Price, however, used these professional meetings to introduce continental research on TB to Irish doctors.

Dr Ella Webb, a former student at Alexandra College, Dublin, who had been medical inspector at St Paul's Girls' School between 1904 and 1923[50] while Dorothy was a student there, was another influence.[51] Dr Price enthused about her work in Dublin: 'she lets me go down and help her in her slum dispensary on Tuesday evenings and shows what simply wonderful things a person can do besides doctoring'. She contrasted Dr Webb with another colleague in St Ultan's: '[Dr Kathleen Lynn was] a lady of an old-fashioned type, if you can imagine the exact reverse of Dr Webb, who, indeed, is much more the Sinn Féin sort, you'd think.'[52] Her enthusiasm for Dr Webb's work was enhanced further when they both worked in the Sunshine Home for Children in Stillorgan, sharing an interest with Katherine Maguire in diseases which were exacerbated by socio-economic deprivation.

Dr Price's interest in tuberculosis can be attributed to her colleague, Dr Nora O'Leary. She recounts how the disease was not foremost in her mind: 'until 1932 when Nora O'Leary came as house-physician to St Ultan's'.[53] Dr O'Leary had a 'very good analytical brain and an inquiring turn of mind', and once they began testing the patients both Dr's Price and O'Leary read as much

**47** Price, *Dr D. Price*, 4-5. **48** *ACM* (January 1893), 38. **49** *British Medical Journal* (August 1931). **50** *ACM* (June 1926), 53. **51** Dr Ella Webb like Dr Maguire graduated with first place in her medical degree from the Royal University of Ireland much to the delight of 'Speranza' of *St Stephen's* (the student magazine of the Catholic University) who declared: 'it was a record to gain it over the heads of so many competitors of the sterner sex, which, until recent years, regarded medicine as exclusively its own ground'. She graduated with her MD in 1906. Her work commitments included the Adelaide, the Stillorgan Children's Sunshine Home (which she helped found) as well as St Ultan's. In 1924 Dr Webb wrote a paper on 'Sunshine and health' for the Alexandra Guild Conference and this interest coincided with her research on rickets, Kirkpatrick Biographical Archive; *Irish Times*, 26 and 27 Aug 1946; *Irish Press*, 26 Aug. 1946; *British Medical Journal* 7 (Sept. 1946); *St Stephen's* (Nov. 1904), 111; ACM (June 1924), 33. **52** Quoted in Ó Broin, *Stopford connection*, 138-9. **53** Price, *Dr D. Price*, 6.

as they could about TB.[54] Dr O'Leary was to travel to Germany with two St
Ultan's patients, who were cured there. Her visit helped immensely as Dr Price
was warmly welcomed in Germany subsequently. She felt that 'Dr O'Leary
must have written to every one and asked them to be nice.'[55] Another influence was Dr Bob Collis who had worked with Professor Wallgren in
Gothenburg.[56] When Dr Collis founded the Irish Paediatric Club in 1933 (it
later became the Irish Paediatric Association), its first meeting was held at Dr
Price's home in 10 Fitzwilliam Place.[57]

As stated earlier the scale of the TB problem in Ireland was enormous.
While the tuberculosis rate in Ireland was declining the Free State still had the
'highest incidence of tuberculosis mortality in young adults among twenty-four
European and North American countries'.[58] Evidence that Irish and Welsh
nurses were 250 per cent more likely to 'develop lesions' than their English
colleagues suggested that Celtic nations seemed to be far more likely to suffer
from the disease.[59] While the tuberculosis death rate continued to decline gradually in the 1930s with the lowest rate ever being recorded in 1938 (1.09 per
thousand), it remained a major killer of young people.[60] This state of affairs was
likely to continue as long as the Irish medical profession remained aloof from
continental research on tuberculosis.

Dr Price played an extremely important role in changing this situation by
gaining experience on the Continent. She completed a postgraduate course in
Bavaria in 1934 where her colleagues were 'mostly Danish, German and Swiss'.[61]
Given the increasing tensions prior to the outbreak of World War Two it was
rare to see English-speaking doctors benefit from continental ideas, particularly
in Germany. Her international experience continued and in the summer of 1935
she represented St Ultan's with Dr Rose O'Doherty in Rome at an International
Hospitals Federation Congress. She inspected Italian hospitals and noted that,
like Ireland, they did little to prevent TB. All of this research and activity ultimately led to the introduction of BCG in 1937 by Dorothy Price.

Given the amount of international scepticism regarding BCG, the need for
clinical testing of the vaccine was paramount in order to convince the medical establishment prior to introducing it in Ireland. As a physician in the Royal
City of Dublin Hospital, Baggot St in the 1930s and 1940s Dr Price was able
to conduct these tests. She also tested healthy students from Colaiste Moibhi,
a Protestant preparatory college for primary teachers. As Medical Officer at

54 Ibid., 3 and 5.  55 Ibid., 11.  56 Ibid., 6.  57 Coakley, *Irish Masters of Medicine*, 325-6.
Coakley believes that Dr Price 'was largely responsible for the elimination of childhood
tuberculosis in Ireland', 326.  58 Annual Reports of the Local Government and Public
Health; see also James Deeny 'Development of Irish Tuberculosis Services', Talk given to
the Royal Academy of Medicine in Ireland 26 Mar 1982, Deeny Papers, Royal College of
Surgeons, Tuberculosis box. There is no reference to Dr Price in his talk.  59 Smith, *Retreat
of TB*, 220-1.  60 *Annual Report of the Dept of Local Government and Public Health 1938-9*, 32.
61 Price, *Dr D. Price*, 6.

the college she 'knew the family and personal history of each pupil' which facilitated her work. Dr Alice Barry who had come to work at Peamount Sanatorium, which was established by the Women's National Health Association to cater for TB patients, also contributed by introducing the tuberculin test, which could diagnose the presence of TB. They actually discovered that contrary to the original diagnosis some of the patients at Peamount were not suffering from TB at all.[62]

A further discovery during these tests indicated that it was vital to locate tuberculosis patients as early as possible to avoid further fatalities. Dr Price noted:

> Our success with the diagnostic employment of tuberculin allowed us further to differentiate between curable and incurable cases; treatment proved most successful in primary lesions, but [was] completely ineffective where the disease had already progressed to a later stage.[63]

She further argued that 'early recognition of the primary infection followed by immediate treatment would do more to lower the death-rate from tuberculosis than perfectly equipped sanatoriums dealing with the established disease'.[64] This waste of sanatorium space could therefore have been prevented by wider use of the tuberculin test, but it was treated with 'scepticism'.

While she was a student at TCD the tuberculin test had been considered to be 'faddy and useless'.[65] In the mid-1930s Price noted:

> some slight interest in the subject [tuberculin testing] was evinced, but in general I do not think anyone regarded it as having any relation to reality and certainly the Department of Health and the local authorities showed no enthusiasm for skin-testing as a public health measure by their TB officers.[66]

None the less, aided by her republican connections and those of St Ultan's, the hospital received funding from the hospitals' sweepstakes which went, in part, towards providing tuberculosis cots.[67] Her efforts to combat the disease did not focus purely on medical research. She was a member of the Irish Clean Milk Society, which sought to prevent infections through milk consumption. However, she was frustrated at the lax attitude towards those who were convicted under the legislation against dirty milk, and people continued to be infected with TB from contaminated milk.[68]

Dr Price's thesis on 'Primary Tuberculosis of the Lungs of Children' was accepted for an MD degree by TCD in 1935 and was subsequently published in the *Irish Journal of Medical Science*. However, her views, though widely

**62** Ibid., 8–9. **63** Dorothy Price, 'The Prevention of Tuberculosis in Infancy', *Irish Journal of Medical Science* (July 1942), 252–5. **64** Price, *Dr D. Price*, 27. **65** Ibid., 12. **66** Ibid., 10. **67** St Ultan's Annual Reports 1930s in St Ultan's Archives. **68** Price, *Dr D. Price*, 7.

endorsed on the Continent, were not immediately accepted by Irish doctors. The *Irish Journal of Medical Science* was not read by many GPs who were the front-line troops in the fight against tuberculosis, but even academics did not take her work on board.

To counteract medical ignorance Dr Price invited Dr Pagel, a childhood tuberculosis expert whom she had befriended on the Continent, to come to Ireland in 1937 to give a talk to the Royal College of Physicians. According to Dr Price his talk 'marked an advance in the development of modern views on tuberculosis among Dublin doctors.' Furthermore, Pagel examined specimens in St Ultan's which provided further illumination for Dr Price, and taught her how to recognise TB. Her published work also brought others in contact with her work on tuberculosis. For example, in 1938 she published a paper in the *British Medical Journal* based on the seventy-eight cases who had received BCG in St Ultan's, and she wrote on the 'Hospital Treatment for Tuberculous Children' for the *Journal of the Irish Free State Medical Union*. This publication was received by all members of the union therefore her views finally reached a wide medical audience. In this article she argued that a provision for paediatric beds should be a priority in the spending of funds allocated towards the elimination of tuberculosis.[69] This would ensure that the disease was treated in its early stages thereby increasing the chances of eliminating it.

As well as medical intransigence she faced the woolly thinking of those whose approach to medicine was not as scientific as her own. Part of her task was changing the perceptions of the medical profession and, according to her husband, her 'work in producing statistical proof of the value of tuberculin testing and of the correctness of the continental views helped to convert the Dublin medical schools'.[70] This was a slow process however, and was not complete until a decade after she conducted her tests in St Ultan's and elsewhere.

Dr Price also took practical steps to combat the disease in Ireland. In 1935, she started a weekly tuberculosis clinic at St Ultan's and by 1936 its TB unit had ten cots. This was however insufficient, as there was a big demand for tuberculosis infant beds.[71] In the same year she was granted permission by the Department of Local Government and Public Health to import the BCG vaccine. It arrived at St Ultan's hospital on 26 January 1937.[72] This made St Ultan's the first hospital in Great Britain and Ireland to use it.[73] As a result of the vaccine St Ultan's drastically reduced its TB mortality rate from 77 per cent to 28 per cent.[74] Between 1933 and 1936 she treated seventy-eight tuberculous patients, sixty of whom died, whereas between 1937 and 1942, 169 were treated and 132 were cured.[75] In 1942 she declared: 'our whole effort is directed towards

**69** Ibid., 17, 22, 24 and 25.   **70** Ibid., 13.   **71** *St Ultan's 50th Annual Report 1968*, 12–13 in, St Ultan's Archives.   **72** Price, *Dr D. Price*, 23–4.   **73** Annual General Meeting of St Ultan's 30 May 1946, Minute Book of the Medical Board of St Ultan's Hospital in St Ultan's Archives.   **74** Price, *Dr D. Price*, 12, 13, 18, and 41.   **75** Price, 'The Prevention of Tuberculosis in Infancy', 252–5.

early diagnosis'.[76] Price wished to inoculate children before they had the chance to contract TB, hence her emphasis on early diagnosis. Poor facilities for paediatrics, which were not a high priority in medicine anyway, retarded her work.[77] She was particularly frustrated by the continued lack of accommodation at St Ultan's. In 1937 she noted: 'our infant hospital is very crowded with pneumonias and gastro-enteritis'. This was, however, not wholly unjustified as the latter was the biggest killer of infants in the hospital throughout the 1930s.[78]

Realising that more space was required in order to implement a full paediatric medical service and to fulfil the need for a fully equipped children's hospital St Ultan's sought to amalgamate with the National Children's Hospital at Harcourt Street. The architect Michael Scott had drawn up plans for the site of a new children's hospital alongside St Ultan's. However, greater powers were at work. The fact that neither of these two hospitals were under the control of the Roman Catholic Church raised some worries in that quarter. In December 1935 St Ultan's received a letter from Dr Byrne, the Roman Catholic archbishop of Dublin. He expressed his fear that 'in such a united institution the faith of Catholic children (who will be 99 per cent of the total treated) would not be safe'.[79] He also outlined his suspicion that sterilisations might take place in the hospital. These objections were passed on to Dr Price, as secretary of the medical board of St Ultan's, by the hospital's administrator, Madeline Ffrench-Mullen.[80] The Roman Catholic Church managed large Dublin hospitals like St Vincent's and the Mater and was keen to control medical activity particularly where it involved children.* St Ultan's plans for extension came to naught and instead a large children's hospital was built in Crumlin with the Church's blessing. The implementation of Price's plans were thus put on hold for a decade, and St Ultan's remained too small to cater for all childhood tuberculosis cases.

Despite this setback, Dr Price continued to promote continental approaches for the elimination of childhood tuberculosis. In March 1939 Professor Wallgren was in England and Dr Price invited him to speak to the Irish Paediatric Club hoping his voice would influence the reluctant government. She wrote: 'childhood Tuberculosis is as yet untouched here by the Government, and when they start to do something I hope that it will be on Gothenburg lines and not on English'. Dr Price wrote to Sean T. O'Kelly, the Minister for Local Government and Public Health, and invited him to Wallgren's talk. He declined. Wallgren visited St Ultan's and his lectures were published in the *Irish*

---

* For a discussion of the Catholic nature of the Free State in the 1930s and the Roman Catholic Church's influence in government activities, see Kieren Mullarkey's and Gillian McIntosh's articles in this collection. **76** Ibid, 254. **77** Price, *Dr D. Price*, 12-13, and 20. **78** Ibid., 19; *St Ultan's Annual Reports*, St Ultan's Archives. **79** Archbishop Byrne to St Ultan's, 20 Dec. 1935, Joint Committee Report St Ultan's Archives. **80** Ffrench-Mullen to Price, 8 Jan. 1936, Joint Committee Report St Ultan's Archives.

*Journal of Medical Science* in 1939.[81] In the same year Dr Price spoke in Belfast on tuberculosis in adolescents and her talk was reported in the national papers. The process of educating both the profession and the public was a long one but dividends were gradually becoming evident. Dr P.F. Fitzpatrick, a regular correspondent of Dr Price and the Cork tuberculosis officer, began 'routine tuberculin testing' in the late 1930s. Meanwhile the physician at Crooksling (the Dublin Corporation Sanatorium) finally forbade infants and children on visits thereby diminishing the risk of infection.[82]

FINAL SUCCESS

Dr Price's work was interrupted by World War Two when it was impossible to obtain BCG. However, in 1942 her book *Tuberculosis in childhood* was published which enhanced her 'international reputation' and such was its success that a second edition was published in 1948.[83] Subsequently she was nominated for the World Health Organisation Leon Bernard Prize for contribution to social medicine. After the war her campaign for the treatment of TB was finally successful. The BCG vaccine again became available and records indicate that Dr Wallgren supplied St Ultan's with it three times a week via airmail. Dr Price noted that in Ireland BCG was used exclusively at St Ultan's.[84] By 1946 the TB unit at St Ultan's had finally been extended to thirty cots and Dr Price reported 'remarkable progress in the prevention and cure of tuberculosis in children up to five years'. By the late forties her work was accepted by others working with infants. Dr Alan Browne, the master of the Rotunda between 1960 and 1966, noted:

> O'Donel Browne [master 1947-1952] supported the introduction of BCG infant vaccination as prophylactics against tuberculosis, which was initiated as a public health measure in the Rotunda in 1949, under the supervision of Dr Pearl Dunleavy. It *gradually* [my emphasis] became widely accepted with long term benefits that still prevail in Ireland.[85]

Her work in researching BCG and propagating the results in Ireland paved the way for 'official recognition' of the value of the vaccine from the state. This became clear when the new Minister of Health, Dr Noel Browne, located the new National BCG Centre at St Ultan's in 1949. In a letter to her Crowley

81 Price, Dr D. *Price*, 28-31.   82 Ibid., 31-2.   83 T.G.M., 'In Memoriam. Dorothy Price M.D.', *Irish Journal of Medical Science* (1954), 95.   84 Annual General Meeting of St Ultan's 30 May 1946, Minute Book of the Medical Board of St Ultan's Hospital in, St Ultan's Archives.   85 Alan Browne, 'Mastership in Action at the Rotunda 1945-95', in Alan Browne, E.W. Lillie, Ian Dalrymple, George Henry and Michael Darling (eds.), *Masters, midwives and ladies-in-waiting* (Dublin, 1995), 21-65, 34 and 38.

friends from Kilbrittain, Co. Cork, she mentioned she had been 'trying to push this new BCG vaccination against tuberculosis', and that they were 'lucky' with the new Minister of Health: 'he is a splendid young fellow & doing a lot for tuberculosis'. Despite her appreciation for the new Clann na Poblachta minister she remained committed to the anti-Treaty side as she 'still voted for Dev'.[86] Dr John Cowell, the medical director of the new national BCG scheme, pointed out that 'the energetic work of Dorothy Price … [may be seen] as a landmark in the history of Irish preventative medicine'.[87] The first report of the National BCG Committee stated:

> The initiation of BCG vaccination will always be linked with the name of Dr Dorothy Price. Due to her conviction of the value of this preventive measure and to her individual endeavour sufficient clinical evidence was made available to her in her work at St Ultan's Hospital to warrant the adoption of BCG vaccination on a larger scale in Ireland.[88]

Dr Price's hectic schedule, her many hospital appointments (she was consulting physician to the Royal Hospital for Consumptives in Ireland as well as Baggot St, St Ultan's and Sunshine Home commitments) and the demands of her private practice had caught up with her. In 1939 she got an attack of 'muscular rheumatism', which continued to affect her over the subsequent years. Despite her ill health her enthusiasm never waned. In a letter to Dr Wassen she admitted that she did not obey the doctor's orders to stop work at five o'clock 'but it was worth it to get the BCG across'. Determined to have her methods adopted she reported to Dr Wassen: 'I had the Minister [Dr Noel Browne] here twice & finally persuaded him to do what I wanted.' In 1948 Dr Price said she was looking forward to 'the day when BCG vaccination will be given to all infants (irrespective of contact) at an early age, thus affording protection from nurse, milk, casual contact and unknown source'.[89] That day finally arrived in the 1950s. The nation-wide BCG vaccination programme ensured that one hundred thousand vaccinations were administered by 1955 while the target was half a million.[90] Subsequently the incidence of TB in Ireland was reduced to an absolute minimum.

**86** Dorothy Price to Bridie Crowley, 27 Dec. 1948, NLI, Accession 4767.  **87** *The National BCG Committee St Ultan's Hospital, Dublin, July 1949-50*, 2, in Royal College of Physician's Archives.  **88** Ibid. BCG meetings were held at Dr Price's home in Fitzwilliam Square and her old friend Dr Wassen of Sweden gave free supplies of BCG between July 1949 and August 1950: cf. ibid., 20.  **89** Dorothy Stopford Price, 'The Need for BCG Vaccination in Infants', *Tubercule* Vol. xxx, no. 1 (Jan. 1949), 11-13. Paper read at the conference of the British Tuberculosis Association on 1 July 1948. I am very grateful to Dr Barbara Stokes for giving me a copy of this paper.  **90** James Deeny, *Tuberculosis in Ireland. Report of the National Tuberculosis Survey* (Dublin, 1954), 240 and 254.

CONCLUSION

It is easy to be critical of the human wastage which resulted from the slow acceptance of BCG. However, Ireland was not unique in its tardy attitude to medical research. In 1971 the editor of *Tubercle* remarked in reviewing fifty years of BCG that 'future historians will find the story of BCG vaccination a strange mixture of endeavour, inertia and ineptitude'.[91] By 1950 there was a worldwide acceptance of the value of BCG. Mass vaccination under the auspices of the World Health Organisation (WHO), which had been established in 1948, was begun internationally in the late 1940s and early 1950s.[92] In Ireland the experience gained as a result of Dr Price's endeavours paved the way for a relatively speedy introduction. When vaccination was instituted on a nation-wide basis in Britain in the 1950s as well, some medical staff there benefited from her work when they came to Ireland in order to train.[93] The state-driven BCG campaign in Ireland also benefited from the co-operation it then received from church leaders who gave access to schools and allowed local clergymen to announce the arrival of the vaccination team in the locality. This facilitated the dissemination of information and the ultimate acceptance of BCG by both the profession and the public.[94]

Dr Price's efforts show that while 1930s Ireland appeared increasingly self-obsessed and stagnant there was still room for energetic and determined individuals to make their mark. Her travels abroad, her international reputation as well as the vital part she played in the elimination of childhood TB indicate that the insular Ireland of the popular consciousness is not entirely valid. Furthermore, the focus on church-state relations and the Noel Browne saga have clouded the achievements of lesser known and possibly more quietly effective individuals such as Dr Dorothy Stopford-Price. The state programme of BCG vaccination was part of 1950s and 1960s Ireland, but the crucial process of gaining medical acceptance for the vaccine was begun in the 1930s. Although Dr Price claimed that 'doctoresses' were as common as pebbles on a beach, the ripples of this particular pebble were felt long after her passing in 1954.

91 Smith, *Retreat of TB*, 203.   92 WHO Monograph series, *BCG vaccination. Studies by the WHO TB. Research Office, Copenhagen* (Geneva, 1953), 13, 14 and 29.   93 Interview with Dr John Cowell, Medical Director of BCG Committee in the 1950s, Dec. 1997.   94 In 1952 Dr Price noted that Czechoslovakia introduced mass BCG vaccination in 1950, though in Ireland she thought this would 'take time'. More optimistically she noted that 'the increasing number of vaccinations performed adds to our efficiency and experience; in December 1950, over 18,000 persons had been vaccinated by the committee's vaccination'. In her paper Dr Price also acknowledged the help of 'Dr Noel Browne, who, as Minister for Health, established the National BCG Committee under the auspices of St Ultan's Hospital' and 'Dr Cowell, Medical Director of the Committee, who placed at my disposal his great knowledge of tuberculin tests in Ireland, gained whilst putting through BCG programmes in nearly every county.' Stopford Price, Dorothy, 'A Tuberculin Survey in Ireland', *Irish Journal of Medical Science* (Feb. 1952), 85-91, 88 and 91.

GILLIAN McINTOSH

# Acts of 'national communion': the centenary celebrations for Catholic Emancipation, the forerunnner of the Eucharistic Congress

> Politics and ceremonial are not separate subjects, the one seri-
> ous, the other superficial. Ritual is not the mask of force, but
> is itself a type of power.[1]
>
> David Cannadine

The celebration in Dublin's Phoenix Park, marking the centenary of Catholic Emancipation in 1929, was the first large-scale theatrical and high profile expression of the Free State's identity performed for a domestic and a foreign audience. Smaller celebrations were held throughout the country to mark the centenary, particularly at O'Connell's home in Derrynane, but it was the events in Dublin which the organisers represented as the nation's main commemoration of the centenary. Organised by the Catholic Truth Society on behalf of the Catholic hierarchy it combined the civic and religious expression of the new state. For observers the weight of Ireland's nationalist past and the burden of that past on the present were visibly affecting those present. This was made clear in the official commemorative book:

> They were motionless, overwhelmed by the majesty of the gathering;
> many of them conscious of a still mightier multitude of adorers, the ghosts
> of our fathers who had come, as an eloquent preacher has pictured it, to
> worship the King and to rejoice that their children have no longer to
> keep watch for the redcoat while He holds court.[2]

The centenary of Catholic Emancipation, and the grander Eucharistic Congress which followed it in 1932,[3] can be analysed in an attempt to understand not only the links and bonds within Irish society, north and south, but also their

---

1 David Cannadine, 'Introduction: divine rites of kings', in David Cannadine and Simon Price (eds.), *Rituals of royalty: power and ceremonial in traditional societies* (Cambridge, 1987), 3. 2 *Catholic Emancipation Centenary Record* (Dublin, 1929) 37. 3 For a fuller discussion of the Eucharistic Congress see, Gill McIntosh, *The force of culture: Unionist identities in twentieth century Ireland* (Cork University Press, forthcoming).

inherent tensions and strains, particularly in the North. Both events represented a very distinctive and selective version of life in the Free State, imposing an image of unity (civic and religious) and success upon the society which the organisers sought to represent. Fractures in that image could be exposed however. For instance a writer to the *Belfast Newsletter*, who stated he was a Catholic, was critical of the money spent on the centenary, and argued that it should have been

> more usefully and profitably and more fittingly employed in providing some of the material necessaries [*sic*] of life for those of my unfortunate fellow-countrymen with their wives and children – wretched victims of another kind of 'emancipation' – who in hundreds to-day are almost naked and starving in the Irish Free State.[4]

With this state-building occasion the centenary organisers were self-consciously 'attempting something that had never before been attempted in Ireland'.[5] This was the public identification of the new state with an apparently unified and triumphant Catholicism. Those in charge of the celebrations were, according to the official literature: 'conscious right from the beginning that they were carrying in their hands the reputation of Catholic Ireland: they realised that failure would reflect upon the whole Catholic body'.[6] They were determined that the event would be a success. To that end they reminded the people of the Free State that if the centenary celebration was to be executed properly it would be expensive. As part of the funding of the occasion all participants were obliged to buy and wear the specially created centenary badge. The public were encouraged in addition to buy the advance programme and the commemorative book (see pp 11-28 above); the latter was highlighted and publicised as a unique publication, reflecting in some ways the organisers' feelings about the uniqueness of this centenary celebration: 'it will not be reprinted, and the value of each copy will thus be likely to become enhanced as a rare book.'[7]

By the late 1920s the Free State was beginning to settle into a distinctive rhythm of its own, its character being moulded by the men who had fought for an independent republic and were left to carve a future and articulate an identity for the infant state. After the perceived nationalist failure surrounding the proceedings of the Boundary Commission, the centenary provided an opportunity to articulate such an identity. O'Connell, the central figure of the centenary, was the ideal symbol for constitutional nationalists in Ireland in 1929, a Catholic champion recognised as 'one who roused the people from a state of

---

4 *Belfast Newsletter*, 25 June 1929.   5 *Catholic Emancipation Centenary Record* , 9.   6 Ibid. The organisers were led by the Catholic Truth Society, which was invited by the Irish archbishops and bishops in October 1926 to organise the event.   7 *Centenary of Catholic Emancipation, Advance Programme*, 39.

political and social servitude and made them realise that they were an ancient and noble nation' through constitutional means.[8] Against the background of civil strife in the early years of the state's life and the renewed activity of the IRA at the end of the 1920s this emphasis on constitutionality comes as little surprise.

Attended by 'the clergy, the representatives of the state, the governor-general, the President of the Executive Council, the parties of Government, the universities, civic administration, the professions, commerce and trade',[9] the centenary of Catholic Emancipation provided the state's political and religious leaders with the opportunity to project the image of the Free State which they desired. That image was of a Catholic state, historically rooted, now 'freed' from English rule and confident in itself and its future. Importantly this ritual (and that which followed it in 1932) allowed the powerful and the elite in the Free State (in particular political leaders and the hierarchy of the Catholic Church) to legitimise their position in southern society by providing them with star billing in this state building performance in view of the public at large. With this in mind it is interesting to note the prominent presence of de Valera and by extension Fianna Fáil in the 1929 proceedings only two years after they had entered the Dáil. The desire to associate themselves with the emancipation of Catholics was apparently sufficiently strong to make them accept the leading role of Cumann na nGaedheal and the governor-general in the proceedings. This legitimisation by the political and religious elite was achieved both in person in the Phoenix Park and also through the extensive press coverage, which monitored the week's events, excited interest in the centenary, and thus extended its scope. The centenary ceremonies, which included a series of lectures,[10] were also put on the air by the Dublin Broadcasting Service, although that would have been to a significantly smaller (and more elite) audience.[11] In general, however, both the 1929 and the 1932 rituals provided the public with the opportunity to express their approval of the new state in a high profile manner and, in a symbolic mirror, to be presented with an image of

---

8 'In O'Connell's Day. When will Northern Ireland see its new deliverer?', *Irish News*, 18 June 1929. 9 *Cork Examiner*, 24 June 1929. 10 The lectures were the following: 19 June 1929: 'St Patrick's Apostleship', J.M. O'Sullivan, Minister for Education; 'The Church of St Patrick', Rev. Myles V. Ronan. 20 June 1929: 'The Elizabethan persecution', Rev. P.J. Gannon; 'The Cromwellian persecution', Louis Walsh, District Justice. 21 June 1929: 'Pre-Emancipation Catholic Associations', Rev. P. Canon Monaghan; 'An teanga agus an creideamh', An t-Athair Séamus Mac Leanacháin; 'The Emancipation struggle', Rev. A.H. Ryan (QUB); 'The Irish Language and the faith', Rev. Clenaghan: *Catholic Emancipation Centenary Record*, 12; *Irish News*, 15 June 1929. 11 The broadcast of the 1929 event was the forerunner in broadcasting terms to the 1932 Congress: 'There had been one experience of the same sort, but on a smaller scale, when the centenary of Catholic Emancipation was celebrated in 1929 and Clandillon himself did a remarkable commentary on the celebrations, identifying everybody present without the help of a programme and talking for hours under a blazing sun', Maurice Gorman, *Forty years of Irish broadcasting* (Dublin, 1967), 84.

themselves. De Valera's Fianna Fáil administration would develop this self-image further by enshrining the Catholic Church in the 1937 constitution.[12] As Cardinal MacRory declared, the 'occasion was, indeed, nothing less than the celebration of the re-birth of a nation ... everything imaginable was done to ensure that the celebrations would be worthy of the Catholic name and worthy, too, of Catholic Ireland'.[13]

This 1929 ritual affirmed that the Free State had survived, despite the multiple traumas of the early 1920s – the War of Independence, the Treaty split, the Civil War and the Boundary Commission.

> The presence of the governor-general, the President of the Executive Council, the Leaders of the Opposition and of the Labour Party, of outstanding Catholics from the North-East, indicated, not indeed any weakening in political loyalties, but a strengthening of Catholic charity; the assuagement of bitterness born in civil strife, and the probability that a sad chapter in our history has been closed.[14]

The Rev. A.M. Crofts, speaking at the Mansion House, articulated this very point: 'The Irish people have survived, and once again have power to shape the destinies of this nation.'[15]

Not surprisingly this theme (the possibility of unity among previously warring Irish factions) was to re-emerge often in the events surrounding the centenary. Although primarily referring to pro- and anti-Treaty factions, it is important, in this context, to note that the official centenary publication also drew attention to the presence of 'outstanding Catholics' from Northern Ireland. Their plight was to be a dominant feature of events in June 1929. A strong northern involvement was present in the week of lectures broadcast on the Dublin radio, which were held in the Mansion House as part of the centenary celebrations. Papers during that week were read by the Professor of Scholastic Philosophy at Queen's, the Rev. A.H. Ryan, Louis J. Walsh, the District Justice for Donegal and former Sinn Féin candidate for South Derry in the 1918 elections, and the Rev. J. Clenaghan from Carnlough.[16] There was therefore a solid and significant northern presence at the proceedings.

The centenary of Catholic Emancipation was held in the final years of the Cosgrave administration. It was a period marked by low-key efforts to modify the constitutional relationship with Britain, leading to the signing of the Statute of Westminster at the 1931 Commonwealth Conference, attempts to curb the

---

12 See David Chaney, 'A symbolic mirror of ourselves: civic ritual in mass society', in R. Collins et al. (eds.) *Media, culture and society: a critical reader* (London, 1986), 247. 13 *Catholic Emancipation Centenary Record*, 13. 14 Ibid., 29. 15 *Irish Independent*, 21 June 1929. 16 See note 10.

activities of republican extremists and harsh action against what was perceived as the menace of communism.[17] The centenary was not only an opportunity for the Catholic Church to proclaim its increasingly important role in the new state,[18] but for the new state to proclaim its permanence, its separate identity from England and to give a high profile to its image as a Catholic nation. The emphasis on the Free State's Catholic identity had become more important due to the perceived failure of its attempts to make itself constitutionally more independent from Britain. This first major state building ritual was covered comprehensively by the press. Reporters highlighted the obvious symbols used; for instance the 'chalice of an Irish martyr', that of Oliver Plunkett, was used in the mass in the Phoenix Park,[19] and Clery's department store displayed Daniel O'Connell's sword.[20]

The emphasis in press reports in the run up to the Phoenix Park mass was on order and obeying the requests of the stewards, highlighting the organisers' expectations that a large crowd would attend the event. Twenty-seven loud speakers were also installed to enable the entire congregation to follow the mass in detail.[21] The hymns for the Phoenix Park mass were noted in the press days in advance and were also available for purchase. Interestingly there was a note to the effect that those who could not sing in Irish should sing in English.* The householders and owners of premises in the centre of Dublin were asked by the Centenary Committee to decorate their premises appropriately. This was apparently successful as the bishop of Waterford and Lismore, Dr Hackett, observed that 'never, indeed, in the memory of any living person in Dublin' had the decorations 'for any purpose been so extensive or so general'.[22] Flowers decorated most places in the city centre; baskets were hung from the lampposts, flags representing the four provinces were hung from the four corners of O'Connell bridge, 'shields bearing symbols of the Most Holy Eucharist, specially designed for the occasion, were artistically grouped at various points in

* On the lack of success in the reintroduction of the Irish language see pp 29–46 above.

**17** On 18 October 1931 a pastoral was read in every Catholic Church regarding the threat of communism.   **18** Dr Harty, archbishop of Cashel, speaking at the Mansion House, observed that 'In truth Catholic ideals in Ireland were endowed with renewed life and Catholic action was gaining strength from day to day', *Irish Independent*, 20 June 1929. Rev. Myles Ronan, editor of the official centenary record, wrote in his prologue: 'The Catholic Emancipation Act marks the end of the English State's pretence that the Catholic Church was dead in Ireland', *Catholic Emancipation centenary record*, prologue.   **19** *Irish Independent*, 19 June 1929.   **20** 'The incense boat and thurible bears the name of Patrick Russell, archbishop of Dublin, who ended his days in an underground cell in Dublin Castle. He died on July 14, 1692, from hardships endured as a prisoner for the Faith.' *Catholic Emancipation Centenary Record*, 31.   **21** Ibid., 35.   **22** J.J. Robinson was the architect for the event, Charles O'Connor was the chairman of the decorations committee and Charles Travers was the honorary secretary of the decorations committee: *Irish Independent*, 19 June 1929. Dr Hackett cited in *Irish Independent*, 21 June 1929.

the City'.[23] As the detailed organisation indicates, never before in the history
of the state had such an ambitious gathering of people been conceived.

The centenary indeed attracted huge numbers; eighty trains arrived in
Dublin, ferrying those who had come to the capital to celebrate the occasion.[24]
Return tickets for train journeys to Dublin were sold for the price of singles
to encourage attendance, and in addition selected trains left stations around the
country before midnight in order that more people would be able to travel by
train, and arrive in time for the proceedings. Accommodating participants, trav-
ellers by train could also buy a 'ration bag' when they arrived in Dublin. All
of this indicated the distances people were willing to travel to attend the centenary.[25] Although the *Independent* noted that the biggest contingents had come
from Cork and Limerick, it also observed the large representation from the
North, whose Catholics were uniting with the 'rest of the country around the
great bulwark of the Faith.'[26] The *Irish News* also noted the presence of visitors
from America, those emigrants who took the occasion of the centenary to come
home: 'many of the grandchildren of those self same exiles of '45 are now
returning to the home of their sires, but under what altered conditions'.[27]

There was therefore a huge public participation in events and while the
involvement of the poor was remarked on repeatedly ('but profuse and brilliant as the display in the centres of fashion, that made by the poor in the back
streets was of surpassing excellence')[28] there was also an elite element to the
centenary proceedings. At the opening mass for instance it was noted that 'all
elements of the public, professional, and commercial life' of Dublin were represented,[29] while in the grounds of Blackrock College a garden party was held
for the church hierarchy and other dignitaries. Some four thousand people
attended the event, for which tickets were available at five shillings.[30] In contrast to the Eucharistic Congress three years later when de Valera snubbed him,
the governor-general was a prominent guest at this and the other events associated with the centenary. Described as 'brilliant and impressive' it was not
quite 'of the people'.[31]

On the day of the Phoenix Park mass itself one hundred loud-hailers
reminded the people that they should conduct themselves as they would in
church.[32] Those attending mass were also reminded not to smoke from the
time they assembled in the Phoenix Park to the conclusion of Benediction on
Watling Street Bridge. It was added, however, that while participants could

**23** *Catholic Emancipation Centenary Record*, 43.   **24** *Irish Independent*, 24 June 1929.   **25** Ration
bags contained two ham sandwiches, an apple, banana, currant bun, packet of biscuits, and
a portion of cheese. All for 1*s.*, *Irish News*, 15 June 1929.   **26** *Irish Independent*, 24 June 1929.
It suggested that 5,000 people had come from the north for the mass.   **27** *Irish News*, 17
June 1929.   **28** *Catholic Emancipation Centenary Record*, 43.   **29** It was attended by, among
others, the Governor General, Professor Eoin MacNeill and General Eoin O'Duffy. *Irish
Independent*, 20 June 1929.   **30** *Catholic Emancipation Centenary Record, Advance Programme*,
5.   **31** Ibid., 19.   **32** *Irish Independent*, 24 June 1929.

not get a smoke they could get a cup of tea in one of the marquees set up in the park.[33] Maps were also published in the papers, outlining the areas designated for men, women and the children (who were also segregated); the men were located on the gospel side, the women on the epistle side. The Taoiseach was given a special place on the gospel side in front of the high altar.[34]

One thousand two hundred troops lined the route to the Phoenix Park. The mass was marshalled by eight thousand stewards (two thousand five hundred of whom were members of the GAA)[35] who gathered in the Phoenix Park in the days before the mass to rehearse, under the direction of General Eoin O'Duffy, the Garda Commissioner. O'Duffy's hope was that the stewards would 'carry out their duties in such a way as would reflect credit on themselves and on their great Catholic country'.[36] The number of stewards reflects the crowd expected by the organisers, and their concerns for safety and order. The stewards also symbolised the attempts to emphasise national unity through the medium of the performance; as the *Irish News* outlined:

> One of the most noteworthy side-issues of the Emancipation Centenary arrangements has been the gathering together of thousands of stewards for the great Procession, and men are now standing shoulder to shoulder on the training ground who formerly served in the National Army, the IRA, and the British military and naval forces. What a triumph for the Faith![37]

Continuing this theme of unity the article concluded: 'They have forgotten past political bitterness and only remember that in the sacred cause of the Faith they are one.'[38] In some way then the centenary was being viewed (or used) as an opportunity for reconciliation between the various factions within the Free State: 'At the feet of the King every barrier separating our people, the poor from the rich, politician from politician, was swept aside.'[39] The editor of the *Irish News* argued that there was no room for division in Ireland: 'We are all united before the Altar of faith, where no mundane differences may intrude.'[40] For the *Cork Examiner*: 'The whole country has been galvanised into a new life and vigour by the recital of what our ancestors endured and overcame.'[41] Similar rhetoric calling for unity in their ranks had been used by unionists in relation to their history and their state. In the North, by way of contrast, the unionist rank and file was called upon to unite behind the figure of Edward Carson and the image of a glorious unionist past which he had come to represent, in the face of economic disturbance and civil unrest in the 1930s.[42]

---

**33** Ibid., 21 June 1929. **34** Ibid., 25 June 1929. **35** Ibid., 24 June 1929. **36** Ibid., 19 June 1929. **37** *Irish News*, 18 June 1929. **38** Ibid. **39** *Catholic Emancipation Centenary Record*, 29. **40** *Irish News*, 21 June 1929. **41** *Cork Examiner*, 24 June 1929. **42** For a discussion of unionist rituals in the 1930s, see Gillian McIntosh, 'Symbolic mirrors: commemorations of Edward Carson in the 1930s', *Irish Historical Studies* (forthcoming).

Reacting to de Valera's election victory in 1933, for instance, the *Belfast Telegraph* reminded its readers that unionism could only be 'assailed by the enemy with any hope of success' when there was 'weakness and dissension in the garrison inside'.[43]

Certainly the penultimate moment of the week of celebrations in Dublin was the mass in the Phoenix Park, attended by twelve hundred priests.[44] Under the headline 'Faith of Our Fathers Triumphant', the leader writer in the *Independent* wrote: 'Ireland has made a glorious Act of Thanksgiving to God for a hundred years of religious freedom. The whole nation was represented in a remarkable demonstration, for the fervour and dimensions of which there has rarely been any equal.'[45] The writer went on to suggest that such an occasion would never come again for those who had had the privilege of taking part, but on the contrary, the 1929 celebrations were but a modest forerunner of the enthusiasm which greeted the presence of the papal legate at the 1932 Eucharistic Congress.[46] The mass in the Phoenix Park was presided over by the archbishop of Dublin, Dr Byrne, with Cardinal MacRory acting as celebrant. The altar 'in white and gold dominated the scene': 'The Celtic cross surmounting the lofty baldachino, the Roman crosses on the slope of the roof, proclaimed the Irish and Catholic significance of the erection.'[47] The impact of the occasion was not lost on observers; the *Independent*'s reporter wrote:

> There were moments yesterday when one felt how feeble words are to convey the thoughts that arise in the mind. One such moment was that which followed the Elevation at the Solemn Pontifical Mass of the Holy Trinity in the fifteen acres in the Phoenix Park.[48]

Following the mass the procession to Watling Street Bridge for Benediction began with the Minister for Justice, Fitzgerald-Kennedy, and de Valera acting as canopy bearers, the first of the various dignitaries who took turns in this role.[49] The procession was impressive, it was estimated it took three hours to pass any one point, and was at times twenty-five people deep:

**43** *Belfast Telegraph*, 26 Jan. 1933.   **44** The children's mass was held on 22 June 1929 in St Andrew's, and was attended by 2,500 children. *Irish Independent*, 24 June 1929.   **45** Ibid.; the *Irish News*' editorial over a week earlier was in a similar vein: 'They [the celebrations] will represent the solemn spirit of a Catholic country dedicating itself anew to the glorious faith to which its people have clung through good times and bad. They will be a great challenge in the face of modern materialism', 17 June 1929.   **46** There's a link here; among the organisers (Sir Joseph Glynn, chairman of the Catholic Truth Society, and the assistant secretary of the committee, H. Allen) was F. O'Reilly, who acted in 1929 as general secretary and was also the secretary of the committee for the organisation of the Eucharistic Congress in 1932.   **47** *Catholic Emancipation Centenary Record*, 35.   **48** *Irish Independent*, 24 June 1929.   **49** The chancellor of the National University, Howley, and the chairman of the city commissioners, Seamus Murphy, also acted as canopy bearers. In addition, four Belfast men acted as canopy bearers: Senator T.J. Campbell, Dr J.B. Moore, P. Flanagan and Councillor James

> As far as the eye could reach citywards were long unbroken columns of
> men on either side of the river, under the most bounteous and brilliant
> display of flags and bunting ever made in a city that has seen in the course
> of its long history pageantry as gorgeous as has ever been presented. And
> yet it was not pageantry: it was prayer, and, mainly, the prayer of the
> poor and the lowly.[50]

Once the procession had reached the bridge 'the Hierarchy, the Ministers, led
by President Cosgrave, the representatives of the Irish Corporations in their
brilliant robes, and the Guard of Honour of the National Army, only were
admitted behind the barriers erected both sides of the Bridge'.[51]

Contrary to the image put forward by the organisers the years that preceded
the centenary did not reveal the Free State as an 'ancient and noble nation' or
a homogenous Catholic community, which had freed itself from the 'old
oppressor'. Rather this was a period of change in the state; by 1927 the Shannon
Scheme had been launched bringing electricity to the whole of Ireland, Kevin
O'Higgins had been assassinated, de Valera had entered the Free State Dáil, the
introduction of a national broadcasting service had been announced, and in
addition to the centenary 1929 also witnessed the introduction of the Censorship
of Publications Act.[52] The Free State was on the eve of the 1930s, a decade in
which its Catholic identity (given dramatic embodiment in 1929 and 1932) was
formally crystallised in the state's constitution. By deliberately identifying itself
as a Catholic state in 1929 the Free State cast itself not only in opposition to
Britain but also to Northern Ireland; the presence of so many northerners as
both performers and as audience at the centenary celebrations ensured that such
a comparison would be made.

The 1929 celebration of the centenary of Catholic Emancipation, taken
together with the Eucharistic Congress, increased the identification of the Irish
Free State with Catholicism, emphasised the widening gap between north and
south, and threw the northern Irish state's Protestant identity into sharper relief.
Unionists in Northern Ireland viewed the event as confirmation of the inter-
connectedness of Catholicism and nationalism, while in the pages of the nation-

Kilpatrick, *Irish News*, 21 June 1929. **50** *Catholic Emancipation Centenary Record*, 39. **51** The
altar on Watling Bridge was a smaller replica of that at the Phoenix Park, *Irish Independent*,
24 June 1929. **52** 'First, it set up a Censorship Board of five persons (originally one
Protestant and three Catholic laymen with a Catholic priest as chairman) with power to
prohibit the sale and distribution of any book or periodical which it considered "in its general tendency indecent or obscene" ... Secondly, the act made the publication, sale, or distribution of literature advocating birth control an offence', Terence de Vere White, 'Social
life in Ireland, 1927-1937', in F. McManus (ed.), *The years of the great test, 1926-39* (Dublin,
1967), 19-29, 19, 151.

alist *Irish News* it was taken as an opportunity to express the grievances of the
Catholic hierarchy against the Northern Irish government. The centenary allowed
for historical allusions to Ireland's perceived Catholic past and its sufferings; there
were references to St Patrick, the Elizabethan and Cromwellian eras, the Famine,
the Protestant ascendancy and of course centrally the 'struggle' for Catholic
Emancipation. Northern nationalists asserted that the struggle for emancipation
had not yet been completed. 'The Dublin celebrations', wrote the editor of the
*Irish News*, 'throw our penal code into sharp relief. It is time another O'Connell,
aggressive and determined as the Emancipator of old, arose to lead us towards
emancipation'.[53] In an editorial which accused the Northern Ireland government
of trying to mitigate the religious freedom of Catholics ('the spirit that animates
them is neither a jot nor title different from that of the earlier enemies of Irish
Catholicity [sic]') the writer concluded that the bigotry which had begotten the
pogrom was not yet dead.[54] He expressed the hope that the tolerance that was
being shown towards Protestants in the south would be mimicked by the
Northern Irish government in their treatment of Catholics. In this context, it is
worth remembering the hostility towards Protestants articulated throughout the
centenary, particularly in papers read in the Mansion House (reminding
Protestants of their oppressive ancestors and their culpability for their actions).
There were attempts then to blame Protestants in the past while exonerating
Protestants in the present; for instance, the Rev. A.M. Crofts argued:

> Let us show the descendants of the minority who fashioned so skilfully
> the unjust laws of oppression, even though the existence of a Boundary
> is still proof that their own methods have never changed, that intoler-
> ance forms no part in the life of a Catholic people.[55]

While the bishop of Ardagh, Dr McNamee reminded those attending the
garden party of the contribution to the cause of 'Catholic freedom' of 'such
great Protestants as Grattan, Burke, and Tone', and he continued:

> fain would we hope that, animated by their spirit of justice and fair play
> Irish Protestants of to-day would rejoice with us in celebrating an event
> that dealt a death blow to that odious ascendancy which, if it was a source
> of cruel wrong to us, was a stigma of shame and reproach to them.[56]

Although ironically the message of the archbishops and bishops to 'the Catholic
people of Ireland' noted that

> It would not be gracious on our part to conclude this message without
> a word of appreciation of the sympathetic attitude of our fellow-coun-
> trymen, who are not of our faith, towards our Centennial Celebrations.[57]

**53** *Irish News*, 24 June 1929.   **54** Ibid.   **55** Rev. A.M. Crofts, cited in the *Irish Independent*,
21 June 1929.   **56** *Irish Independent*, 20 June 1929.   **57** 'Message of the Archbishops and

Mary Harris in her book on the Catholic Church and the foundation of the Northern Irish state argues that 'the Catholic Emancipation celebrations of 1929 provided the Church with an opportunity to assess their position under the Northern Irish government'.[58] Rev. Myles Ronan in his introduction to the official centenary record reminded the reader that although:

> we glory in the wondrous achievements of Ireland's spiritual sons and daughters in foreign countries, yet our victorious struggle for religious liberty in our own land must be our chief concern on the present occasion.[59]

The 1929 centenary provided an opportunity for nationalists to draw attention to the northern Irish state and the perceived injustices being meted out to Catholics in that jurisdiction. It was the perfect context for northern nationalists who saw their grievances in terms of the 'past struggles of the Irish Catholic Church against a hostile British state'.[60] These 'struggles' were highlighted in the Mansion House lectures and contradicted in the pages of the *Belfast Newsletter*: 'we cannot', wrote the paper's editor, 'comment on the week's perversions of history except to say that history must be perverted if the monstrous claims of the Papacy are to find any defence or excuse.' This followed an editorial which accused the Free State of lacking toleration towards Protestants, before detailing the historic crimes of the papacy against Protestantism – among them, the burning of Protestants by 'Bloody Mary', the massacre of St Bartholemew, and the horrors of the Inquisition.[61]

By 1929 the state in Northern Ireland had settled into its Protestant character, with Protestants dominating the government, civil service and police force. That same year proportional representation was abolished and the Catholic population settled into their position as recalcitrant minority. The presence of many northerners in the proceedings for the centenary week made the North an issue; the presence of Cardinal MacRory as celebrant of the Phoenix Park mass ensured that it would be a high profile point of debate.[62] The presence of northern Catholics in addition allowed for the weaving of the historical with the contemporary, a feature of the centenary generally. Under a newspaper headline which read 'Northern Catholics struggle for justice', the *Irish Independent* quoted MacRory as saying that 'in the Six Counties Ascendancy was fighting its last battle in the trenches carefully dug for it by Partition'.[63]

Bishops to the Catholic people of Ireland', issued after the meeting of the Hierarchy at Maynooth, Tuesday 25 June, *Catholic Emancipation Centenary Record*, 67. **58** Mary Harris, *The Catholic Church and the foundation of the Northern Irish State* (Cork, 1993), 264. **59** Rev. Myles Ronan, *Catholic Emancipation Centenary Record*, 11-17. **60** Harris, *The Catholic Church*, 264. **61** *Belfast Newsletter*, 24 June 1929. **62** However, as Harris has argued, 'the fact that Catholic specific grievances arising from legislation were not always clearly differentiated from objections to the state per se rendered the Church's protests less plausible': Harris, *The Catholic Church*, 263. **63** *Irish Independent*, 22 June 1929. This was juxtaposed with the obser-

Referring to the ongoing conflict regarding the religious control over education in the North MacRory reminded his audience that there was 'just one
consideration' that was 'calculated to modify' their 'joy' and that was that in
one part of the country the Catholics were not enjoying 'the full fruits of
Emancipation'.[64] His remarks at the Mansion House were met with 'sympathetic applause', the centenary committee noted.[65]

In the context of claim and counter-claim by nationalists and unionists, Dr
Arthur Ryan of Queen's University Belfast also focused on the plight of the
northern Catholics in his contribution to the week's lectures in the Mansion
House: 'We are once more the victims of the ascendancy – less cruel, indeed,
but more subtle than that which was shaken a hundred years ago.'[66] The *Belfast
Newsletter* was particularly critical of Ryan, arguing that control of scholastic
philosophy at Queen's had apparently been given to the Catholic Church to
satisfy its demands.[67] Ryan's complaints about the discrimination against
Catholics was therefore incorrect, the editor argued, and was merely part of
the claim of the Catholic Church 'as ever' for ascendancy, which it never ceased
to strive for 'by fair means and foul'.[68] Education, as Harris' book makes clear,
was the enduring cause of conflict between the Catholic Church and the
Northern Irish government in this period. Beyond issues of power and politics, it was for Catholics the means by which their identity was to be trans-
mitted, and therefore was an emotive issue. These were factors in the centenary celebrations also, as the new state through it's civic and religious leaders
sought to forge and transmit an identity for the Free State.

In form and style, although on a much greater scale, the 1932 Eucharistic
Congress owed much to the 1929 centenary; and in its similarities reminded
the audience and participants of the previous drama of the centenary of Catholic
Emancipation, and by extension of a Catholic and nationalist interpretation of
Ireland's past, which was the stated intent of the Mansion House lectures.

> In the Papers and Addresses that form a special feature in the Centenary
> Celebrations it is one of our objects to emphasise our Catholic continuity,
> through the vicissitudes of centuries, with the Church of St Patrick, and
> through our Apostle, with the One, Holy, Catholic and Apostolic Church.[69]

In this way the Eucharistic Congress reinforced the memory of the centenary
for its audience, and was itself reinforced by it. The parallels between the two

vation that the Phoenix Park mass was 'a great national act of faith'. **64** Ibid. **65** *Catholic
Emancipation Centenary Record*, 23. **66** *Irish News*, 22 June 1929. **67** There is a background
to this issue, centring around the question whether to establish an honours school in
Scholastic Philosophy or not. Dr Ryan was involved in this dispute, although an honours
school was established in Queen's in 1928. See T.W. Moody and J.C. Beckett, *Queen's,
Belfast 1845-1949. The history of a university*, vol. II (London, 1959), 492-93. **68** *Belfast
Newsletter*, 25 June 1929. **69** *Catholic Emancipation Centenary Record*, 23.

are obvious, but can be usefully highlighted to underline the level of repetition. Carefully organised and choreographed both rituals were preceded by a week of events, including a week of high masses and a special children's mass, building to the climax of the Phoenix Park mass. Both masses were followed by a procession to the centre of the capital where benediction was held on Watling Street Bridge in the first instance and O'Connell Bridge in the second.[70] Both events were meticulously planned. For the 1929 ceremony the organisers provided an advance programme in 1928. In addition there was extensive press coverage and information was provided through parishes. Throughout Ireland the centenary was the subject of Lenten lectures and parish priests were asked to help in the organisation of parish groups wishing to attend the ceremony.[71] Participants were, therefore, kept very well informed of arrangements and of their duties in relation to events. So, while 'nothing was left to take care of itself'[72] this is not to say that the centenary, or the Eucharistic Congress, were prepared for or performed cynically: they were above all genuine expressions of a Catholic state which tentatively felt that it was coming into its own. With these two events the marriage of church and state in the Free State was being formally acknowledged and affirmed in the modern age; in an almost literal way they were (or were presented as) acts of 'national communion'.[73]

**70** Watling Street Bridge was chosen perhaps because it is 'the first bridge spanning the Liffey from Knightsbridge and nearest to the Church of S.S. Michael and John, where the first church bell sounded on the winning of Emancipation.' *Cork Examiner*, 24 June 1929. **71** *Catholic Emancipation Centenary Record*, 9. 'It is realised that many persons will attend other than with their organised Parish or Church units – though this is to be discouraged in every way', *Centenary of Catholic Emancipation, Advance Programme*, 25. **72** *Catholic Emancipation Centenary Record*, 13. **73** Elizabeth Hammerton and David Cannadine, 'Conflict and consensus on a ceremonial occasion: the Diamond Jubilee in Cambridge in 1897', *Historical Journal*, xxiv, 1 (1981), 112. 'The supreme and most insidious exercise of power [is] to prevent people, to whatever degree, from having grievances by shaping their perceptions, cognitions and preferences in such a way that they accept their role in the existing order of things either because they can see or imagine no alternative to it, or because they see it as natural and unchangeable, or because they value it as divinely ordained and beneficial': Steven Lukes, *Power: a radical view* (London, 1974), 42.

# Ireland, the pope and vocationalism: the impact of the encyclical *Quadragesimo Anno*

On 15 May 1931 Pope Pius XI issued the encyclical *Quadragesimo Anno*. At that time Europe was in the midst of the Depression following the Wall Street Crash of 1929 which had severely shaken people's trust in the capitalist economic system and made socialism and totalitarianism increasingly attractive. Governments in an effort to shield their countries from economic crisis and ward off social and political upheaval raised tariffs and imposed stiffer quotas on imports. The problem, however, as far as the pope was concerned was much more fundamental and required the 'reconstruction of the social order'. In *Quadragesimo Anno* Pius argued that what was wrong with society was the way in which it was divided into opposing classes. In order to bring about much needed reform and avoid the 'class warfare' that was becoming increasingly evident in industrialised nations, he stated that a total overhaul of the institutions and a general moral revival were necessary.[1]

*Quadragesimo Anno* is divided into three parts. Part I reviews Pope Leo XIII's encyclical *Rerum Novarum* whose fortieth anniversary Pius' encyclical was commemorating. *Rerum Novarum*, dealing with the condition of the working classes in a capitalistic society, tackled the issue of workers rights and laid out the responsibilities that employers had towards them. Leo had challenged both liberalism and socialism, showing special concern about the latter's growing popularity with the less well-off. *Quadragesimo Anno* was modelled on *Rerum Novarum*:

> Leo set the agenda and the pattern for future social encyclicals: in his analysis of the social conflict, in his challenge to the economic system of the day, in his condemnation of the false doctrine of socialism, in his insistence that Catholic teaching alone provides the solution, and in his defence of basic human rights in the economic sphere.[2]

In *Quadragesimo Anno* Pius XI refers to *Rerum Novarum* as the 'Magna Charta upon which all Christian activity in the social field ought to be based, as on a

---

1 *Quadragesimo Anno* (QA), 15 May 1931, par. 77.   2 Liam Ryan, 'The modern popes as social reformers', *Furrow*, May 1991, 92.

foundation'.[3] Part II of the new encyclical outlines the Vatican's contemporary views on economic and social affairs, while Part III looks at how economic life has changed since *Rerum Novarum*. Pius noted that during those forty years 'an immense power and despotic economic dictatorship is consolidated in the hands of a few, who often are not owners but only the trustees and managing directors of invested funds which they administer according to their own arbitrary will and pleasure'.[4] Having criticised the liberal capitalist ideology, Pius then attacks socialism in even stronger terms. While acknowledging that socialism inclined toward Christian principles he announced that 'Religious socialism, [or] Christian socialism are contradictory terms; no one can be at the same time a good Catholic and a true socialist.'[5] Even stronger language was reserved for communism, which according to the pope sought two objectives: 'Unrelenting class warfare and absolute extermination of private ownership.'[6]

In his call for reform Pius XI focused on the ever growing importance of the state in all spheres of human activity. Referring to the demise of the old medieval guild system through the evils of 'individualism', he contended that 'there remains virtually only individuals and the State.'[7] That powerful authoritarian governments now tried to dominate all aspects of national life was, as David Thomson argues, a result of the abandonment in the face of economic uncertainty of the nineteenth-century separation between political and economic activity, enshrined in the doctrines of free trade and laissez-faire.[8] Pope Pius argued:

> Just as it is gravely wrong to take from individuals what they can accomplish by their own initiative and industry and give it to the community, so it is also an injustice and at the same time a grave evil and disturbance of right order to assign to a greater and higher association what lesser and subordinate organisations can do.[9]

In his view the state's role should be limited to 'directing, watching, urging, restraining, as occasion requires and necessity demands'.[10] He proposed that the state and its citizens work together so that 'the conflict between the hostile classes be abolished and harmonious co-operation of the industries and professions be encouraged'.[11] Ultimately he hoped that members from each industry or profession could be organised into 'vocational groups' or 'corporations' where employers and workers would collaborate to further their common interests.[12] Recognising the danger of occupational groups following their own selfish interest he balanced this up by referring to the need to ensure that the 'common good' of society was always given pre-eminence. Pius somewhat ide-

---

**3** QA par. 39. **4** QA par. 108. **5** QA par. 120. **6** QA par. 112. **7** QA par. 77. **8** D. Thomson, *Europe since Napoleon* (London, 1966), 698. **9** QA par. 79. **10** QA par. 80. **11** QA par. 81. **12** J.H. Whyte, *The Church and State in modern Ireland 1923-1970* (Dublin 1971), 67.

alistically went on to explain that: 'associations or corporations are composed of delegates from the two syndicates (i.e. of workers and employers) respectively of the same industry or profession and as true and proper organs and institutions of the State they direct syndicates and co-ordinate their activities in matters of common interest toward one and the same ends'.[13]

To make this institutional reform workable Pius stressed the need for moral reform: 'preceding this ardently desired social restoration there must be a renewal of the Christian spirit'. He encouraged Catholics to become involved in 'Catholic action' and to 'strive according to the talent, powers, and position of each to contribute something to the Christian reconstruction of human society'.[14] By arguing for such reform the Pope was not merely adding to the ideas of Leo XIII's *Rerum Novarum* but to those Catholic social thinkers who had proposed a constructive response to a world that was becoming more modern, liberal and secular.[15] It was this moral conservatism and the desire to go back to a more community based society that gave *Quadragesimo Anno* part of its appeal in the Irish Free State.

This chapter examines the impact *Quadragesimo Anno* had on southern Irish society from its publication in 1931 to the early 1940s. It endeavours to explain why its message affected political discourse in Ireland as much as it did, despite the fact that the country was not in the throes of industrialisation or class warfare. It explores the verbal support that was given to the pope's recommendations in newspapers and journals as exemplified in the likes of the *Standard* in the late 1930s, as well as the apparently positive actions of politicians. It concludes, however, by explaining why this support was ultimately limited and why it was not translated into the kind of action 'vocationalists' desired.

### INITIAL RESPONSES IN IRELAND

J.H. Whyte argues that *Quadragesimo Anno*'s publication can be regarded as the date when the Catholic social movement finally took off in Ireland.[16] There can be little doubt that it gave a great impetus to organisations like Muintir na Tire, which was originally set up in 1931 as a producers co-operative but now began to hold rural weekends where participants discussed and sought Catholic remedies for the problems of Irish rural life. Another organisation strongly affected was the Guilds of Regnum Christi, set up to encourage personal sanctification, it decided, in response to the encyclical, to divide its members into their respective 'vocational' groupings.

Above all the intensity of the debate on Catholic social thought was raised considerably. The Catholic Young Men's Society, founded in Dublin in 1928,

**13** QA par. 93.    **14** QA par. 147.    **15** For a background to these Catholic social thinkers, read E.J. Coyne, 'Corporative organisation of society', *Studies*, vol. xxiii, March 1934.    **16** J.H. Whyte, *The Church and State*, op. cit., 67.

played a crucial role in this. Its growing educational work included study weeks in the countryside. The most famous of these study weeks was the Social Order Summer School, which was held in the Jesuit college of Clongowes Wood from 1935 until 1940. These attracted influential individuals from the world of politics, the professions and trade unions. At these weekends men earnestly sought solutions to the problems that affected Irish working life. These solutions were, needless to say, based on Catholic social principles. Clergymen like Fr Michael Hayes, the founder of Muintir na Tire, also began to play an important role in their support of vocationalism.

One thing that is clearly evident is that the ideas of *Quadragesimo Anno* and the vocational organisation it espoused was strongly supported by those who were keen to associate Catholicism with the new Free State. Catholic social thinkers generally favoured a social and moral order that was based on small-scale capitalism, family, property, farms and small business.[17] They also desired to see the social, economic and political realms develop along Catholic lines. Under W.T. Cosgrave this desire to recognise the Catholic nature of the state had already been strengthened by legislation on film censorship in 1923, a ban on divorce in 1925 and the Censorship of Publications Act of 1929. While the attempts to revive the Irish language as a second vernacular remained unsuccessful (cf. pp 29-46 above), Catholicism became the most distinctive national badge that an Irishman in Free State Ireland could wear. In their efforts to distinguish themselves from their former rulers, Irish nationalists tended to exclude their Protestant countrymen from full citizenship (cf. pp 83-95 above). *Quadragesimo Anno* and other papal encyclicals when combined with the legislation of the Irish State encouraged people to be socially conservative in their outlook. As well as Protestants those who found themselves increasingly excluded from this Catholic ethos now included socialists, communists and liberals. Free State Ireland was beginning to subtly and not so subtly assert that its citizens be ideally Gaelic by blood and Catholic by nature.

The appeal of the papal encyclicals was also clearly recognised by the new Fianna Fáil administration. After the general election victory of 1932, Sean T. O'Kelly announced that: 'the Fianna Fáil policy was the policy of Pope Pius XI'.[18] In January 1933, Eamon de Valera called a snap general election in the hope of gaining an overall majority which had eluded him in the 1932 elections. The Fianna Fáil paper, the *Irish Press*, underlined the growing importance of appealing to Catholic sensibilities when it declared in its pre-election message: 'there is not a social or economic change Fianna Fáil has proposed or brought about which has not its fullest justification in the encyclicals of either Leo XIII or the present pontiff'.[19] Fianna Fáil duly won their desired overall

**17** A. Cochrane and J. Clarke, *Ireland: Catholic corporatism in company welfare states* (Milton Keynes, 1995). **18** *Irish Independent*, 11 February 1932, cited in J.J. Lee, *Ireland 1912-1985. Politics and society* (Cambridge, 1989), 170. **19** *Irish Press*, 11 January 1933, cited in Tim Pat Coogan, *De Valera: Long Fellow, Long Shadow* (London, 1995), 455.

majority. With the reception of de Valera in Rome by the pope in May 1933 and of his vice-president Sean T. O'Kelly later that year the new administration publicly consolidated the nation's Catholic association.[20] On 4 October 1933 O'Kelly speaking at the Cercle Catholique in Geneva stressed that the Fianna Fáil government was 'inspired in its very administrative action by Catholic principles and Catholic doctrine'.[21] Referring to the encyclical *Quadragesimo Anno*, he added: 'in no country was this inspiring pronouncement read and studied with greater eagerness and interest than in Ireland'.[22] The question was whether this eagerness extended to the Fianna Fáil administration itself and what they were going to do about the encyclical's recommendations.

Certainly Eamon de Valera had some interest in the ideas of Catholic social reconstruction, as he sought the advice of J.W. Dulanty, the Irish High Commissioner in London, on the matter. On 27 September 1933 Dulanty wrote a letter to Maurice Moynihan, (de Valera's private secretary) with a report on 'The Corporative System applied to Ireland'.[23] In his report Dulanty applied the Italian 'corporative' model of Mussolini to the Free State. He believed that a scheme of vocationally organised councils if adopted would be beneficial to the country, and recommended that a 'General Economic Council' (representing the various vocational groups) would replace the existing senate. He pointed out that employers and employees would both be separately represented in the new council under the categories of industry; agriculture; commerce; internal communication; credit and insurance; and sea and transport. Dulanty was keen to stress that the vocational system in Mussolini's Italy was not fascist and referred to the history of vocationalism as expounded in the writings of Catholic social thinkers like Bishop Von Kettler and Baron de Vogelsang.

No doubt Dulanty's suggestion to replace the senate interested de Valera, who was beginning to lose patience with this body's delaying of legislation. He was particularly displeased when it rejected his bill to have the oath of fidelity to the king abolished. He indeed introduced a bill in March 1934 to have the senate itself abolished and, although delayed in the senate, it eventually happened in May 1936.[24] However, apart from the moves to abolish the senate, little concrete was done by the Fianna Fáil administration in the wake of this report.

It seems that Fianna Fáil had no real interest in making the necessary structural changes that Dulanty had suggested to. De Valera clearly had his own personal vision of how the nation should progress, and if there were to be any socio-economic restructuring it would be solely on his terms. While clinging

20 D. Keogh, *The Vatican, the bishops and Irish politics, 1919-1939* (Cambridge, 1986), 202. 21 Ibid. 22 Ibid. 23 Department of an Taoiseach, NA, S10813, J.W. Dulanty to M. Moynihan, 27 September 1933. 24 M.E. Collins, *An outline of modern Irish history 1850-1966* (Dublin, 1985), 371.

to an idealised image of a noble rural nation, it was in industry rather than agriculture that de Valera put his hopes for economic development. Fianna Fáil's economic planning supported the development of native manufacturing industries. In 1933 the Industrial Credit Corporation was set up to make capital available to new industries, investing £6 million by 1937.[25] Rather than letting industries and agricultural groups have a more active say in their own affairs as vocationalism advocated, the government became more and more interventionist by introducing quotas, licenses and tariffs as a means of regulating business. The government's role in the economy was increasing as it was in other countries on account of the economic depression of the 1930s. De Valera's economic war with Britain, which started over his refusal to pay the land annuities, only exacerbated the situation.

## FINE GAEL AND VOCATIONALISM

Although the IRA decided at its General Army Convention of March 1933 to consider the introduction of some form of 'classification and distribution of electors, on a vocational basis',[26] it was the National Guard (popularly known as the Blueshirts) under their leader General Eoin O'Duffy who were the first organisation to publicly adopt vocationalism (see pp 117-42 below). In their policy document of July 1933 they announced a commitment to the vocational order of society.[27] This became more significant when in September of that year Cumann na nGaedheal, the National Guard and the National Centre Party merged to form the United Ireland Party or Fine Gael. General O'Duffy assumed overall party leadership while W.T. Cosgrave became its parliamentary leader. Fine Gael now adopted as part of their policy: 'the planning of our national economic life with a view to increased industrialised efficiency and harmony by the organisation of industrial corporations with statutory powers, assisted by industrial courts and functioning under the guidance of a national economic council'.[28]

This commitment to vocationalism was a recent one for most Fine Gaelers. When an article in the Cumann na nGaedheal paper *United Irishman* of 22 April 1933 argued that parliament's role should be made less extensive and that the task of examining details of legislation should pass from deputies to vocational organisations representing economic and professional interest,[29] the paper's editorial quickly rejected it: 'it should be obvious that a proposal for a revolutionary change in the constitution of the State which is likely to commend itself as being practical politics to relatively few people cannot be allowed to occupy any substantial fraction of our very limited space'.[30] However, after the found-

**25** Ibid., 361. **26** Governmental Policy and Constitution of Óglaigh na h-Éireann. **27** M. Manning, *The Blueshirts* (Dublin 1970), 217. **28** Ibid., 214. **29** *United Irishman*, 22 April 1933 cited in Manning, *The Blueshirts*, 215. **30** Ibid.

ing of Fine Gael such practical concerns got left behind. Maurice Manning argues this sudden conversion was at least partly due to the growing interest in the development of vocational or corporative ideas and their application to Irish politics.[31]

Nevertheless, Fine Gael's association with the vocationalist ideal proved to be short lived. General O'Duffy's outlandish speeches, his general political inexperience and his growing identification with Mussolini and what in reality was a totalitarian corporatist state embarrassed the more conservative elements of the new party. On 21 September 1934 O'Duffy was forced to resign and W.T. Cosgrave took over the party leadership. With O'Duffy went Fine Gael's brief flirtation with vocationalism. The likelihood of it being introduced in Ireland had been dealt a severe blow as many now associated it with fascism. The quick abandonment of vocationalist thought proved that the concept had no real grass root-support in the Fine Gael organisation or in Ireland as a whole. The openly corporatist party set up by Eoin O'Duffy after leaving Fine Gael, the National Corporate Party never had any electoral success (see pp 117-42 below). It was this lack of support from the political parties which ultimately proved to be the Achilles heels of the vocationalist ideal in Ireland.

There were nevertheless more genuine and level-headed followers of Pius XI's proposals in the Fine Gael Party than O'Duffy. Professor James Hogan of University College, Cork, and Professor Michael Tierney of University College, Dublin, wrote a number of articles on vocationalism for the *United Irishman* paper during 1933 and 1934 when the concept had still some credibility among their party colleagues. Both men contributed much to vocationalist thought in Ireland by laying out how such a system would affect the Free State. At the same time several articles on vocationalism appeared in the journals *Studies* and the *Irish Ecclesiastical Record*. Reading these, one is particularly struck by the dramatic tone of those who advocated the adoption of vocationalist principles.

In the *United Irishman* of 14 October 1933 Professor Hogan wrote on 'The need for vocational corporations.' He argued with great strength that laissez-faire capitalism was outdated and that parliamentary democracy was equally unable to deal with what was being expected from it. He proposed the setting up of vocational councils which would resemble the former guild system from the Middle Ages: 'built upon a conception of society in close accord with the social teaching of the papal encyclicals *Rerum Novarum* and *Quadragesimo Anno*'.[32] He felt that this would bridge the gap that existed between politics and economics, which had discredited parliamentarianism.[33] In a later article he contended that a corporative economy would also act as a safeguard against excessive state centralisation.[34] The dislike of parliamentarianism and central government control became a common feature in the writings of Irish voca-

**31** Manning, *The Blueshirts*, 217.  **32** *United Irishman*, 14 October 1933.  **33** Ibid.  **34** Ibid.,
4 November 1933.

tionalists. Hogan believed that the introduction of a vocational structure would unify society:

> the family, the occupational group, the State, each having its own sphere of influence and activity would nevertheless be organically linked with each other by the fact that all would tend to the same social ends namely the highest possible development of the individual within society.[35]

This rather idyllic notion belies much of the vocationalist writings of the time. As far as Hogan and other vocationalists were concerned this was the 'natural' form of social organisation. Vocationalism they argued would help create a society where party politics would become less partisan: 'such a society would give us the principle of unity and peace which we so desperately need in our national life.'[36] Hogan along with other advocates of vocational organisation also believed that the new system would make the new State truly independent in the social, economic and political sphere, in particular from Britain. He admitted that the proposals were revolutionary in so far as they demanded the establishment of a new societal structure. However, he pointed out that 'revolutionary proposals are in the air of every country,'[37] and that it would bring a safe alternative to what he called 'Statism' – something he felt extreme republicans in particular and Fianna Fáilers by association were guilty of: 'revolutionary republicanism is committed to Statism in its most extreme form, State socialism.'[38]

Michael Tierney the other notable intellectual in Fine Gael who advocated vocationalism was equally passionate in the rhetoric he used. As far back as 1919 he had argued that 'we must have a national philosophy in government, in the shaping of that philosophy must go not only a few chosen intellectuals in some urban libraries or debating societies, but the collective genius of the Irish people'.[39] Now with the papal blessing of *Quadragesimo Anno* on the vocational system he believed he had found such a philosophy. In an article in *United Irishman* of 16 December 1933 he noted the influence of vocationalist principles throughout Europe and referred to the developments made under Mussolini in Italy, Hitler in Germany, Dollfuss in Austria, and to the progress made in France. Noting a general move to corporatism he emphatically stated in an almost dialectic materialist way: 'the Corporate State must come in the end in Ireland as elsewhere'.[40]

Tierney also attacked the dominance of parliament in the existing political system. He argued that the vocational system would replace the 'inherited defects and disorders' that were 'inseparable from individualistic capitalism'.[41]

---

**35** Ibid., 19 May 1934. **36** Ibid. **37** Ibid., 31 March 1934. **38** Ibid., 2 June 1934. **39** Cited in M. O'Callaghan, 'Language, Nationality, and Cultural Identity in the Irish Free State 1922-7', *Irish Historical Studies*, vol. xxiv, 94, November 1984. **40** *United Irishman*, 16 December 1933. **41** Ibid.

In his hope for future reforms he consoled himself with the fact that the Irish Free State had 'been too short a time in the enjoyment of political autonomy to have developed many native or organic institutions'.[42] He challenged the role of parliamentary democracy and surmised that the introduction of vocational organisation, while not bringing the abolition of parliament would reduce the number of parliamentary members: 'Parliament must cease to monopolise all national activity and we must abandon the grotesque idea that the whole work of rebuilding the nation can be done by a combination of ignorant ministers and mechanised civil servants.'[43] For him, vocationalism, or as he termed it 'representative democracy', was the only possible basis for an Irish government.[44] He too proposed (like J.W. Dulanty) that an economic council should replace the senate and that it be given the right to initiate and control legislation that affected the economic life of the country.[45]

From the writings of Irish vocationalists it becomes clear that certain disagreements were beginning to emerge. E.J. Coyne writing on 'The corporative organisation of society' in 1934 attacked the much praised Italian model.[46] With great foresight he pointed out: 'a corporative organisation which is merely a means to establish and maintain the "totalitarian's State" could never be accepted as being in accord with Catholic social philosophy.' Challenging Tierney's conception of vocationalism, he argued, that what was required was a corporative society and not a corporative State. Coyne explained that vocationalism was based on the philosophy of 'Soldarism', which was developed by a German Jesuit, Heinrich Pesch: 'Soldarism is a complete economic and social doctrine, and as such takes its stand beside Individualism on the one hand and Collectivism on the other.' While being a vocationalist himself, Coyne was also aware of the inherent difficulties within vocationalist thought. He referred to a conference attended by Catholic sociologists in Germany where five different 'corporative' plans were put forward in a report. He admitted that none of these were entirely satisfactory and conceded that 'to the practical statesman and administration the whole discussion and report would seem fantastic and unreal'. These words proved strangely prophetic in relation to the fate of the report of the Irish Commission on Vocational Organisation written mostly by Coyne, which was presented to the government in 1944.

## DE VALERA AND VOCATIONALISM

The suggestion that vocationalism might limit the power of parliament was something that particularly appealed to Cumann na nGaedheal which had just lost power and two general elections within one year. However, de Valera who had just won an overall majority in the Dail was unlikely to welcome it. While

42 Ibid., 24 March 1934.  43 Ibid.  44 Ibid., 7 April 1934.  45 Ibid.  46 E.J. Coyne, op. cit., 193.

de Valera was trying to assert the sovereignty of the Irish Free State by challenging the terms of the 1921 Anglo-Irish Treaty, he did not need any internal upheaval, which might delay or hinder this. However, de Valera's vision of the Irish people as being self-sufficient, industrious, Gaelic and anti-materialist,[47] rested comfortably beside those Catholic social theorists who lauded vocationalism, derided capitalism and lamented about the bygone day of an 'uncorrupted' medieval guild system. Like them the Fianna Fáil leader was keen to show that the State he was helping to build would be very much Catholic in nature.

This became clear from several pieces of legislation introduced by the new Fianna Fáil government. In 1933 it introduced a tax on imported papers as a means of guarding against secular foreign influences. This was followed in 1935 by the criminalisation of the sale of contraceptive devices. In the same year the Dance Halls Act was passed in the wake of a long clerical campaign against 'company keeping' and 'immodest deportment'.[48] Like those advocates of vocational organisation, it was an image of a nation set apart that de Valera clung to: 'Alone among the countries of western Europe, she never came under the sway of Imperial Rome. When all her neighbours were in tutelage, she was independent, building up her own civilisation undisturbed.'[49] De Valera saw the Irish as a people content with frugal comfort who were willing to suppress their individual ambitions in favour of those of the state, Church and community: 'The Irish genius has always stressed spiritual and intellectual rather than material values.'[50] This message was reinforced by Aodh de Blacam, a close associate of de Valera and an important propagandist for the Fianna Fáil party, who argued that the day of industrialism and urbanism was past and that a new decentralised agrarian order was at hand.[51]

Such a vision of Ireland seemed closely akin to the vocationalist ideal. However, Fianna Fáil's efforts to make the nation more industrialised showed the difference between rhetoric and economic reality. De Valera himself skilfully maintained his distance from vocationalism while at the same time never publicly disassociating himself from the concept. To do so would have proved very unpopular with the Catholic hierarchy. At the Fianna Fáil Ard Fheis of 1936 he stated:

> I would like personally to see such an organisation for our society developed, but I want it quite clearly understood that I would like to see it developed voluntarily. I don't believe in a State-inspired organisation of that kind; a regime may support them in its power but once the regime

---

**47** R.F. Foster, *Modern Ireland 1600-1972* (London, 1988), 538. **48** T.K. Hoppen, *Ireland since 1800. Conflict and conformity* (London, 1989), 235. **49** De Valera at the opening of the Athlone broadcasting station on 6 February 1933, M. Moynihan, *Speeches and statements by Eamon de Valera 1917-73* (Dublin and New York, 1980), 231. **50** Ibid. **51** Foster, *Modern Ireland*, op. cit., 547.

> breaks, they break, and there is nothing permanent about them because
> they are not natural.[52]

Of course de Valera was proved correct in his analysis if one is to look at the
fate of Mussolini's regime, but his concept of vocationalism developing 'voluntarily' indicated his lack of enthusiasm for doing anything constructive in
that direction. The paradox was that vocationalists despite their calls for less
State interference in economic and social affairs actually needed the State to
introduce structures to get the vocational idea up and running. It is hardly surprising that the politically secure Fianna Fáil administration were less than forthcoming in doing so.

The new constitution of 1937 was an opportunity for Catholic vocationalists to affect the structure of the state in line with Pope Pius's suggestions. Its
content was no doubt affected by de Valera's loyalty to the Catholic Church,
and heavily influenced by the Holy Ghost father John Charles MacQuaid and
the Jesuit father Edward Cahill who had provided their own drafts.[53] Article
44 quite clearly recognised the special position of the Holy Catholic and Roman
Church in the State.[54] A Catholic social philosophy was indeed very evident
especially in the constitution's attitude towards the family, divorce, education
and the role of women. For vocationalists there was indeed some recognition
of their principles in that the formation of the new senate would be partially
vocationalist, with forty-three of the sixty senators representing five vocational
categories. In this way, de Valera was partly implementing what J.W. Dulanty
had suggested to him in 1933 (a National Vocational Assembly) and what was
put forward in a minority report from a government commission to look into
the future of the senate, presented in 1936.[55] Of course this fell far short of what
vocationalists had wanted, and the potential influence of vocational groups was
undermined by Article 19 which stated that these members of the senate could
be elected if the Oireachtas so decided. To make matters worse Article 18 provided for alternative election procedures of these forty-three candidates through
election by TDs or councillors.[56] Having abolished the Free State Senate on
account of its obstructionist policies, it was inevitable that de Valera would not
give occupational groups even more opportunity to disrupt government policy
in a National Vocational Assembly. What he did introduce by way of the new
senate was merely a token gesture to the vocational ideal.

De Valera's apparent commitment to vocationalism was taken further. On
New Year's Day 1938 the Taoiseach suggested to Radio Éireann's director of
broadcasting, T.J. Kiernan, that a series of broadcasts should be given on radio
to discuss vocational organisation.[57] One can only guess why de Valera made

**52** Lee, *Ireland*, op. cit., 193.  **53** Coogan, *De Valera*, 489.  **54** Ibid., 490.  **55** J.J. Lee,
'Aspects of corporatist thought in Ireland: The Commission on Vocational Organisation,
1939-1943,', in A. Cosgrave and D. McCartney (eds.), *Studies in Irish history* (Dublin, 1979),
325.  **56** Lee, *Ireland*, 272.  **57** Department of An Taoiseach, NA, S10812A, T.J. Kiernan

such a suggestion, although placating the powerful Catholic hierarchy would be the most likely reason. Archdeacon John Kelleher in a reply to a letter from Kiernan responded enthusiastically: 'I approve wholeheartedly of the suggested broadcast talks on vocational organisation. I am particularly pleased that the suggestion has come from Mr De Valera himself.'[58] Kelleher's enthusiastic endorsement again showed up the contradictions within vocationalist thought concerning the role of the state: 'While the organisation must come from below upward and cannot be imposed by the State, still without sympathetic support and perhaps even initiative from the State, I see no basis for hope that it can ever be realised in this country.'[59] At this stage seven years after *Quadragesimo Anno*'s publication the need for some definite government action was becoming more and more crucial for vocationalists.

The series of talks on vocationalism took place from the GPO and were broadcast between 20 March and 15 May 1938. In all there were nine broadcasts which covered a broad range of issues on vocational organisation:

| Date | Subject | Speaker |
|------|---------|---------|
| 20 March | Vocational Organisation in the Past. | Alfred O'Rahilly |
| 27 March | The Encyclicals and Vocational Organisation. | Archd. John Kelleher |
| 3 April | Vocationalism and Parliamentary Democracy – Are they reconcilable? | Michael Tierney |
| 10 April | How Vocational Organisation would Promote Social Justice. | Hugh O'Neill |
| 17 April | Vocational Organisation for Wage Earners. | M.P. Linehan |
| 24 April | Vocational Organisation for Industrialists. | C.P. McCarthy |
| 1 May | Vocational Organisation for Farmers and Farm Labourers. | Fr John Hayes |
| 8 May | A Vocational Second Chamber. | J.J. Horgan |
| 15 May | How Farmers can organise. | J.J. McElligott.[60] |

Most of these were later published in the *Irish Monthly* and they give us a good insight into the vocationalist mind. In his talk, Archdeacon John Kelleher showed the idealism of some vocationalists when he asserted that *Quadragesimo Anno* 'might well serve as a basis for a complete programme of practical reform, perfectly consistent and comfortable to man's nature, with all its virtues and vices'.[61]

State bureaucracy comes to the fore as a pet hate of Irish vocationalists, painting a picture of unqualified civil servants interfering in other people's busi-

to M. Moynihan, 29 January 1938. **58** Ibid., J. Kelleher to M. Moynihan, 6 February 1938. **59** Ibid. **60** Department of An Taoiseach, NA, S10812A. **61** Archdeacon J. Kelleher, 'The encyclicals and vocational organisation', *Irish Monthly*, vol. lxvi (May 1938).

ness. In his talk Alfred O'Rahilly argued that 'any attempt to control price, quality or conditions of employment by unqualified outsiders is sure to be clumsy, irritating and ineffective. Besides, it is extremely dangerous, for it creates a huge State machine with large and almost autocratic powers of interference with every phase of business life.'[62] Vocationalists wanted those who were directly involved in various occupational groupings to have a direct say in the decisions that affected them. As Michael Tierney contended, this was being prevented by: 'the attribution to the State of supreme power in moral as well as in political questions'. The purpose of vocationalist organisation, he said, was 'to complete the return to a healthier state of society by at one and the same time abolishing economic class distinctions and providing all citizens with a series of organic barriers both against individualist exploitation and the soulless domination of the State'.[63] Clearly this type of rhetoric would have won little support from the Fianna Fáil Government. De Valera himself was asked by T.J. Kiernan to give a talk at the end of the series. Maurice Moynihan, his private secretary, refused on his behalf, explaining that the Taoiseach wanted to address the nation on the inauguration of the new President, but that he might speak at a later date. This, however, never happened.

Nonetheless the feeling that something practical had to be done following the talks culminated in July 1938 in the request by Senator MacDermot and Senator Michael Tierney to have a commission set up to examine the suitability of vocational organisation for Ireland. MacDermot (a co-founder of the National Centre Party) astutely claimed that *Quadragesimo Anno* 'has been more praised in this country than it has been read, more read than it has been understood and more understood than it has been put into practice'.[64] He was nevertheless critical, questioning whether the sweeping social reorganisation necessary was practicable and challenging the hagiography of the guild system. Such guilds he contended 'were often terribly quarrelsome amongst themselves, almost as much inclined to scrap with each other as capital and labour are inclined to scrap with each other today'.[65] He also stressed that western democracy was fundamentally right and that he did not want vocationalism used here as in Italy 'simply to buttress dictatorship, to give a facade of consultation with the people'.[66] However, he desired to see once and for all, whether vocationalism could work in this country. Predictably, Michael Tierney's call for a commission stemmed more from a conviction than a curiosity in vocationalism.

De Valera could hardly have refused the request for a commission, especially in the light of his expressed interest in vocationalism and after instigating a series of radio talks on it. Therefore on 10 July 1939 a commission was duly appointed. It was asked to examine and report on: (a) the practicability of developing functional or vocational organisation; (b) the means best calculated

---

62 M. Tierney, 'Vocationalism and parliamentary democracy: are they reconcilable', *Irish Monthly*, vol. lxvi (June 1938), 371.  63 Ibid.  64 Seanad Debates, vol. xxi, no. 7, 13 July 1938.  65 Ibid.  66 Ibid.

to promote such development; (c) the rights and powers which should be imposed on functional or vocational bodies and generally the relations of such bodies to the Oireachtas and the Government; and (d) the legislative and administrative measures that would be required.[67] The vocationalists finally had an opportunity to examine the practicalities of such a system in Ireland.

## PUBLIC DISCOURSE

Meanwhile the public discussion on vocationalism continued. One paper that avidly supported the vocationalist cause was the *Standard*. Founded originally in 1928 it had always been supportive of Catholic social teaching but with its re-launch in 1938 this became even more apparent. The first new issue of 2 December declared: 'The new *Standard*, an independent organ of Catholic news and views has for its first object the creation of a united public opinion in the case of Catholic reconstruction.' It identified the Catholic Church as 'the last stronghold of corporative freedom, the only force that could stand out against the modern State'.

Eight years after its publication in 1931 there was however still uncertainty among the public about what *Quadragesimo Anno* exactly said. One of the paper's readers wrote to the paper in December 1938 to ask whether Pius XI had declared himself in favour of the 'Corporate State'.[68] In its response the paper emphasised that what the pope actually advocated was a vocational society, but that he stayed out of the political realm. In order to help people understand exactly what this and other encyclicals entailed the *Standard* began a series of articles on 6 January 1939 called 'The encyclicals simplified'. The paper explained that the lack of knowledge among ordinary Irishman about the Pope's proposals was caused by the fact that the encyclicals were 'written in a traditional and formal style, which is full of dignity but is not conducive to easy reading'. To justify this belated attempt to find support for the vocational idea it argued: 'The message of *Quadragesimo Anno* is of such importance today that every means should be taken to spread it as widely as possible.'

The *Standard* also challenged the 'essentially English character' of the government's economic policy and argued that the country needed a new vocationalist one. With this it hoped to tap into the belief in some nationalist circles that Ireland's economic misfortune was linked to what was regarded as misguided British policies, and the desire to develop a more native approach to economics. Pius XI's suggestions in *Quadragesimo Anno* were to be the starting point. Writing in the *Standard*, Stephen Ward, an economic correspondent, asked: '[when] are we going to have the social order outlined in the Papal Encyclicals and desired by all decent people'.[69] On 2 June 1939 the editorial

**67** Lee, 'Aspects of corporatist thought', 326. **68** *Standard*, 30 December 1938. **69** Ibid., 17 March 1939.

'The Catholic Press – its urgent duty' stated: 'To urge the energetic application of remedies which His Holiness declared to be urgent, is not only per-
missible, but is a foremost duty of the Catholic press.' Referring back to Britain's
influence on the country's economy it continued: 'Ireland is still weighed down
by this economic system imposed on us in the past. It is the evils of this condition which we have actually to reform and not the opposite abuse of communism.' In a similar vein, Hugh O'Neill, in his radio talk on 'How vocationalism would promote social justice', argued that monetary reform would
be needed: 'before we can hope to see the vocationalist order in being we must
recognise the fact that our present social monetary system is dominated by the
necessity of money profit as its sole activating motive and therefore interests
are inevitable and groups impossible'.[70]

In this regard vocationalists and nationalists had pinned their hopes on the
banking commission set up by de Valera in 1934:

> to examine and report on the system in Saorstat Éireann of currency,
> banking, credit, public borrowing and lending, and pledging of state credit
> on behalf of agriculture, industry and the social services, and to consider
> and report what changes, if any, are necessary or desirable to promote
> the social and economic welfare of the community and the interest of
> agriculture and industry.[71]

However, the Commission's report published in 1938 merely endorsed the
economic status quo. This it seems pleased de Valera, who had indicated to the
governor of the Bank of Ireland, back in 1934 that he did not favour changes
in Irish financial affairs, but had merely gone along with the appointment of a
commission to placate the extremists in his own party.[72] P.J. O'Loghlen voiced
the concerns of nationalists and vocationalists alike in his minority report: 'is it
right and necessary that in a country in which over 92 per cent of the people
profess the Catholic faith, due regard should be had to the pronouncement of
the Papacy on the subject of socio-economics.' He challenged the commission's recommendations 'that the Irish currency should not be managed by an
Irish authority to suit the particular needs of Ireland but should be attached at
a fixed parity to the currency of Great Britain and should follow in whatever
direction Great Britain will lead'.[73] De Valera had seemed to support such ideas
when he headed the opposition back in 1928. Criticising Cumann na
nGaedheal's economic policies he had stated: 'I see them letting things go on.
I see them hanging on following a system which they have inherited from outside.'[74] Now de Valera seemed to be doing exactly the same thing much to the
dismay of vocationalists. The fact that the banking commission supported such

**70** *Irish Monthly*, vol. lxvi.   **71** Coogan, *De Valera*, 506.   **72** Ibid., 505.   **73** P.J. O'Loughlen,
'Commission of Inquiry into Banking, Currency, and Credit 1938', Minority Report no.
III, 4. Copy in the National Library of Ireland.   **74** Moynihan, *Speeches and statements*, 161.

'inherited economics' proved that in spite of nationalist rhetoric the death of British style capitalism had been greatly exaggerated.

THE REPORT OF THE
COMMISSION ON VOCATIONAL ORGANISATION

All hopes for thorough reform now rested with the vocationalist commission. In their request for it, Senators Tierney and MacDermot had asked that it be a small one of about ten people in order to be efficient and effective. However, perhaps to delay the report, De Valera had twenty-five members assigned and stated this was necessary 'in order that persons with a knowledge and experience covering a wide field may be included'.[75] The Commission on Vocational Organisation met for the first time on 3 March 1939 to 'determine whether in the circumstances of this moment, it was practicable to develop here a general form of organisation of that character'.[76] It was chaired by Dr Michael Browne, the bishop of Galway, and included various influential people representing the church, universities, labour, employers, agriculture and other miscellaneous groups. Familiar names included Senator Michael Tierney, Dr Alfred O'Rahilly (of the *Standard*), Fr E.J. Coyne (of the Society of Jesus), Fr John Hayes (the founder of Muintir na Tire) and 'Big Jim' Larkin. Altogether the commission met for 164 days from 10 March 1939 until 4 November 1943 and sat for a mammoth 312 sessions. It collected both oral and documentary evidence, sending out a questionnaire to 333 organisations.[77]

The commission's first meeting was well covered in the press and de Valera announced at the opening session that 'if the commission could evolve a scheme that would work, it would have conferred the greatest benefit that could be given to the nation at the present time'.[78] Claiming that he 'did not think that there had been set up in this country since they had got the right to govern themselves a commission that was so important from the point of view of the public well-being'.[79] However, in typical fashion he stressed that the commission's function would not be political but would only be of a social and economic nature.[80] De Valera was clearly adamant from the start that no proposals made would limit him or his government's political authority.

The commission's report was initially presented to the government in November 1943 but it was not until August 1944 that it was officially published as an extensive 540-page examination of the vocational system as it applied to Ireland.[81] The commission achieved a high degree of unanimity, out of the twenty-five members only three refused to put their names to the report.

---

**75** Letters to member of the Commission on Vocational Organisation from de Valera, in Department of an Taoiseach, NA, S10677B. **76** *Irish Times*, 3 March 1939. **77** Lee, 'Aspects of corporatist thought', 327; *Irish Independent*, 18 August 1944. **78** Ibid. **79** Ibid. **80** *Irish Press*, 3 March 1939. **81** Lee, 'Aspects of corporatist thought', 328.

J.H. Whyte contends that the report was important as an analysis of what was deemed to be wrong with Irish society and the remedies it proposed for these.[82] The report was indeed very critical of government's role in socio-economic affairs, but for those who had followed or supported the rhetoric of Irish vocationalists, the commission's proposals would have caused little surprise.[83]

The setting up of a 'National Vocational Assembly' representing the various occupational group was once again suggested. It should have a three-fold function of co-ordinating, planning and advising on Irish socio-economic policy. It proposed the assembly should have a co-ordinating role in industrial relations, social security and economic regulation of the country. It would also act as a final court of appeal in any dispute between vocational groups. In relation to its planning capacity it was suggested that it would seek solutions for the problems of unemployment and emigration. Finally in its advisory role it should be considered 'the only body to which the government should apply for information or suggestions on the best means of attaining national policy'.[84] Furthermore, it was argued that the assembly should have the right to obtain information from government departments on regulations, quotas, licences, tariffs and exemptions, and to submit reports to the government on its own initiative and have them published.[85] In addition the report suggested that a governing body of twenty-four people should be set up to work alongside a new National Vocational Office, which would be a separate and distinct entity from the civil service.[86] Clearly the report was very ambitious in its proposals and the potential for construing their suggestions as being 'political' was very much in evidence. There was no doubt that politicians would have had to justify their decisions much more to an independent vocational assembly and its governing body than to a partisan Dáil and dependent civil service.

Prior to the release of the report the *Irish Press* announced that: 'the publication of the report will be eagerly awaited. It comes at a time when the air is full of plans for post-war reconstruction and development and when national and local authorities are preparing schemes to deal with the post-war requirements.' However, they added a cautionary note: 'if feasible proposals are made, which can be adopted they will naturally influence the plans that are being made.'[87] The *Irish Independent* reacted to the report by asserting that the commission's recommendations were 'a desirable antidote to bureaucracy and to the menacing increase in government affairs'.[88] However, it astutely pointed out that the commission's proposal that the National Vocational Assembly should act as an advisory body to the government would 'inevitably be setting its opinions and advice against those of the permanent officials, and in a con-

82 Whyte, *The Church and State*, op. cit., 97.   83 Lee, 'Aspects of corporatist thought', 328. 84 'Report of the Commission on Vocational Organisation in Ireland', *International Labour Review* (January 1945), Department of An Taoiseach, NA, S13556.   85 Ibid.   86 Lee, 'Aspects of corporatist thought', 325.   87 *Irish Press*, 18 August 1944.   88 *Irish Independent*, 18 August 1944.

flict between a purely advisory body on the one hand and bureaucracy on the other, bureaucracy is bound to win, unless the legislature shows a desire not hitherto perceptible, to curb the bureaucrats'. The paper concluded, nonetheless, that the Commission's recommendations were sound and could be given effect in the social system of the nation.

What ultimately mattered however was how the Fianna Fáil administration would react. Just prior to the publication of the report on 28 October 1943, Sean Lemass, the Minister for Supplies and for Industry and Commerce, spoke at the TCD Philosophy Society on 'Planned society'.[89] The talk turned out to be a defence of the present political structure and directly challenged some of the criticisms that vocationalists had thrown at it. Pre-empting the likely criticism his department would receive from the vocational commission's report, Lemass argued that a great deal of nonsense had been talked about bureaucracy. He stressed that it was untrue to suggest that all extensions of government control were forced on an unwilling population and that the government only intervened when public interest so required. In a reference to the type of distorted vocationalism of the likes of Mussolini, he argued that politicians were necessary if the advantages of a planned economy were to be secured without the risk of a dictatorship. He also felt that the government should retain the emergency powers it had even when the present war was over. This talk made clear that even before the publication of the report it was obvious that the government and the vocational commission were at opposite poles as far as the State's role in society was concerned.

The vocational commission indeed challenged Lemass and his department head on. In its report it argued that the Department of Industry and Commerce had failed to consult with vocational groups on issues that directly affected those groups. It also contended that the department had no overall economic plan and that 'such planning as appeared was sectional, local, piecemeal and unbalanced. It neglected one overriding factor, namely the necessary unity of the economic structure.'[90] The report rather predictably challenged the centralised authority of the state: 'when extensive powers of control over practically every phase of economic life are exercised by officials, true liberty is seriously diminished as the individual citizen finds his activity circumscribed and regulated by an anonymous power'.[91]

Certainly the state in general had become more involved in people's lives and may have seemed overpowering compared to the separation that existed between politics and economics in nineteenth-century governments. But times had moved on and the Depression had forced governments to take interventionist action to protect their citizens as much as possible from uncertain economic trends. While some abused the situation and formed totalitarian regimes others merely tried to adapt to a time of economic and even political uncer-

**89** *Irish Press*, 29 October 1943. **90** Report of the Commission on Vocational Organisation, cited in Lee, 'Aspects of corporatist thought', 337. **91** Ibid., 336.

tainty. To charge the Fianna Fáil government with being an overbearing power was frankly unfair. It ignored the strong connection the party had with its grass-roots and its ultimate adherence to democratic principles.

Not surprisingly there was extreme criticism of the commission's report from within the civil service. The Department of Finance in particular voiced its strong opposition to some of its proposals, claiming the report gave no critical exami-nation of vocational organisation but took for granted the supposed desirability of vocationalism. This of course was also clearly evident in the articles written by vocationalists up to this time. The difference now was that vocationalists had by way of the commission been given an official platform to air their views, which consequently had to be taken seriously. Up until this point politicians had merely paid lip service to the concept hinting approval while doing nothing con-structive, but now the practicalities of vocationalism were scrutinised like never before and a response was necessary. The department rightly pointed out that if new bodies were set up as outlined in the report they would ultimately assume functions that were now being carried out by the government, and would there-fore result in a 'political' change. It also noted the potential for conflict and the danger that economic groups would have undue powers over the community at large. They understandably claimed that the proposal for vocational bodies to be set up would in fact lead to an even bigger and more expensive bureaucracy, which would have totally contradicted the vocationalist philosophy. The report's rough estimate that the new structure would cost between £100,000 and £200,000 only heightened the department's disdain.[92]

This strong and well-argued objection seems to have summed up the feel-ing in the civil service. One civil servant wrote to de Valera's private secretary on 12 July 1945 saying,

> I do not think that I have ever come across a report which annoyed me more. [...] I sincerely hope that the government ministers will at best give as good as they've got when the report comes up for discussion. If someone in authority does not prick the balloon in good time, there is a danger that all the sillybillies through the country who have neither seen nor heard the theological support and blessing it has been receiving, will be passing resolutions calling for its adoption.[93]

Criticism from outside government circles was also evident. H.M. Dockrell, chairman of the Federated Manufacturers, challenged the whole concept of the 'common good' on which vocationalism was based. He told Dr Browne the chairman during the commission's inquiry: 'You are really a bit altruistic in the suggestion that the Federation should act for business in general, rather than

**92** Preliminary Examination by Department of Finance on Vocational Report, Department of An Taoiseach, NA, S13552.   **93** Civil Servant to M. Moynihan, 12 January 1945, Department of An Taoiseach, NA, S13552.

for the vital concerns of the specific interests it represents.'[94] Vocationalist somewhat naively seemed to believe that those motivated by self-interest in a capitalist system would suddenly be reformed in a vocationalist one!

The commission's report was keen to stress that their vocational system could
operate alongside the present system of parliamentary democracy. However,
the reforms that were requested in order to make this possible made the idea
unpalatable to politicians in general. Ultimately what was needed were changes
in the political structures that no one in government was willing to make. As a
result, the Fianna Fáil administration simply chose to ignore the report and only
referred to it in a critical capacity.[95] The commission had probably anticipated
this, but the frustration with the lack of movement towards vocational structures since 1931 meant that the report had become a protest document against
the government's socio-economic policy. Its resulting critical tone meant that
even de Valera himself was unable to give token respect to the document.

## CONCLUSION

The reaction to the commission's report clearly proved beyond doubt that the
whole concept of vocationalism was not regarded as a feasible option by those
in power. It seems that its rhetoric and the image of Ireland as a nation set free
from its British past were appealing, but the practicalities of a less centrally controlled society were not. The rhetoric of vocationalism was allowed to remain
unchallenged for over a decade in a nation keen to enhance its Catholic identity. In reality, however, Irish society was becoming more modern and the association with capitalism was as firm as ever. In fact the nation's economic depen-
dence on Britain was clearly shown by the hardship endured during the economic
war with Britain and the Emergency. Instead of a decrease in State interference
in the nation's economy de Valera's first years in office saw a substantial increase,
as the government tried to deal in turn with the general economic depression,
economic sanctions from Britain, and the consequences of a world war.

As Peter J. Williamson argues, vocationalist thought emerged as a response
to the disappearance of the *ancien régime* in many continental European countries during the nineteenth century and initially came from those who had lost ·
out most with the emergence of capitalism and the liberal political institutions
that followed. Little wonder then, he notes, that the earliest theorists were
either exclusively aristocrats or Catholics, or both.[96] In Ireland the situation
was no different except that intellectuals (rather than aristocrats) along with the
Catholic clergy advocated this system based on the medieval guilds. They too
looked back to a bygone age when Ireland was free from British influence.
Vocationalism would restore this order, or so they thought. But the vocation-

**94** Lee, 'Aspects of corporatist thought', 338.  **95** Whyte, *The Church and State*, op. cit., 106.
**96** P. Williamson, *Varieties of corporatism* (Cambridge, 1985), 19.

alists never received enough public support for their ideas and so were constantly beholding to a government whose interest was minimal.

In countries like Italy attempts were made to make the concept more populist and Mussolini succeeded for a while. His ultimate failure, however, and the distortion of the vocationalist ideal by fascists caused the concept to lose much of its credibility. It seemed that the only way vocational organisation would take place in a capitalist democracy was if a dictator forced it on the people. The contradictions within the ideology meant that in spite of its disdain for centralised government, it needed a sympathetic government to introduce the reforms they required. This was especially true in Ireland due to the lack of grass root support and vocationalism's rather exclusive appeal to Catholic clergy and certain intellectual figures. De Valera had the charisma to get mass support for the vocationalist ideal if he believed in it. The fact was he did not. While he spoke about the merits of vocationalism, as he did about comely maidens and honest farmers, the reality was he was moving the nation forward as a capitalist democracy. As John A. Murphy argues: 'Fianna Fáil's anxiety to establish its Catholic credentials faded according as its electoral strength grew, and the challenge to vocationalism came at a time when it was securely established in power.'[97]

The message of *Quadragesimo Anno* and the vocationalism it espoused strengthened the nation's Catholic consciousness. However, its idealism and impracticalities, shown in the vocational commission's report, meant it would have no substantial influence on Irish political or economic life. During World War Two and its aftermath governments needed to manage their resources and develop a more rational economy. In a radio broadcast in 1940, de Valera indicated his belief in the State's control of all areas of the nation's affairs: 'The very notion of the State is futile if it not be conceded that there exists within the State one single and sovereign directing power having the supreme right effectively to co-ordinate all wills in the pursuit of the common end.'[98] The Commission on Vocational Organisation was ultimately just going through the motions in preparing their report. Although forcing the government and its civil servants to at least reflect on a possible different way of conducting the nation's affairs, it was clear that de Valera was not going to concede any government power to occupational groupings. *Quadragesimo Anno* and the commission's report were out of step with the direction de Valera's government was going. The reality was that Ireland and Europe were moving further and further away from the medieval guild system on which vocationalism was based. In that system the Roman Catholic Church had played a powerful role. Now, in post-war Europe it was the State who wielded most control and influence over people's lives. That influence was something that Eamon de Valera and Fianna Fáil were loath to give up.

---

97 John A. Murphy, 'The achievement of Eamon de Valera', in John P. O'Carroll and John A. Murphy (eds.), *De Valera and his times* (Cork, 1983), 7.   98 Moynihan, *Speeches and statements*, 423.

FEARGHAL McGARRY

# General O'Duffy, the National Corporate Party and the Irish Brigade

> We are leaving for a battlefield, and now words seem in a sense to have no great significance, for we have entered on that phase when action will speak far louder. Intensely conscious of my own responsibilities and, moved by the realisation of the personal sacrifice and the consequent individual greatness of every Volunteer, I am reminded of Lincoln's simple words at Gettysburg: 'The world will little note nor long remember what we say here, but it can never forget what they did here'.
>
> General O'Duffy, 20 November 1936[1]

While the world may not remember what the Irish Brigade did in Spain, the short-lived involvement of General Franco's Irish volunteers in the Spanish Civil War has ever since proved a source of amusement for Irish wits. Brendan Behan famously remarked that 'the Irish who fought for Franco appeared to achieve the remarkable military feat of coming home with more men than they went out with'.[2] Folk songs like Christy Moore's *Vive el Quinte Brigada* contrast the bravery of the Irish 'comradeship of heroes' in the International Brigades with the Blueshirts who 'sailed beneath the Swastika to Spain'. The republican ballad, *O'Duffy's Ironsides*, later recorded by Ronnie Drew, satirises 'the fierce Crusaders' who went 'off to slaughter workers in the sunny land of Spain'. It is only recently that historians have begun to look at the story of the Irish Brigade and attempted to discover the reality behind the popular myth.[3] The focus of this article is the role of Eoin O'Duffy[4] in the brigade. Irish historians have generally considered O'Duffy's participation in the Spanish Civil War as a well-meaning if risible epilogue to his controversial leadership of the Blueshirt movement – the semi-fascist organisation of the early 1930s – which

---

1 *Irish Independent*, 20 February 1937. 2 Brendan Behan, *Confessions of an Irish rebel* (London, 1991 ed.), 135. 3 In particular see, Dermot Keogh, *Ireland and Europe – 1919-89* (Cork, Dublin, 1990) and, R.A. Stradling, 'Battleground of Reputations: Ireland and the Spanish Civil War', in *The Republic besieged: civil war in Spain* (Edinburgh, 1996).

ended (at least as far as most Blueshirts were concerned) following his resignation from Fine Gael in 1934. However, to understand what led to the Irish
Brigade's participation in the Spanish Civil War a detailed study of O'Duffy's
political career after his resignation from the presidency of Fine Gael is necessary. O'Duffy's activities during this period, centred on the marginal and politically unrewarding fringes of far-right politics, have received little attention.
But the history of his short-lived fascist organisation, the National Corporate
Party, in particular, provides a useful insight into the origins of the Irish Brigade.
Aside from O'Duffy's political career, the experiences of the seven hundred
volunteers who followed him to Spain are also considered. What motivated so
many Irishmen to fight for General Franco? Was their military performance
really as disastrous as has been popularly depicted?

O'DUFFY AND IRISH FASCISM

General O'Duffy is best known for his leadership of the Blueshirts. Following
his dismissal as Garda Commissioner by Eamon de Valera in February 1933,
O'Duffy was invited to assume command of the recently founded anti-communist Army Comrades Association (ACA). This was a veteran organisation,
open to ex-Irish Army men, which was the forerunner of the Blueshirt movement. Under O'Duffy's control, the National Guard (as the ACA was renamed)
became extremely popular espousing increasingly radical views particularly in
its opposition to the IRA and the payment of land annuities to the government. Following its proscription by de Valera in 1933, the National Guard
amalgamated with the Centre Party and the main opposition party, Cumann
na nGaedheal, to form Fine Gael. Despite his lack of political experience and
apparent distaste for parliamentary democracy, General O'Duffy became the
first president of Fine Gael while W.T. Cosgrave, the leader of Cumann na
nGaedheal, led the party in the Dáil. It was an arrangement which most of the
more moderate leaders within Fine Gael soon came to regret. Following
increasing criticism of his violent rhetoric and unconventional leadership,
O'Duffy dramatically resigned from Fine Gael in September 1934.

Following the shock resignation, the Blueshirt movement was thrown into
further disarray when O'Duffy insisted that his resignation applied only to the
presidency of Fine Gael and not to his leadership of the League of Youth (formerly the National Guard) which had maintained a semi-autonomous status
within Fine Gael. Ned Cronin,[5] who had been appointed O'Duffy's successor

4 Eoin O'Duffy (1892-1944): b. Co. Monaghan; auctioneer; secretary, GAA Ulster Council;
director of organisation, IRA, 1921; Monaghan TD 1921-2; chief of staff, National Army,
1922; Garda Commissioner 1922-33; leader, Army Comrades Association (ACA), 1933; first
president of Fine Gael, 1933; resigned September 1934.  5 Edmund Cronin: b. Charleville,
Co. Cork; farmer and landowner; ACA founder, 1932; Fine Gael vice-president, 1933;

as director-general of the League by Fine Gael's executive committee, responded by suspending O'Duffy's supporters within the organisation. Most senior Blueshirts and almost all of the Cumann na nGaedheal/Centre Party section of Fine Gael sided with Cronin against O'Duffy. By late 1934 the controversy receded as it became apparent that O'Duffy had failed to retain the loyalty of the vast majority of Blueshirt activists. However, there were now two organisations styling themselves the League of Youth and many activists preferred to leave the movement rather than choose sides.

Relieved of his responsibilities as leader of the opposition, O'Duffy became increasingly involved in international fascism. In December 1934 he attended the Nazi-sponsored International Action of Nationalisms conference in Zurich and the Italian-controlled Comitati d'azione per l'Universalità di Roma at Montreaux. The latter appointed O'Duffy to the secretariat of the Fascist International – a co-ordinating committee for fascist propaganda. In January 1935 he met Mussolini in Rome and attended a meeting organised by the right-wing Catholic Italia e fede to establish the Centre for Corporative Studies. As leader of the Blueshirts, O'Duffy had promoted corporatism – the belief that workers and employers form bodies to regulate industry and economic activity in order to eliminate class conflict – and succeeded in persuading Fine Gael to adopt it as party policy in 1934.[6] The corporate society, as envisaged by the papal encyclical *Quadragesimo Anno* and many Irish Catholic intellectuals was not necessarily incompatible with parliamentary democracy, but in practice, corporatism, or more precisely the corporate state, was associated with fascist or authoritarian European regimes such as Mussolini's Italy. The variety espoused by O'Duffy clearly owed more to Mussolini than Pius XI.

Back in Ireland, Special Branch reports reveal that O'Duffy's section of the League of Youth adopted a radical change of tactics during 1935, presumably to attract more support. In early 1935 O'Duffy still displayed the traditional Blueshirt hostility towards republicans – belligerently telling supporters in Bandon, 'we have as much guns as the IRA'.[7] By May, though, there were indications that O'Duffy was courting republican support. He announced his intention to establish a new constitution based on the 1916 Proclamation and instructed his supporters not to inform on republicans. When O'Duffy visited Cashel the gardaí reported that two Blueshirts visited a local republican to set up a meeting with the IRA:

> General O'Duffy is now most anxious to draw as many as possible of the extreme Republican element into the new Organisation, and the rank

replaced O'Duffy as director-general, (official) League of Youth, 1934; expelled from Fine Gael, October 1936; attempted to lead rival brigade to Spain, November 1936. **6** Eugene Broderick, 'The corporate labour policy of Fine Gael, 1934', *Irish Historical Studies*, vol. xxix, no. 113 (May 1994), 88–99. **7** Garda report, 17 March 1935, NA, D/Jus., D32/36 (1993 release series, now re-indexed as Justice 8 series).

and file of his supporters are instructed to cultivate the utmost friendliness with the IRA.[8]

The report astutely continued: 'it can safely be assumed that this new pose will not have a very long life' – a supposition based on the legacy of civil war bitterness which divided Blueshirts and republicans. The IRA in Cashel, at any rate, declined to meet O'Duffy.

During the same period O'Duffy proposed another unlikely initiative. In May, his newspaper, the *Blueshirt*, announced the formation of the 32 Club in Northern Ireland. The 32 Club had many of the features typical of O'Duffy's idiosyncratic political style – the avowal of non-political intentions (a common theme among European corporatist leaders during this period), the attempt to identify corporatism with Gaelic medieval guilds, and the planning of the most minor organisational details (pp 96-116 above). By O'Duffy's extremist standards, however, the 32 Club was tempered by an uncharacteristically conciliatory policy on Northern Ireland. The 32 Club aimed to cultivate cross-border relations to achieve the voluntary re-unification of Ireland through 'the reinstitution of an independent Irish Monarchy linked by dynastic ties to the British Commonwealth of Nations'. By 'giving a new emphasis to our millennial culture and historic traditions' the organisation would 'satisfy the dual aspirations of humanity for an arbitral paternal authority and democratic social reforms'. Each branch organiser would be known as a Pioneer and wear a silver badge provided by the organisation. (The latter details perhaps inspired by O'Duffy's admiration for the Pioneer Total Abstinence Association.)[9] The discussion of 'party politics' would be 'rigidly discouraged'. The most curious detail was the instruction that at each meeting 'a chair shall be left vacant in a prominent position reserved for the personage who is to give embodiment to the idea of National unity'. This 'personage' was not identified but it seems likely that O'Duffy's ambitions had now risen from dictatorial to monarchic.

The main purpose of the 32 Club was to forge an alliance with the Ulster Fascists, one of Northern Ireland's several tiny fascist organisations. The Ulster Fascists – who claimed 'no connection with British Fascists Limited of Kilkeel fame'[10] – were led by Job Stott, a B Special and director of the Ulster Centre of Fascist Studies. Stott's organisation had close links with the British Union of Fascists. Established in the autumn of 1933, the Ulster Fascists aimed to replace both existing Irish states with a united fascist dominion within the British Empire. In April 1935 a delegation of O'Duffy's Blueshirts led by Captain The

---

8 Ibid., 1 May 1935, NA, D/Jus., B9/35. For a description of corporatism and its wider response in the Free State see pp 96-116 above.  **9** *Garda Review*, March 1930, 318.  **10** Ulster Centre of Fascist Studies, *A brief introduction to Fascism in Ulster* (pamphlet, n.d.). The Kilkeel section of the British Fascists, led by Dorothy Harnett since the mid-1920s, combined extreme loyalism and fascist ideology, but, in contrast to the Ulster Fascists, was not closely linked to Oswald Mosley's British Union of Fascists.

O'Donovan met Stott and other Ulster Fascists at the Grand Central Hotel in Belfast. The negotiations foundered and Stott's motion to establish a branch of the 32 Club was defeated by two Blueshirts, Brendan Kielty[11] and Jack Hewitt. The reasons for the failure of what was probably Ireland's only cross-border fascist initiative are not clear but RUC Special Branch reports indicate considerable disunity and incompetence among both Blueshirt delegations:

> From what can be ascertained the meeting resolved itself into a huge farce, no one apparently taking the proceedings seriously. McKeaveney [an Ulster Fascist] is described as a 'mental case' and The O'Donovan may be described as falling within the same category. No attempts have been made to hold further meetings.[12]

Although O'Duffy's attempts to forge alliances with the IRA and Ulster Fascists appear ill-conceived they were not without some logic. The gulf between the Blueshirts and the IRA was not as wide as their mutual animosity would suggest. Much of the Blueshirt movement, in contrast to Fine Gael, was fervently nationalistic and irredentist. Their support for Cumann na nGaedheal and the merger with them into Fine Gael resulted from their allegiance to Collins and Griffith during the Treaty split and a virulent enmity towards de Valera rather than any strong belief in Cumann na nGaedheal's policies. Many Blueshirts disapproved of the moderate nationalism of Cumann na nGaedheal/Fine Gael. The militancy of their nationalism was a significant factor in O'Duffy's forced resignation from Fine Gael.

Colonel P.J. Coughlan's[13] personal account of the Cork Blueshirts illustrates this extreme nationalism. Coughlan, like O'Duffy, was deeply scornful of the moderate section of Fine Gael personified by politicians such as James Dillon and Frank MacDermot – 'who never lost even an hour's sleep for the freedom of this country.' Coughlan sided with Collins because of de Valera's 'trickery' during the Treaty negotiations. Although he emphatically rejected the perfidy

---

11 Kielty, a chemist's assistant from Plumbridge, Co. Tyrone, and former engineer with the IRA, later served in the Irish Brigade. 12 RUC report, 12 June 1935, PRONI, Home Affairs 32/1/615. The reports do not suggest why two Blueshirts should vote against establishing a branch of what was apparently intended by O'Duffy as either a Blueshirt 'front' or a unifying organisation for southern and northern fascists. Interestingly, a previous abortive initiative to link the Blueshirts and Ulster Fascists in September 1934 had proved disastrous for both organisations – resulting in the latter group splitting and contributing further to the tensions between O'Duffy and the Fine Gael leadership. See James Loughlin, 'Northern Ireland and British fascism in the inter-war years', *Irish Historical Studies*, vol. xxix, no. 116 (November 1995), 548 and Maurice Manning, *The Blueshirts* (Dublin, 1987), 151. 13 P.J. Coughlan: ex-National Army officer; leading Blueshirt activist in the Cork area; remained loyal to O'Duffy following split with Fine Gael; appointed deputy director-general of O'Duffy's League of Youth/NCP; organised recruitment of Irish Brigade volunteers in Cork.

of Fianna Fáil, Coughlan opposed the 1930s IRA only because of their inef-
fectual idealism. In a revealing passage, written during the height of the Blueshirt
conflict with the IRA, Coughlan declared:

> I say here straight to you if I had only my choice of two stands to take
> up tomorrow in the Public Life of this country, well – I'd stand by [Tom]
> Barry and [Sean] Buckley, because I'd be a hypocrite to my own princi-
> ple if I stood with de Valera, and yet I know Barry could not get me any-
> where.[14]

Apart from this nationalistic affinity, the ideological differences between the
IRA and the Blueshirts had diminished after most of the left-wing membership of the IRA broke away in 1934 to form Republican Congress.[15] The
potential for co-operation was later demonstrated by the IRA's willingness to
aid Germany's inept espionage missions in Ireland during World War Two.
Another motive for some form of co-operation was de Valera's application of
coercion against both organisations. By 1935 the Blueshirts were largely a van-
quished force and de Valera was effectively targeting his public safety powers
against the IRA.

The alliance between O'Duffy's irredentist Blueshirts and the Ulster Fascists
('the most British Organisation in the Empire') was also not as unlikely as might
appear. The latter's assertion that the 'Red Hand of Ulster is the Grasping Hand
of Communism and the Grabbing Fist of Party Government' indicates they
shared O'Duffy's hostility towards Unionists and liberal democracy, and a pro-
clivity to invent communist threats. More significantly, the Ulster Fascists
declared:

> The BLUESHIRT movement in the Free State is to a great extent FASCIST
> minded. From a FASCIST viewpoint IT'S ONLY HOPE for the SALVATION
> OF IRELAND is to remain WITHIN THE EMPIRE … A DOMINION OF IRE-
> LAND within the British Empire of FASCIST NATIONS would receive our
> full support.[16]

Although imbued with a thoroughly British and Imperialist ethos – and hostile to the idea of an independent Irish Republic – the Ulster Fascists were
opposed to Stormont and Ulster Unionism. In this context O'Duffy's decision
to manoeuvre the Blueshirts into a broader coalition of anti-Free State forces

14 P.J. Coughlan, *The truth. The story of the Blueshirts* (Skibbereen, 1934), 26. Barry and
Buckley were prominent republicans.  15 The short-lived Republican Congress was established following tensions between left-wing republicans and the militaristic leadership of the
IRA when a substantial minority of activists under the leadership of Peadar O'Donnell and
George Gilmore formed the new organisation to create a united front of socialist and republican forces.  16 Ulster Centre of Fascist Studies, *A brief introduction to Fascism in Ulster* (n.p.,
n.d.), 13.

should not be dismissed as ridiculous. However, O'Duffy's resounding lack of success in implementing this strategy suggests that his ambitions far outweighed his political competence.

O'Duffy followed these attempts to realign his dwindling section of the League of Youth by establishing a new political organisation. In November 1934 it had been rumoured that O'Duffy was planning a new political party with Patrick Belton,[17] a former Fine Gael colleague, to promote farming interests. However, O'Duffy's National Corporate Party (NCP), formed without Belton's support, did not appear until June 1935. At the inaugural convention on 8 June O'Duffy outlined the NCP's objectives; the abolition of 'party politics', the establishment of a united Irish corporate state, and the protection of liberties against communism, capitalism and dictatorships. Three hundred and fifty delegates attended the meeting, which nevertheless lacked the Blueshirt movement's previous dynamism. (The organisation was essentially comprised of those Blueshirts who had remained loyal to O'Duffy). The meeting was devoted to recriminations over the Blueshirt split and lengthy procedural wrangling between O'Duffy and his executive committee. Special Branch (curiously adopting the same phrase as their colleagues in Northern Ireland) described the convention as 'little better than a huge farce' and felt there was 'little to fear from this Movement'.[18] Events during the rest of the year confirm this. O'Duffy made little attempt to establish branches or attract publicity.[19] This may have been due to his involvement with European fascism or, more likely, a reflection of the lack of Irish support for fascism. The opposition of Cronin's Blueshirts was also an important factor. O'Duffy's attempts to set up branches in Co. Cork were violently disrupted by pro-Cronin Blueshirts. By late 1935 the gardaí noted that O'Duffy's support in the important Blueshirt region of west Cork – which had equalled Cronin's following the split – was now far weaker.[20]

The NCP soon found itself in trouble. During the summer of 1935 financial difficulties compelled O'Duffy to cease publication of the *Nation* and the party could no longer afford to retain Thomas Gunning[21] as full-time general secretary. As the NCP slipped further into obscurity O'Duffy's plans grew increasingly ambitious. He appeared unable to appreciate the marginal position of his party. At the next general election the NCP executive expected to

**17** Patrick Belton (1885-1945): born Lanesborough, Co. Longford; fought in 1916; farmer, publican and property developer; elected Fianna Fáil TD but left to enter Dáil, 1927; re-elected Cumann na nGaedheal but soon resigned; co-founder National Centre Party which merged into Fine Gael; expelled for support of O'Duffy, 1934; Irish Christian Front founder, 1936; re-admitted and left Fine Gael once again; lost seat in 1943 general election. **18** Special Branch report, 8 June 1935, NA, D/Jus., B23/35. **19** Manning, *The Blueshirts*, 200. **20** Garda report, 29 October 1935, NA, D/Jus., B9/35. **21** Thomas Gunning: studied for priesthood at Freiburg University but took up journalism; edited *Catholic Standard* newspaper; O'Duffy's personal secretary, 1933-6; enlisted in the Irish Brigade and remained in Spain as Nationalist advisor during the war; employed by Propaganda Ministry in Berlin (writing broadcasts for William Joyce), 1939-40; died of TB in Breslau, Germany, June 1940.

'secure one seat in each of the twenty constituencies, two seats in one con-
stituency, and no seat in 13 constituencies.'[22] O'Duffy, moreover, believed that
'the estimate was not an optimistic one' and formulated far-reaching policies,
including finance reform, a national credit system and a vocational parliament,
to be introduced when his party gained an over-all majority.[23]

Significantly, the only burst of activity within the NCP occurred following the Italian invasion of Abyssinia in 1935. O'Duffy was extremely critical of
the government's support for League of Nations sanctions against Italy. In
September he announced: 'several Blueshirts have volunteered for service, not
for Italy or against Abyssinia, but for the principles of the Corporate system.'
An internal party bulletin claimed that 'hundreds' of Blueshirts volunteered.
Two months later, however, the NCP executive committee rejected the proposal declaring that Italy needed moral rather than military support.[24] The NCP
continued to decline during 1936. In March the party adopted a new uniform
of green shirts, green ties, and '1916 Volunteer' hats. During the long-running
internal debate on the need for a new uniform, O'Duffy had defensively
declared: 'Blue is not our national colour no more than yellow or red. All over
the world green is, and ever shall be recognised as the national colour of the
*Emerald Isle.*'[25] However, the change of shirts symbolised a belated acceptance
that the NCP had failed to gain control of the Blueshirt movement.

In June O'Duffy visited the small number of towns where NCP branches
still existed to generate enthusiasm for the forthcoming annual convention. A
meeting in the formerly strong Roscarbery area, described by gardaí as 'a tame
affair, devoid of any interest' attracted only six members. The second, and final,
NCP convention was held on 18 July, the first day of the Spanish Civil War.
Attendance had dropped to two hundred and fifty and the mood was subdued:

> Nothing of a revolutionary nature was proposed or discussed at the
> Convention ... The proceedings did not occasion much public interest
> ... Even the presence of the delegates attired in green shirts did not excite
> attention on the part of the few onlookers.[26]

The air of apathy surrounding the National Corporate Party was, however,
soon to change.


THE ORIGINS OF THE IRISH BRIGADE

The Spanish Civil War, particularly the news of widespread anti-clerical atroc-
ities sensationally reported in the *Irish Independent*, had an enormous impact in

---

22 *NCP Bulletin*, No. 5 (December 1935), NA, D/Jus., B9/35.  23 Garda report, 17
December 1935, NA, D/Jus., B9/35.  24 O'Duffy to John McCarthy, 29 October 1935,
NA, D/Jus., B9/35.  25 NCP Circular No. 14, November 1935, NA, D/Jus., B9/35.  26
Special Branch report, 20 July 1936, NA, D/Jus., B9/35.

Ireland. The Irish Christian Front, led by O'Duffy's former ally, Paddy Belton, organised a series of pro-Franco meetings around Ireland in the autumn of 1936. Over forty thousand people attended a rally at College Green. Fine Gael vigorously supported Franco in the Dáil. The Hierarchy urged Irish Catholics to raise funds for Nationalist Spain,[27] while Cardinal MacRory, the Primate of All-Ireland, secretly helped to organise more direct support for the military rebels.

Three weeks after the start of the war, General O'Duffy was contacted by Ramirez de Arellano, a Carlist aristocrat based in London, who urged him to raise a volunteer militia – 'What a glorious example Ireland could give the whole of Christendom!'[28] O'Duffy had been recommended by Cardinal MacRory who described him to Arellano as 'a chivalrous, courageous, upright man and a good Catholic, and above all a fine organiser'.[29] O'Duffy's letter to the *Irish Independent* on 10 August proposing the idea of an Irish Brigade met with enthusiastic support. On 15 August, the Cashel branch of the NCP opened a recruiting office. The Catholic Young Men's Society in Listowel followed several days later. The Irish Town Tenants' Association urged men to join. Eamon Horan told Tralee Urban District Council that he would lead the Kerry contingent. O'Duffy opened a fund to support his new military organisation – the Irish Crusade Against Communism – and claimed to have received seven thousand applications from potential volunteers by the end of the month.

Why did O'Duffy agree to organise the Irish Brigade? In his autobiographical account, *Crusade in Spain*, he offers several reasons – the historic links between Ireland and Spain, anti-communism and, most importantly, the defence of the Catholic Church.[30] The Irish Crusade against Communism (the name itself embodying the latter two motives) repeatedly emphasised these motives. On the eve of his departure O'Duffy declared: 'the motive is born of Christianity, and the object is defence of Christianity; both are deep-rooted in the traditions of our race and inseparable from any true conception of the Irish nature'. He stressed the non-political nature of both his brigade and the Spanish Nationalists and claimed that the NCP had 'ceased all social and political manifestations'.[31] This explanation by O'Duffy has generally been accepted by historians. Maurice Manning stated:

> The Spanish situation was, from the outset, calculated to appeal to O'Duffy's enthusiasm and to his imagination. Here before his very eyes the conflict between the forces of Christianity and Communism was being fought out in bloody battle for possession of one of the oldest countries of Europe – a country moreover bound to Ireland by many strong ties of history and religion.[32]

**27** See, Keogh, *Ireland and Europe*, 79-85. **28** Eoin O'Duffy, *Crusade in Spain* (Dublin 1938), 12. **29** Capt. Liam Walsh, 'General O'Duffy – his life and battle' (ms., n.d.), 205. Copy in National Library of Ireland. **30** O'Duffy, *Crusade in Spain*, 1, 40. **31** *Irish Independent*, 21 November 1936. **32** Manning, *The Blueshirts*, 200.

Dr R.A. Stradling, the most recent historian to consider the Irish Brigade, concluded: 'For O'Duffy Irish Catholicism was inevitably implicated in the fate of
Spain; he saw his mission as purely and simply, a Crusade against Communism.'[33]

Although anti-communism and militant Catholicism were clearly important motives it is doubtful that O'Duffy's participation was based solely on these
terms. O'Duffy's other attempts to intervene on the side of fascist powers suggest that his participation in the Spanish Civil War should be viewed in the
context of his commitment to international fascism as well as his chosen image
of a Christian crusader. The fact that there was no question of either a communist threat or a danger to the Catholic Church in Abyssinia did not deter
O'Duffy from proposing to lead a brigade there. Similarly, the plight of the
Catholic Church was not a motive – although anti-communism obviously was
– to offer the anti-clerical Nazis a 'Green Legion' for the Russian front in 1943.
Political considerations were therefore central to O'Duffy's decision to fight
in Spain. Several trends were apparent in O'Duffy's post-Fine Gael political
career; increasing participation in international fascism, a shift towards more
extreme domestic political views and a corresponding decline in his political
influence in Ireland. His decision to fight in Spain was a logical outcome of
these trends.

O'Duffy's description of the Spanish Civil War as 'the first massed attack of
International Communism against Christianity' appears incongruous given his
knowledge of Spain's right-wing movements. O'Duffy knew Franco was not the
non-political crusader he described to the *Irish Independent* – indeed his later summary of Franco's political plans (a 'non-political' corporatist state partly inspired
by papal encyclicals) bear a striking resemblance to his own.[34] By 'non-political'
O'Duffy, like Franco, meant the suppression of political parties in a state ruled
by benevolent dictatorship with the co-operation of vocational committees and
other groups deemed less socially divisive than political organisations. O'Duffy
belonged to the 'reactionary, ultramontanist element of the [Fascist] International'
and perceived Franco – who similarly styled himself as a Catholic crusader against
communism and advocate of corporatism – as an ideological ally.[35]

The efforts made by O'Duffy to render the Irish Brigade non-political were
rather superficial. His assertion that he suspended the NCP to preserve the
'non-political character of the brigade' is contradicted by his original statement
(and that of other NCP members) that the party – struggling to exist before
the war – was disbanded because of 'the volume of work connected with the
Crusade against Communism.'[36] Similarly, his concern about the political
appearance of the brigade did not prevent him from purchasing one thousand
green shirts, the uniform of the NCP, for his volunteers.

33 R.A. Stradling, 'Franco's Irish volunteers', *History Today* (March 1995), 44. 34 O'Duffy,
*Crusade in Spain*, 227. 35 Michael Ledeen, *Universal Fascism* (New York, 1972), 128. 36
O'Duffy, *Crusade in Spain*, 60; *Irish Independent*, 13, 16 September 1936.

O'Duffy's decision to organise the Irish Brigade should also be seen as a response to his marginal position in Irish politics. His involvement in Spain halted what appeared to be an irreversible decline into political obscurity. O'Duffy regained his status as a dynamic leader and even managed to recruit substantial numbers of Ned Cronin's Blueshirts. Cronin's concern that his old rival would again overshadow him is evident from his initial statement that the brigade 'has as much prospect of reaching Zaragoza as it has of reaching the moon' followed by his later unsuccessful attempts to organise his own brigade.[37]

In September O'Duffy travelled to London to discuss his proposal with Nationalist officials. Despite elaborate cloak and dagger precautions on O'Duffy's part, the English Special Branch observed him meeting Count de Arellano, who proposed the brigade, and Juan de la Cierva, Franco's unofficial agent in London who organised the transport of the volunteers.[38] The British government was concerned about the implications for Anglo-Irish relations of O'Duffy's venture. A representative of the British Union of Fascists had previously contacted the War Office to enquire whether English fascists could legally enlist in the Irish Brigade. Moreover, the Foreign Office felt that 'it would be particularly unfortunate if United Kingdom Communists found themselves fighting opposite Irish Catholics'.[39]

O'Duffy then travelled to Spain to discuss his proposal. According to press reports General Cabanellas, the nominal head of the Burgos junta, rejected the idea, but General Mola was more enthusiastic. The following day, as the Nationalists were celebrating the relief of the *Alcazar* – the fortress in Toledo which had been besieged by Republicans for over two months and became a symbol of heroic resistance for Nationalist Spain – General Franco telegraphed his approval to O'Duffy.[40] Irish volunteers would form *banderas* (battalions) of the *Tercio* (Foreign Legion) commanded by Colonel Yagüe. Each *bandera* would be a distinctly Irish unit with its own drill, medical staff, chaplains and cooks. The volunteers would receive the same rate of pay as the rest of the elite *Tercio*, twice that of a regular Spanish soldier, but O'Duffy agreed with Franco's stipulation that Irish volunteers would not qualify for compensation or pensions. O'Duffy originally insisted the brigade could not be deployed against the Catholic Basque forces but later decided the Basques were 'no more entitled to partition from Spain than the six counties of Ulster are to partition from Ireland'.

The next problem facing O'Duffy was the transport of volunteers to Spain. The brigade received no support from the Irish Government, which was alarmed by O'Duffy's activities for various reasons. The brigade was an embarrassing testament to the ineffectiveness of the non-intervention policy supported by the government. Also, the thought of O'Duffy returning to Ireland

**37** *Irish Independent*, 22 August, 26 November 1936. **38** PRO, W 12847/9549/41, Foreign Office series (FO). **39** Memo, 14 December 1936, PRO, W 18567/9549/41 (FO). **40** O'Duffy, *Crusade in Spain*, 16-23.

with an experienced militia was not attractive. An External Affairs memo revealed more paternalistic concerns including 'the consequence to the general well-being of the country of the return from a foreign war of this terrible character of groups of men whose moral outlook but cannot be seriously altered for the worse'.[41] The government could nevertheless do little to stop the volunteers going to Spain. Although the *Irish Times* claimed they were breaking the Non-Intervention Agreement,[42] O'Duffy correctly predicted the government could not legally stop them under current legislation. Although passport endorsements for Spain were withheld, volunteers could not be prevented from travelling to countries contiguous to Spain. The Department of External Affairs passport files contain numerous applications from Blueshirts intending to holiday in Portugal and, even less plausibly, from known communists hoping to visit Lourdes.[43] O'Duffy also exploited a legal loophole by sailing a contingent of men to the boundary of Irish territorial waters before transferring them to a foreign-registered ship.

Juan de la Cierva liaised between O'Duffy and the Nationalist headquarters in Salamanca. However, a ship intended to pick up the first group of volunteers at Passage East, near Waterford, on 16 October was postponed due to difficulties with the Non-Intervention Committee, putting a question mark over the whole project. O'Duffy, against the wishes of the Nationalist agents in London, returned to Spain while Franco considered the brigade's viability. There was some opposition to the Irish Brigade in Salamanca, but the brigade also had influential supporters, including some aristocratic descendants of the Wild Geese.[44] Moreover, the support of the Irish volunteers, unlike that of German and Italian soldiers, embellished Franco's image as a defender of Catholicism. Consequently Franco allowed O'Duffy to continue organising the brigade.

The transportation of the recruits remained beset with difficulties. During November, Franco's agents in London pressed Salamanca to authorise the transport of groups of at least three hundred Irish volunteers. However, fearing Non-Intervention difficulties, Franco instructed them to bring the volunteers over in small groups. O'Duffy's chagrin was made known to Franco by telegram: 'We have O'Duffy here very angry of difficulties he has all his men who have lost their employment in a very awkward situation stop O'Duffy wishes to be categorically and finally told whether or not we wish to use them.'[45]

41 Memo, 18 December 1936, NA, D/FA 241/12 (Restricted).   42 The Non-Intervention Agreement was proposed by France and Britain in August 1936 and had been accepted by most European States including Ireland by the end of the month. The agreement attempted to limit military intervention in Spain by external powers but was openly flouted by Germany, Italy and the Soviet Union. A further non-intervention initiative to prevent foreign volunteers fighting in Spain in February 1937 proved somewhat more successful.   43 Passports and Endorsements, NA, D/FA 102/21.   44 Keogh, *Ireland and Europe*, 73.   45 Telegram, London to Salamanca, 14 November 1936, Archivo de Burgos, Ministerio de Asuntos Exteriores, Madrid, L. 1105-10.

Another ship was cancelled in late November. Nonetheless, a telegram from London suggests that plans for an impressive force were near completion:

> Next Irish contingent of 1,000 leaving 1st January [followed by] 1,000 every week until total of 5.000. Italian Minister at Dublin offers Italian ship gratis for January ... General McNeill very distinguished soldier and second Chief of the General Staff of the Irish Army will arrive Salamanca to join volunteers before 31st of this month. American-Irish offer cavalry squadron 500 men and horses completely equipped except for arms they will pay all expenses.[46]

The soldier referred to, Major General Hugo McNeill[47] – the Assistant Chief of Staff Adjutant-General of the Irish Army – never arrived. Considering McNeill's rank and O'Duffy's tendency to exaggerate, it is possible he never agreed to enlist. However, given McNeill's close relationship with O'Duffy, his pro-Nazi sympathies and mercurial reputation, it is plausible that he intended to fight in Spain.[48] The loss of such an accomplished officer was a blow to the military efficiency of the brigade. The squadron of American-Irish cavalry also failed to arrive. The telegram indicates possible reasons for later friction between O'Duffy and Franco. O'Duffy clearly exaggerated the resources at his disposal when he met Franco as the Nationalist anticipation of five thousand volunteers was over-optimistic. According to Fr McCabe, the rector of the Irish College at Salamanca, the Nationalists expected some ten thousand Irish volunteers.[49] Conversely, Franco's inability or reluctance to arrange transport for the Irish volunteers, and there were at least twelve hundred, clearly frustrated O'Duffy.

Finally, on 13 December 1936, approximately six hundred volunteers boarded the German ship *Domingo* off the coast of Galway. However, to the anger of the Irishmen, two more ships were cancelled at the last moment. Non-Intervention legislation rushed through the Dáil in February precluded the possibility of large numbers of volunteers arriving in Spain. Franco's indecision and the co-ordination difficulties resulted in only seven hundred volunteers reaching Spain. Consequently, relations between O'Duffy and Franco were strained from the outset and the under-strength Irish *bandera* never performed effectively as an autonomous unit.

The volunteers, as Map 1 illustrates, were predominantly drawn from rural Ireland particularly the strongly Blueshirt south-west and midlands.[50] Per capita,

---

**46** Ibid., 7 December 1936.   **47** Hugo McNeill: National Army colonel during Civil War; appointed Adjutant General following army mutiny, 1924; first director of Irish Military College, 1927; Commandant, Military College, 1930-32; Assistant Chief of Staff, 1932-37; commanded 2nd Division, 1942-46; Eastern Command, 1946-51.   **48** See, John P. Duggan, *Neutral Ireland and the Third Reich* (Dublin, 1989), 180-92. On Christmas eve, the Nationalists in London informed Salamanca that McNeill was unable to go to Spain.   **49** Fr Alexander McCabe diary, 17 June 1937, NLI, McCabe papers.   **50** The geographical and socio-economic statistics are drawn from a wide range of sources including Department of Foreign

Map 1  Distribution of the Irish Brigade

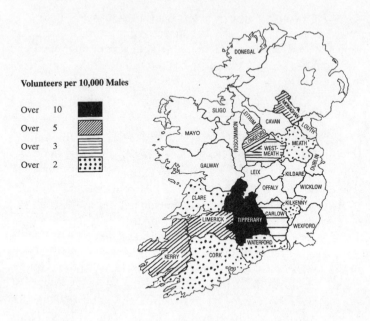

Map 2  Distribution of Blueshirts (August 1934)

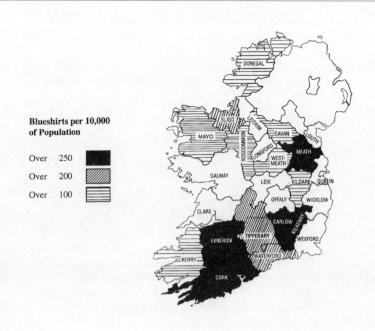

Tipperary, Longford, Limerick, Kerry, Westmeath and Carlow were the best represented counties. The Irish Brigade, like the Blueshirt movement, benefited from the support of individuals discontent with de Valera's Ireland. A substantial proportion – O'Duffy claimed over half – were the sons of farmers. Due to the economic war and international depression, most of these would have been un- or under-employed. Former gardaí and soldiers were also prominently represented. A substantial proportion of the volunteers, probably over a third, were former National Army soldiers.[51] A Department of Justice report noted the high number of National Army members among one group of volunteers.[52] Many had served only three or four years but there was no shortage of senior officers including Commandant Dermot O'Sullivan, Commandant Sean Cunningham, Major Patrick Dalton, and Brigadier-General Eamon Horan. The brigade also attracted what could be described as a mercenary contingent including Irish veterans of the British Army, United States Navy, and French and Spanish Foreign Legions. Many of the volunteers had left the Irish army as a result of demobilisation in the 1920s but some of the security force members prominently associated with Cumann na nGaedheal had faced demotion or dismissal when Fianna Fáil gained power in 1932. O'Duffy was the most famous political casualty of the new regime. Another volunteer, Dave Tormey from Co. Westmeath, previously a sergeant in the Detective Branch, resigned when he was demoted to uniform duties by the new government.[53]

The recruits came from a diverse range of economic backgrounds. An analysis of the occupations of seventy-eight volunteers (excluding ex-soldiers and the sons of farmers) shows that roughly one third were farmers (9), business proprietors (9) and professionals (16), another third were tradesmen and semi-skilled workers (27) and the remainder unskilled workers (26). The geographical and socio-economic backgrounds of the Irish Brigade differed substantially from Irish volunteers in the International Brigades. The majority of the Irish Brigade came from small towns and villages in rural Ireland. Over two-thirds of the International Brigaders were from Dublin, Belfast, Cork and Waterford. Approximately 60 per cent of the International Brigade recruits were unskilled workers compared to 30 per cent of the Irish Brigade. But political beliefs naturally formed the greatest difference between both contingents. The International Brigade was predominantly composed of communists, IRA volunteers and Republican Congress activists. O'Duffy's description of the Irish Brigade as non-political is inaccurate – he had a tendency to describe every movement he headed as non-political. There was a small proportion of republicans, Fianna Fáil and Labour Party supporters but Blueshirts were clearly the most dominant political grouping within the brigade. For example, of the five

Affairs and Department of Justice records, national and regional newspapers and memoirs. **51** Victor Ennis, 'Some Spanish Moors' (ms, n.d.), 2, copy in Military Archives, Dublin. Maps 1 and Map 2 respectively are based on samples of 430 volunteers and 47,923 Blueshirts. **52** UCDA, Sean MacEntee papers, P67/534, Calendar of Events, 1930-39, 61-62. **53** *Irish*

local representatives who enlisted in the brigade, all were elected as Fine Gael Blueshirts in the local elections of June 1934.

A substantial proportion of the volunteers described themselves as non-political but despite this many of them were hostile to both Fianna Fáil and the IRA. The geographical origins of the volunteers (see Maps 1 and 2) indicates that even if many were not Blueshirts, they came from areas with a strong Blueshirt tradition. This composition partly reflects the recruiting process, which was secretively directed by O'Duffy's Greenshirts and several of his former Blueshirt colleagues who had remained loyal to Fine Gael. Many of the Blueshirt recruits, such as Captain Padraig Quinn,[54] were members of Cronin's (official) League of Youth. A letter by Quinn to another Kilkenny Blueshirt suggests that although the brigade attracted men from Cronin's organisation it should not be assumed they transferred their political allegiances:

> there is and will be no change in my political views; as far as National life at home is concerned I am and will remain a member of Fine Gael and the Blueshirt Organisations … A number of Blueshirts here and there throughout the counties of Carlow and Kilkenny have volunteered their services for the 'Irish Brigade' to Spain, the motive of such service being for the GLORY OF GOD and the HONOUR OF IRELAND.[55]

Quinn's letter raises the question of volunteer' motives. For Quinn, religious sentiment appears to have been more important than political differences. Only a small number of the brigade, essentially key NCP members such as Thomas Gunning can be readily identified as fascists although many of the volunteers undoubtedly sympathised with European fascist leaders. Fascism, as the failure of the NCP illustrates, did not have a mass following in Ireland. Considering its inherent irredentism and extreme nationalism it is difficult to see how fascism could encompass an internationalist appeal comparable to the International Brigades. The fact that less than twenty volunteers from Britain, which had a far larger number of fascists than Ireland, fought for Franco suggests Irish volunteers were motivated by other factors.[56] For many of the recruits anti-communism appears to have been more important than sympathy for fascism. The Spanish Civil War occurred during a decade of unprecedented anti-communist fervour in Ireland. The conflict was widely presented, not just by extremists, but by the clergy and mainstream politicians as a consequence of the expansion of Russian communism. Mirroring the response of International

*Independent*, 14 December 1936.  **54** Padraig Quinn: Kilkenny Blueshirt leader; appointed to Fine Gael national executive, 1933; jailed for non-payment of rates, 1934; supported Cronin after O'Duffy resigned, 1934; split from Fine Gael with Cronin, 1936.  **55** Padraig Quinn to Joseph Doyle, 22 September 1936, NA, D/Taois S 9179.  **56** One explanation for the low number of British recruits for the Nationalists was that the British Union of Fascists, despite enjoying considerable support from Catholics in Britain, was not sympathetic to Franco who was regarded by Mosley, the BUF leader, as a reactionary rather than a fascist.

Brigade volunteers to fascism, many of the volunteers regarded Spain as the front-line in the war against communism.

Anti-communism was but one aspect of the militant Catholicism central to the appeal of the Irish Brigade. Contemporary newspaper accounts convey a remarkably pious atmosphere. As volunteers left the North Wall during November they were presented with miraculous medals, Sacred Heart badges, prayer books, and blessed by priests while crowds of supporters gathered to sing *Faith of our fathers*. Similar scenes occurred throughout Ireland. In Cork, Col P.J. Coughlan, accompanied by three local priests, declared that 'the hour had come to take their departure for the battlefields of Spain to strike a blow for Christ the King.'[57] A letter from one seventeen-year-old Kerry volunteer to his mother demonstrates this religious motivation:

> I didn't want to tell you I was coming here that day because I was afraid you wouldn't like it. Please tell me how you feel, and that you forgive me, because I treated you rotten and I know it … I have a feeling you hate me for it, but after all what I have done is for Our Lord, and if I die it will be only for the best.[58]

Even the Department of External Affairs noted the importance of religion in the recruitment process:

> The general character of the volunteers already gone to Spain does not appear to be very high, but we have information that some of them are very young men who have been enticed from their families through the impression that they are going to fight for Christianity.[59]

However, this memo also implies that not all the volunteers were so pious. The appeal of the brigade was partly due to the economic depression of the 1930s and the more limited opportunities for emigration, which particularly affected unemployed men from rural Ireland impoverished by the economic war. There were numerous other motives for enlistment. One volunteer 'had fought as a boy in the Irish Civil War, and had liked it so much that he had come out to see what the Spanish Civil War was like,' while George Timlin went for 'the spirit of adventure'.[60] Fr McCabe, the rector of the Irish College in Salamanca, who met many of the volunteers observed:

> As regards the men, a good many of them were idealists, who came out to fight for religion and Spain. Some were of the adventurous type, who, in the old days, would take the English 'bob', and join the British Army

---

**57** *Irish Independent*, 28 November 1936.   **58** NA, D/FA Madrid Embassy 10/2.   **59** Memo, 18 December 1936, NA, D/FA 241/12.   **60** Francis McCullagh, *In Franco's Spain* (London, 1937), 246; Cathal O'Shannon, 'Even the olives are bleeding' (RTE, 1975).

to see the world. It was a change from standing at the corner and staring at the pump.[61]

### THE IRISH BRIGADE IN SPAIN

The volunteers were enthusiastically received in Cáceres, where they were stationed for basic training. Their military parade was the highlight of the town's new year celebrations. Fr McCabe was initially very positive. He found O'Duffy to have 'the simple, friendly, hospitable way of all Irishmen with one another, and especially, of the Irish lay folk with their priests'. The volunteers 'looked athletic, clean, and muscular and seemed to be a crowd that will give a tough account of themselves'. The officers' morale appeared excellent: 'They're manly, cheery, and refined, and they're all good companions, like school-boys going home for a holiday.'[62] The following day, however, McCabe discovered some of the tensions within the brigade. Much of the trouble involved the Irish chaplain; Fr Mulrean. He was engaged in a feud with Thomas Gunning – 'O'Duffy's right-hand man and factotum in Spain'[63] – and he was resented by many of the Irishmen, particularly the officers, for the criticism of their behaviour in his Sunday sermons.[64] Although the Spaniards were impressed with the piety of the volunteers, McCabe believed the Irishmen were less enamoured with the Spanish Church:

> the Irishmen, even the common soldiers, are not very impressed by Spanish Catholicism, even though that's what the whole row is supposed to be about. They have noticed that several women, girls and children, a few professional and middle-class men, and an occasional Spanish officer attend Mass, but the ordinary Spanish male ... believes in a different way of life.[65]

Excessive drinking among the Irish also caused problems. McCabe noted that when the bemused Spaniards 'see these idealists, and frequent church-goers drinking and "having one too many" they are profoundly shocked'.[66] Several sources testify that alcohol was a problem from the outset. According to Captain Tom Smith when the *Domingo* arrived at Lisbon some of the men 'got drunk,

---

61 McCabe diary, 17 June 1937. 62 Ibid., 4, 6 January 1937. 63 Leopold Kerney to Joseph Walshe, secretary, External Affairs, 13 March 1937, NA, D/FA Madrid Embassy 52/1. 64 McCabe commented: '[Mulrean] had a "tough" job, but the officers and men regarded him as a "bully" addicted to gossip, a sneak and mischief maker. He was educated in the seminary in Madrid – and bore the marks of it'. The Irish officers complained that Mulrean inquired into 'intimate and even feminine affairs' at confessions – 'They feel that he sits down in the box and listens eagerly just to satisfy his morbid curiosity', McCabe diary, 7 January 1937. 65 Ibid. 66 For an account of this and other aspects of the Irish in Cáceres, see Keogh, *Ireland and Europe*, 81-3.

fought the police, and caused an awful scandal along the whole water-front'.[67] Lieutenant Pete Lawlor observed similar scenes at the *vin d'honneur* held for the brigade at Salamanca. Fr Mulrean felt it necessary to launch a crusade against the declining moral standards:

> On Sunday week last I preached against drunkenness and the Kips [broth-els] ... The attendance at the Kips has increased to my knowledge from 5 the 1st fortnight to over 40 a week now. O, my work gets more diffi-cult every day. Drunkenness is a curse, I told them they were trying to make a national virtue out of it, and the language vile.[68]

The calibre of the men was varied. O'Duffy admitted that 'a few doubtful characters' had been accepted.[69] McCabe now decided the Irish looked 'soft' compared to the Spanish soldiers. After visiting the barracks he described sev-eral volunteers as 'limp, spineless and worthless'. One volunteer, who believed the Spanish climate would improve his tuberculosis, was hospitalised on arrival in Cáceres. Two deserters were confined 'in a wretched hole of a cell'. In the next cell McCabe discovered two insane volunteers: 'one stripped naked to the waist, was up in the window, and clinging to the bars ... having a sun-bath on a frosty day in January'. McCabe also observed, however, that when the Irishmen were on duty discipline was strict. The training of the men, con-ducted by two British army veterans, appeared to be progressing well. He felt the sooner the brigade reached the front line the better.[70] Fr Mulrean, how-ever, claimed the Spanish authorities were so disappointed with the military expertise of the Irish officers that they delayed the brigade's departure to the front for further training.[71]

On 16 February the Irish Brigade received orders for the Madrid front. The volunteers suffered their first casualties the following day while marching to Ciempozuelos. A Nationalist *bandera* from the Canary Islands, coming across English-speaking volunteers in unusual uniforms, had mistaken them for International Brigaders and opened fire killing two Irishmen, Lieutenant Tom Hyde[72] and Dan Chute. O'Duffy insisted the incident was the fault of the Spanish unit, which failed to follow correct military procedure. The descrip-tion of the Canary Islands *bandera* by another Spanish soldier as 'a gay and feck-less lot who ... regard the war as a joke and anything military as utterly ridicu-

**67** McCullagh, *In Franco's Spain*, 235. **68** Fr Mulrean to Fr McCabe, 9 February 1937, folder 57, McCabe papers. **69** As Fr Mulrean harshly commented: 'Strike me pink, if I know where the old man managed to pick up all the scum he has collected', McCullagh, *In Franco's Spain*, 292. **70** McCabe diary, 7 January 1937. **71** Fr Mulrean to Fr McCabe, 9 February 1937, folder 57, McCabe papers. **72** Tom Hyde (1897-1937): b. Midleton, Co. Cork; Irish volunteer 1916-17; served in Active Service Unit, 4th Battalion, 1st Cork Brigade during Anglo-Irish War; retired from National Army with rank of captain; cinema propri-etor; Cork staff officer of National Corporate Party 1935-6; leader, No. 1 Section, A Coy, Irish Brigade.

lous' supports O'Duffy's statement.[73] However, following the brigade's return
to Ireland several disaffected officers claimed that the incident occurred because
the Irishmen had marched towards the Canary Islands unit in battle formation.[74] Retrospectively much has been made of this incident by the brigade's
detractors, but it does not appear to have ruined the brigade's credibility with
the Spanish command.

The village of Ciempozuelos, fifteen miles from Madrid, had been the scene
of heavy fighting and the brigade's first duty was to bury the corpses scattered
throughout the town. The village was not particularly exposed but it was occasionally shelled and the Irishmen were frequently sniped at by International
Brigaders, some of them Irish, who faced the brigade across the Jarama river.
One veteran of the International Brigades, Tom Murphy from Co. Monaghan,
recalled one, possibly apocryphal, incident:

> Our trenches were maybe a few hundred yards [away]. Frank Ryan used
> to speak on the speaker. He says: 'Irishmen go home! Your fathers would
> turn in their graves if they knew that you'd come to fight for imperial-
> ism. This is the real Republican Army. The real, real men of Ireland.[75]

By March there were signs of tension within the unit when Major Patrick
Dalton, apparently suffering from sciatica, returned to Ireland. O'Duffy
appointed Dermot O'Sullivan, a leading member of his National Corporate
Party, as the new commander of the Irish Brigade. On 12 March Tom Smith,
captain of B Company, also returned home – reportedly due to illness. On the
same day, the Irish *bandera* was strengthened with a company of mixed Spanish
and Moroccan cavalry.[76] The first real military test of the Irish *bandera* occurred
the following day when the Irishmen were ordered to advance on the nearby
village of Titulcia. Amidst heavy shelling, the brigade neither reached the village nor managed to engage any Republican troops in combat.[77] Three volunteers from Tralee died during the assault, and Sergeant Gabriel Lee died
shortly afterwards.[78]

On 14 March, the brigade was ordered to repeat the advance. O'Duffy,
convinced that the attack would not succeed, disobeyed the order. Although
he later claimed that Mola and Franco agreed with his decision this seems
unlikely.[79] It is unacceptable for local commanders to arbitrarily counteract
divisional orders in any army, but in the elite *Tercio* where soldiers were shot

---

**73** Peter Kemp, *Mine were of trouble* (London, 1957), 151.  **74** *Irish Press*, 22 June 1937.  **75**
Tom Murphy interview, Imperial War Museum, London, Sound Archives, International
Brigade collection, 805/2.  **76** Seósamh O'Cuinneagáin, *The war in Spain* (Enniscorthy,
n.d.), 19.  **77** O'Duffy, *Crusade in Spain*, 156-9.  **78** The three Tralee men were Tom Foley
(30) John McSweeney (23) and Bernard Horan (23). Gabriel Lee (1905-37): b. Dublin; IRA
volunteer; served National Army until 1924; North Dublin League of Youth director;
remained loyal to Cronin after O'Duffy split.  **79** O'Duffy, *Crusade in Spain*, 163.

for minor infractions of discipline it was almost inconceivable. O'Duffy's belief in the futility of another assault on Titulcia is not supported by the low casualty rate of 13 March. Also, it is unlikely that Franco supported O'Duffy against General Saliquet, the commander of the forces surrounding Madrid, particularly as the purpose of the assault was not necessarily to capture Titulcia but to form part of a diversionary series of attacks to relieve pressure on Italian forces at Guadalajara.[80] One account suggests that O'Duffy's decision was caused by the refusal of his own officers to fight. Seósamh O'Cuinneagáin recalled that Lieutenant Tom Cahill, captain of A Company, refused to lead his men on 'a fruitless expedition'.[81] The failure at Titulcia was a pivotal event for the brigade. It confirmed the doubts of the Nationalist military command about the military capabilities of the *bandera*. Two years later, Fr Mulrean told Leopold Kerney, the Irish minister to Spain, that when Franco met O'Duffy following this incident, on 17 March at Navalcarnero, to seek an explanation, the two generals argued and O'Duffy threatened to return to Ireland with his men.[82]

### THE DEMISE OF THE IRISH BRIGADE

Soon after the Irish Brigade's assault on Titulcia – and almost certainly as a consequence – the Irish *bandera* was transferred north of Madrid to La Marañosa. They were stationed with the *Requetes*, the Carlist militia, which had originally invited O'Duffy to Spain. The disintegration of the unit soon followed. The antagonism between the Irish officers (which had preceded the failed attack on Titulcia) was central. The most serious rift occurred between O'Duffy and Gunning while the *bandera* was stationed in Cáceres.[83] The transfer of two Anglo-Irish officers serving in the Foreign Legion, Lieutenant Fitzpatrick and Lieutenant Nangle, to the Irish *bandera* shortly after its formation resulted in further acrimony. The Protestant, Sandhurst-educated, ex-British Army officers resented their new commander.[84] Given their background (Fitzpatrick was a Freemason whose favourite author was Kipling) and O'Duffy's anglophobia, there was a certain inevitability about the friction which followed. Further problems had ensued following Dalton's return to Ireland in March when several officers refused to fight under his successor Dermot O'Sullivan. Following this, O'Duffy informed Franco that he had relieved the 'English officers' and

**80** Stradling, 'Battleground of Reputations', 128. **81** O'Cuinneagáin, *The war in Spain*, 21. Cahill was removed from the front-line and sent back to Ireland on March 16. **82** Kerney to Walshe, 19 December 1939, NA, D/FA Madrid Embassy 19/4. **83** McCabe diary, 17 June 1937. McCabe did not record a reason for this falling out but Kerney subsequently reported – '[Gunning] says O'Duffy is very treacherous. O'Duffy seems to have turned on Gunning because latter frequented other officers whom O'Duffy disliked. Gunning thinks O'Duffy is mad and that this Spanish business has actually unbalanced his mind' (Kerney to Walshe, 8 June 1937, NA, D/FA Madrid Embassy 51/1). **84** McCullagh, *In Franco's Spain*, 132; Kemp, *Mine were of trouble*, 90-1.

some of the Irish ones of their command for undermining the loyalty of the Irish soldiers.[85]

Relations between the Irish officers and the Spanish military command were also fractious. After the incident with the Canary Islands *bandera* a large number of Spanish officers were drafted into the brigade. The implication that Spanish leadership was necessary was resented by O'Duffy and his Irish officers. Francis McCullagh, an Irish war correspondent who visited La Marañosa, believed their presence created 'an impossible situation, which could not, I felt, last for many weeks longer'.[86] Moreover, O'Duffy, and Colonel Yagüe, the head of the *Tercio*, disliked each other. Captain Meade, a Spanish officer attached to the Irish *bandera*, told Kerney that the tension between the two existed because Yagüe 'who at the time was only a Colonel ... looked down on O'Duffy, but had to treat him with the respect due to a General'.[87]

The harshness of life at the front and the breakdown of command destroyed morale. McCullagh described the situation:

> I found the Irish unhappy, owing to the isolation, the intense monotony of trench warfare, ignorance of the language, the difficulty of communicating with Ireland, letters taking an incredibly long time owing to the censorship and other delays. The food was unfamiliar and there was no tea, whiskey or humour. What depressed them most was the austere Spanish landscape, wrecked houses and burned villages.

The hatred between the Spanish people shocked even veterans of the Irish Civil War and the regular executions 'shook the nerve of the toughest'. McCullagh formed a low opinion of the military leadership of the *bandera*. O'Duffy knew little of 'modern mechanized war' – his officers 'expected guerrilla fighting, unaware that the aeroplane had killed it'.[88] Fr McCabe learnt of similar complaints. The Nationalists expected that the Irish officers would have been trained at a military academy but found that their experience of war was limited to 'cross-road ambushes during the Black-and-Tan struggle'.[89]

O'Duffy clearly bears much responsibility for the condition of the brigade. His lengthy absences from the front, heavy drinking, and ostentatious lifestyle at the Gran Hotel in Salamanca exacerbated the difficulties. O'Duffy's behaviour in Spain appeared increasingly erratic. In Salamanca he was variously described as 'flippant', 'fantasque' and 'a queer fellow'.[90] McCullagh observed

---

**85** General O'Duffy to General Franco, 9 April 1937, Cuartel General del Generalísimo (CGG), Archivo General Militar de Avila (AGMA), Avila, Spain, L. 156-25. The officers concerned were Fitzpatrick, Nangle, Cahill and probably Tom Smith, a Belfast Protestant. I wish to thank Sr Eithne Corcoran for translating this letter and numerous documents from Spanish military and political archives.  **86** McCullagh, *In Franco's Spain*, 297.  **87** NA, D/FA 119/17, 9 June 1938.  **88** *Irish Press*, 26 May 1937.  **89** McCabe diary, 17 June 1937. **90** Kerney to Walshe, 8 March, 8 April, 12 May 1937, NA, D/FA Madrid Embassy 51/1.

that 'O'Duffy's mentality was an especially interesting study – his vanity, the generosity with which he threw himself into his work, his incompetence, his irritability, and the unevenness of his temper'.[91] The same qualities which resulted in O'Duffy's unsuitability for the presidency of Fine Gael – his bluntness, impetuosity, exuberance and poor judgement – damaged his credibility in Spain.

On 24 March the Irish Brigade was inspected by Yagüe, who reported drunkenness, insubordination and low morale. He concluded that the unit was so inefficient any front they occupied would not be secure. Interestingly, given the harsh criticism directed at the Irish Brigade, it was the Irish officers rather than the volunteers who were blamed for the unit's deficiencies. Nonetheless, the influx of Spanish officers into the brigade had not resulted in significant improvements in its efficiency. Yagüe recommended the redistribution of the men among other *banderas*.[92] The following week a further report claimed that O'Duffy was using the Nationalists for his own political aggrandisement and that the Irish *bandera* was spreading a bad example among other units of the *Tercio*. It also referred to a shooting incident within the Irish Brigade.[93] Furthermore, the Spanish command refused to recognise O'Duffy's appointment of O'Sullivan as commander and insisted that a Spanish officer lead the *bandera*.

On 9 April O'Duffy belatedly responded to Yagüe's demand for a change in the leadership. The uncompromising tone of his letter to Franco made clear he had already decided the brigade should return home:

> I am obliged to believe that unfortunately Your Excellency no longer has the same confidence in the Irish Brigade and we could not stay here unless we were able to enjoy total confidence and neither could we allow you to invite other Irish to Spain … I have no alternative but to ask that you would see fit to provide transport to send the Irish Brigade home. It will be a sad journey that we are obliged to take. We came full of sincere desires to help Spain and to have the honour of raising our flag beside yours as you take Madrid. Unfortunately we leave Spain with pain and distress.

O'Duffy asked Franco to consider letting Irish volunteers who wished to stay form their own company within a *bandera* of the *Tercio*. More surprisingly, given their strained relations, O'Duffy stated that he wished to stay and 'fight for Spain' – albeit as an *attaché* to the Nationalists at the Gran Hotel – to prevent propaganda from their 'mutual enemies in Russia and France'.[94] Franco allowed a small number of Irishmen to remain but declined O'Duffy's offer.

**91** McCullagh, *In Franco's Spain*, 264. **92** Yagüe to General Jefe de la División Reforzada de Madrid, 24 March 1937, CGG, AGMA, L. 156-24. **93** El Teniente Coronel Ayudante to General Segundo Jefe de Estado Mayor del Cuartel General de S.E. el Generalísimo, Salamanca, 29 March 1937. **94** O'Duffy to Franco, 9 April 1937, op. cit.

A further report in April detailed the final decline of the Irish *bandera*. A second shooting had occurred when an Irish officer intervened in a fight seriously wounding another officer. The fact that he had taken sides against an officer to assist a private particularly disgusted the *Tercio* command. The following week Dermot O'Sullivan told a Nationalist officer, Xavier de Silva, that the brigade wished to return home. A clearly distraught O'Sullivan told de Silva he would lead the Irish Brigade – representing *'la gran democracia Irlandesa'* – to fight on the side of the Spanish Republic. When Yagüe learnt of O'Sullivan's outburst, he placed him under arrest and disarmed the Brigade.[95]

During May and early June Franco and O'Duffy argued over the terms of the brigade's return. In his autobiography, O'Duffy recalled that Franco ordered a 'special first-grade train' and 'one of the best ships on the sea' laden with 'first class fare' to repatriate the Irishmen. In fact, these conditions were demanded by O'Duffy who hoped to portray the brigade as returning heroes.[96] Kerney reported, not surprisingly, that 'Franco has difficulty in acceding to this'. On 17 June, two months after the brigade had been disarmed and ordered from the front, approximately six hundred and fifty volunteers left Lisbon on the *Mozambique*.[97] Twelve to fourteen men died in Spain, about half as a result of illness. Around nineteen Irishmen remained in Spain – six recovering in hospitals, the others continuing to fight in the Foreign Legion.

O'Duffy's attempts to portray the Irish Brigade as a success were initially partly effective. It was in the Nationalists' interests to maintain the illusion of a successful Irish Brigade. The brigade was met in Dublin by a small crowd of supporters and a marching band. A reception at the Mansion House was attended by Lord Mayor Alfie Byrne, Monsignor Waters, head of the Catholic Young Men's Society and Patrick Belton, president of the Irish Christian Front.[98] O'Duffy was later made a Freeman of Kilkenny.

Despite such ceremonies, however, O'Duffy could not prevent the real story of the Irish Brigade becoming known. The hostility between O'Duffy and his officers, illustrated by Thomas Gunning's letter to Desmond FitzGerald, the Fine Gael politician, was too deep-seated to allow for much of a show of unity:

> O'Duffy and his entourage of bosthoons have given us a black eye here that will last for generations … We have insulted, swindled and hurt the grandest people on earth who thought of us as the finest soldiers and the most self-sacrificing Christians in the world. I should have known O'Duffy well enough to realise that he could and would make a mess even of this affair, which seemed so foolproof. I was very stupid, and I

95 Report of El Coronel 2° Jefe de E.M., Tavalcarnero, 22 April 1937, CGG, AGMA, L. 335-100, L. 156-24. 96 CGG, AGMA, L. 156-24. 97 This figure does not include the St Mary's Anti-Communist Pipers Band which accompanied the Brigade to Spain. 98 *Irish Press*, 22 May 1937.

did a poor day's work for both Spain and Ireland when I helped the insane, uncultured lout to put his flat and smelly feet across the frontier last October.[99]

The splits within the brigade became apparent as soon as the *Mozambique* reached Dublin. Two factions, a group of Kerrymen led by Horan and some northerners headed by Seán Cunningham, marched away in separate directions. Confirming Spanish Nationalists' concerns about volunteers speaking to the press, they told journalists that the brigade had been politically motivated, that officers had refused to fight, that the only battle they were involved in was with Franco's soldiers and that O'Duffy had been told to leave by the Spanish authorities.[100] Incessant bickering between O'Duffy and Belton during the summer of 1937 over missing Christian Front funds further tarnished the image of the Irish pro-Franco movement.

The failure of the brigade profoundly affected O'Duffy. A year later he declared:

> It would have been better perhaps if the shells of the Communists, which exploded in our trenches and dug-outs everyday and every hour of the day, for eleven weeks on the Jarama front, had effectively found their mark, rather than we should be subjected to such vilifying attacks … on our return to the country for the honour of which we risked everything that held life dear to us. *Hibernia*, April 1938.

O'Duffy, now in declining health, made no attempt to revive the NCP. His only political activity following his return from Spain was with the secretive pro-Nazi People's National Party during World War Two. He died in November 1944 and was buried, as he wished, close to the grave of Michael Collins. O'Duffy's final appraisal of his brigade has not yet proved prophetic: 'We have been criticised, sneered at, slandered, but truth, charity, and justice shall prevail, and time will justify our motives. We seek no praise. We did our duty. We went to Spain.'[101] History has judged the brigade harshly. Although three times as many Irishmen fought for Nationalist Spain as the Republic there are no Irish memorials to the brigade. There is no association to commemorate their participation in the Spanish Civil War. The brigade has also proved too embarrassing for 'official' memory. A memorial to the Irishmen who fought in Spain, unveiled in 1991 by the Lord Mayor at Liberty Hall as part of Dublin's year as 'European City of Culture', commemorates only the International Brigaders.[102] The existence of the brigade has been similarly overlooked in Spain. When the government of King Juan Carlos offered Spanish citizenship

**99** 15 July 1937, UCDA, Desmond FitzGerald papers, P80/627.    **100** *Irish Times*, 23 June 1937.    **101** O'Duffy, *Crusade in Spain*, 248.    **102** See Stradling, 'Battleground of Reputations', 107-110, 130-2 for discussion of commemoration and the Irish volunteers.

to the volunteers of the International Brigades who fought to protect the Spanish Republic in 1996 the soldiers of the Irish Brigade were again forgotten.

While those involved in the 'Connolly Column' (the name retrospectively given to the Irish soldiers of the International Brigades) earned a place in popular Irish culture as heroes, the Irish Brigade are remembered, if at all, with derision. The ineffective military performance of the brigade, the contrast between their low casualty rate and that of the 'Connolly Column' and their early return are partly to blame. The volunteers also fell victim to the shift in public perceptions of right-wing movements which followed World War Two. When the Irish Brigade left for Spain they were fêted by many clerics, politicians and the *Irish Independent* as defenders of the Catholic Church; decades later, they are remembered only as defenders of Franco's fascistic regime. During the last sixty years, as the once condemned 'reds' of the International Brigades gained the proper respect due for their premature anti-fascism, the reputation of the men who offered their services to Spain and the Catholic Church was gradually destroyed.

LABHRAS JOYE

# 'Aiken's slugs': the Reserve of the Irish Army under Fianna Fáil

Today the Irish Defence Forces consist of eleven thousand men and women charged with defending the state and aiding the United Nations in peacekeeping missions. This relatively small professional army is supported by a reserve entitled Foras Cosanta Aituil (FCA), or local defence force. The FCA has its origins in the part-time Volunteer Force established by the Fianna Fáil Government in 1934 as the reserve of the Irish Army. This chapter examines the various reasons for the establishment of this force, assesses its success in military and political terms, and traces the attempts to make it a viable organisation.

The Irish Army was established in the midst of great civil turmoil leading to the Civil War of 1922-3. The need to build it up quickly had made the army according to Tom Garvin: 'a strange hybrid organisation consisting of IRA veterans, British army veterans and young, inexperienced and apolitical mercenaries from the garrison towns who traditionally would have joined the British army'.[1] Its genesis and composition had created a number of problems which had to be dealt with urgently. After the Civil War ended, the permanent army was slowly scaled down from a height of fifty thousand men in 1923 to a peacetime level of five thousand. The tendency to act independently from the government was quelled after the Army Mutiny of 1924 when the army was placed under firm political control. To enhance its low training standards and to enable the establishment of a military college in Ireland officers were sent to the United States for training.

To augment the strength of the remaining tiny army a series of reserve forces were set up, which however all remained too small and experimental in nature to prove adequate. In 1927, the General Reserve Class A and, in 1928, a Class B Reserve consisting of retired soldiers or soldiers who had served at least three months with the army was created. These reservists attended a month-long training camp each year. In addition a relatively small Volunteer Reserve based in Dublin and Cork was formed, in 1929, to train part-time soldiers at nightly parades and at weekends. Finally, an Officers Training Corps was established in several universities to train students as officers.

---

1 Tom Garvin, *1922 The birth of Irish democracy* (Dublin, 1996), 115.

Overall the army was in a poor state by March 1932 when Fianna Fáil took over government. After playing a key role in the Civil War it had been largely neglected; continuously under strength and barely trained. Most of the regular army were confined to garrison duties and the armaments were poor.[2] Ever since the Civil War the Department of Finance had been reluctant to sanction funds for the army and under influence of the recession of the early 1930s the annual grant for warlike stores fell further from an already inadequate £87,523 in 1931 to £51,983 in 1932. Facing a general apathy from the government and the general public the army had lost its appeal and many of its more able men left: 'Low rates of pay made it difficult to recruit and to retain skilled men for the various technical corps, as employment in Britain was a very attractive alternative for anyone with qualifications.'[3]

When Fianna Fáil came to power the most pressing issue was the loyalty of the army and its attitude towards a government representing the Anti-Treaty forces of 1923: 'To shoot or salute was the stark choice some senior officers saw facing them.'[4] Frank Aiken, the last IRA Chief of Staff during the Civil War, was appointed Minister for Defence. He was regarded by many as the link between the hard-line republicans within the Fianna Fáil party and Eamon de Valera. His appointment indicates the importance that was attached to the army's loyalty to the government, and has been described by J.J. Lee as an inspired choice, 'more acceptable to the Free State Officers than any other possible appointment'.[5] In the event the professionalism of the army, under the leadership of the Chief of Staff Major General Michael Brennan, prevailed and the army was soon reconciled to the new regime. The government, nevertheless, continued to have its doubts over the loyalty of the army. It could not dismiss large numbers of Free State officers without affecting the stability of the State, but it could place its supporters in the army by setting up its own volunteer force.

FORMATION OF THE FORCE

In the years before Fianna Fáil formed a government they had expressed their support in the Dáil for the concept of a small professional army combined with a reserve. In this they followed Cumann na nGaedheal which had defined defence policy along this line largely due to financial constraints.[6] During a Dáil Debate in 1927 de Valera identified Britain as the main threat to Irish security: '[that] one power that in the past has been interfering with our rights

2 See John P. Duggan, *A history of the Irish Army* (Dublin, 1991), 163   3 Eunan O'Halpin, 'The Army in independent Ireland', 414, in Thomas Bartlett and Keith Jeffrey, *A military history of Ireland* ( Cambridge, 1996).   4 Duggan, *A history of the Irish Army*, 157.   5 J.J. Lee, *Ireland 1912-1985. Politics and society* (Cambridge, 1989), 176.   6 Government Minutes, 13 November 1925, C2/225, .317, NA, G2/4.

and attacking us'.[7] Drawing on the experience in the Anglo-Irish War he argued: 'Our defence will, I say, in the future lie as in the past, in having a territorial volunteer force which will make it impossible, or at least very costly, for that one power to try to establish its rule here amongst us.'[8] In 1929, Sean Lemass suggested in Dáil Éireann that an invasion by a third country might cause Britain to reoccupy Ireland. To avoid this he argued, the army must be 'so constituted, sufficiently strong, well trained and equipped as to be able to justify our claim to Britain that we would be able, in the event of Britain going to war, to undertake out own defence and thus take from Britain any excuse she might allege for sending troops here' such an army 'must be a volunteer force'.[9]

After coming to power Sean Lemass, now Minister for Industry and Commerce, indicated to his colleagues that there was an even more pressing reason for establishing a new volunteer force. On 23 October 1933 he stated that he saw the reserve primarily as a tool against illegal para-military organisations such as the IRA and the Blueshirts:

> the primary purpose of any Volunteer scheme in the present circum-
> stances of the Saorstat is a political one, i.e. the provision of an opportu-
> nity of military training in a manner beneficial to the State, to young men
> to whom military manoeuvres are an attraction and who if they do not
> get the association they desire in an official organisation may be induced
> to seek it in illegal organisations.

Military considerations were clearly less important to him then: 'The provision of effective military forces to strengthen the existing army and fit in with present or contemplated army organisation is, while important, only a secondary consideration for the present at any rate.'[10]

Before this became widely accepted Lemass thus openly acknowledged that political needs and realities influence the defence policy of a small country such as Ireland. Ever since the Civil War internal security had dominated the minds of Irish politicians when considering matters of defence, with aid to the civil power being the primary role of the Irish Army. The ideals of strategic defence were left to larger European countries. Above all else Sean Lemass foresaw the Volunteers as weakening the IRA, which had again become a serious threat to the government. Recruits had rushed to join its ranks as a result of Fianna Fáil's assent to power.[11] In the public's eyes the IRA and Fianna Fáil were still linked, and joining the former was now considerably less dangerous and might well advance one's career in the long term. In 1933 and 1934 IRA membership and activity further increased partly due to the developing conflict with the

**7** DD, vol. 21, cols. 1455-6. **8** DD, vol. 21, col. 1452. **9** DD, vol. 29, col. 1181. **10** Memorandum to Cabinet from Sean Lemass, 23 Oct 1933, NA, S6327. **11** J. Bowyer Bell, *The secret army* (Dublin, 1979), op. cit., 100.

Blueshirts. By 1934, the membership of the Dublin Brigade alone had swelled to three thousand.

To neutralise the potential threat Fianna Fáil had initially suggested that the IRA would become the new volunteer force. De Valera argued that now that Fianna Fáil formed the government the republic could be achieved through constitutional means and there was no justification for the IRA's continued existence. However, contrary to Fianna Fáil's demands the IRA did not disband. They doubted Fianna Fáil's ability to achieve the republic against British opposition. They asked themselves: '[As Fianna Fáil] would preside over the same army, police and state bureaucracy that had prevailed since the [civil] war. Could this be relied upon in a confrontation with the British?'[12] Unwilling to join their former comrades-in-arms the IRA clearly foresaw the purpose of the proposed militia. Already in June 1932 *An Phoblacht* stated: 'the establishment of such a force is an attempt to divert men of military age from the revolutionary movement.'[13] They, nevertheless, continued to negotiate with the government.

In July 1932 a meeting was held between Eamon de Valera and Tom Barry in Cork discussing 'unity of Republicans and the question of National Defence'.[14] Later that month another meeting took place between Frank Aiken and several IRA leaders, including Tom Barry, Moss Twomey, George Gilmore and Sean Mac Bride. Tom Barry began the meeting expressing support for a volunteer force under the Free State Ministry of Defence 'to steady the country the best gesture would be such a force which the IRA would join'.[15] Frank Aiken's contribution to the meeting was described as

> saying very little and [he] offered no information as to his plans in regard to the new force, except to say that they intended launching it very soon. He said he hoped the IRA will see their way to join it, especially since the Oath question is ended; the Land Annuities being fought, and the Governor General put in his place.[16]

Although no decisions were taken at the meeting, Moss Twomey and George Gilmore visited Tom Barry the next day and 'impressed on him that it would be very bad if at this stage people such as he were to raise the question of the IRA joining the Free State forces'.[17] On 18 February 1933 the Army Council of the IRA sent a directive on the forthcoming General Army Convention 1933 to all commanders. It stated that the Army Council wished to look at the relationship between the IRA and the government and that the 'proposed creation of a Volunteer Reserve Force as an auxiliary to the Free State Army will also require the attention of the convention'.[18]

---

12 Conor Foley, *Legion of the Rearguard The IRA and the modern Irish State* (London, 1992), 103. 13 *An Phoblacht*, June 1932. 14 UCDA, Moss Twomey Papers, P69/52 (60). 15 UCDA, Moss Twomey Papers, P69/52 (56). 16 UCDA, Moss Twomey Papers, P69/52 (56). 17 UCDA, Moss Twomey Papers, P69/52 (57). 18 Tim Pat Coogan, *The IRA*

The support for a new volunteer force in the cabinet also enabled the General Staff of the Irish Army to advance their own ideas for a part-time force. They put their proposals to the cabinet on 18 August 1932 in a document entitled 'The Volunteers'. In this they suggested a nation-wide militia based upon the British Territorial Army. However, the government made no immediate decision in 1932. This delay may have been caused by the ongoing negotiations with the IRA and with the need to ensure the loyalty of the existing state organs. During 1933 the proposal for 'The Volunteers' underwent many changes before implementation and two separate cabinet committees were established to discuss the scheme.

The fact that two cabinet committees were deemed necessary shows the political importance that was bestowed on the proposal. Naturally the Department of Finance queried the need for a new militia when there was a Volunteer Reserve capable of expansion and several OTC's to provide officer material: 'It seems to the Minister that the present cost of these forces is in reality more than commensurate with the resources of the State especially in a period of financial stress and abnormal but necessary expenditure.'[19] These concerns were shared by the opposition parties who realised what was going on behind the scenes. W.T. Cosgrave, leader of the newly formed Fine Gael party, wondered how the government could afford the new reserve and believed that the Volunteer Force served only a political objective and was born out of: 'a desire to try to rehabilitate in a military order some of those who were defeated eight, ten or twelve years ago'.[20]

However, as shown in Lemass' memo quoted above, the Department of Finance's reluctance conflicted with the government's growing perception of the IRA as a security threat. The memo also reveals that the talks with the IRA had reached a dead end in the autumn of 1933. This is confirmed in a statement by the Army Council of the IRA published in *An Phoblacht* on 11 November 1933 referring in a negative way to the new volunteer force: 'on behalf of the army of the Republic, and on behalf, we believe of all who are faithful to the ideal of Sovereign Independence, the Army Council publicly declares its unrelenting hostility to the creation of the new appendage to the Free State Army'.[21]

ORGANISATION AND TRAINING

Failing to entice the IRA into the force, the cabinet decided to give the go ahead to the new force. On 8 December 1933 formally approved the amended scheme first put forward by the General Staff of the Irish Army, 'subject to the limitation of expenditure during the year 1934 to 1935 to a maximum of

(London, 1987), 96. **19** Memorandum from Department of Finance 26 September 1933, NA, S6327. **20** DD, vol. 50, 7 February 1934, col. 1160. **21** *An Phoblacht*, November 1933

£250,000.'[22] Indicating the importance of the new Volunteer Force to the government this sum represented nearly 20 per cent of the annual Defence Budget of £1,318,458. Immediately twenty-one former republicans were commissioned into the army as organisers for the new force. They were known as Area Administration Officers (AAO's), twenty with the rank of captain and one lieutenant. All the new AAO's had been prominent during the Civil War[23] and represented a clear attempt by Fianna Fáil to get republicans established into the higher echelons of the army. The political affiliation of the recently commissioned AAO's worried the opposition. According to Donal O'Sullivan, the debate in the Senate: 'reflected the general uneasiness at the possibility of the creation of a partisan Volunteer Force and the progressive republicanisation of the Forces.'[24] Eamon de Valera admitted in the Dáil that the AAO's 'had taken up arms in defence of the Republic which had been proclaimed at that time'. But he did attempt to allay the opposition's fears: 'every one of them will be expected to make a declaration accepting the authority of the elected representatives'.[25]

The appointment of the AAO's from outside the army circumvented the official promotion procedures. Since 1928 army cadets had to attend a two-year training course at the Irish Military College in the Curragh before being appointed to commissioned rank. The AAO's only received a special three-month course of instruction at the Military College instead, before they took up their duties.

The Area Administrative Officers were responsible for recruiting and acted as the liaison between the regular army and the Volunteer Force. Their appointments were an attempt to make service in the reserves and therefore in the Free State Army itself acceptable to hard-line republicans. There are few personal accounts of members of the Volunteer Force, but according to one of them, Lt Col M. Feehan,[26] joining the Free State Army was a serious problem to republicans: 'we were sons or brothers of people who were on the losing side of the Civil War; for us to join the army of the State at that time was asking quite a lot in view of the recent wounds and bitterness which was very much alive'.[27] The efforts to make the new force attractive to republicans worried the IRA. *An Phoblacht*, the IRA paper, wrote of the AAO's: 'If these new officers were men without courage or intelligence or a record of service to the nation in the past, Republican Ireland would not have much reason to be afraid of their influence.'[28] Despite the apparent independence from the official army the AAO's came under the control of nine regular army officers, the District

22 DD, vol. 53, col. 1149.  23 *Irish Press*, 22 December 1933, contains biographies of eighteen of the new officers.  24 Donal O'Sullivan, *The Irish Free State and its Senate* (London, 1940), 359.  25 DD, vol. 53, 1149.  26 Lt Col Matt Feehan became the highest ranking Volunteer Officer, commanding the 42nd battalion in Collins Barracks during the Emergency. He was also editor of the *Irish Press* for a number of years.  27 Lt Col M. Feehan (retd.), 'A Personal Reminiscence of the Volunteers', *An Cosantóir*, 1978, 42.  28 *An Phoblacht*, December 1933.

Executive Officers (DEO's), who controlled funds and had ultimate responsibility for the Volunteer Force.

To enhance the appearance of independence the government attempted to create a separate identity for the Volunteer Force. They were provided with a distinct uniform modelled on the uniform of the 'Casement Brigade'; a brigade of Irish soldiers raised by Sir Roger Casement in the German prisoner of war camps during World War One. This used the German 'Feldgrau', a green grey colour, which, it was argued, suited the Irish countryside. The boots, leggings and belts were black with a wedge forage cap. This was in contrast with the regular army's green uniform and peaked cap. Lt Col Feehan recalled that 'This Casement Brigade uniform gave us something different and distinctive from what was regarded by us, with some distaste I must admit, as "The Free State Army".'[29] He also mentions that one meeting was held in a local hotel rather than in the stigmatised former British barracks in an attempt to persuade young republicans to enlist.

The strained relation between the new Volunteer Force and the regular army is illustrated by an incident recalled by another volunteer: 'The Volunteers were most unpopular during my early years of service 1934-41. A remarkable incident occurred at the time which gives an indication of this fact. A volunteer and a regular were seen speaking on friendly terms, and this was remarked upon. Later on, however, it was discovered that these two gentlemen were brothers!'[30]

Further developing the separate identity and to make the force more attractive a regimental scheme was established on a local basis. Each regiment was provided with a short history and marching song to create an *esprit de corps*. The Volunteer Force consisted of nine regiments:

The Regiment of Oriel: Counties Louth, Meath and Monaghan.
The Regiment of Leinster: Counties Kildare, West Wicklow, Wexford and Carlow.
The Regiment of Dublin: County and Borough of Dublin and East Wicklow.
The Regiment of Ormond (renamed Ossory in 1935): Counties Kilkenny, Waterford and Tipperary.
The Regiment of Thomond: Counties Limerick and Clare.
The Regiment of Connaught: Counties Galway, Mayo and Roscommon.
The Regiment of Breffni: Counties Cavan, Longford, Leitrim and Sligo.
The Regiment of Tirconnail: County Donegal.
The Regiment of Uisneach: Counties Leix, Offaly and Westmeath.

In order to integrate the Volunteer Force into the local communities, civilian committees, known as 'The Sluagh,' were appointed by the local AAO,

**29** Feehan, 'A personal reminiscence of the Volunteers'. **30** Comdt. J. O'Callahan (retd.), 'Memories of a Volunteer', *An Cosantóir*, 1975, 214

which assisted him in matters not directly of a military character. The members of the committee were not paid but the secretary received an honorarium of £5 a year while the funds of the Sluagh were in the charge of the AAO. The funding of the Sluagh was through grants-in-aid the size of which depended upon the extent of the Sluagh membership. These committees filled an essential role by carrying out the day to day running of the Volunteer Force, which the under-resourced regular army could not do. Frank Aiken outlined their role: 'In each Sluagh area there will be built or hired halls for the purpose of training, administering and promoting the various activities of the Sluagh and the Sluagh Committee will help in seeing that these activities are property co-ordinated and efficiently carried out.'[31] In addition it gave civilians some control over the local units. The Sluaighte soon acquired the nickname 'Aiken Slugs' because the Minister for Defence confirmed all appointees to the committees. The nickname also implies that there was a perception that the Sluaighte were dominated by the local Fianna Fáil cumainn.

The Volunteer Force was organised into three lines. For the 1st Line, volunteers had to be aged between eighteen and twenty-five. Men over twenty-five years with special qualifications or old IRA volunteers with service prior to the Truce in July 1921 could also be taken in the 1st Line. Enlistment was for twelve years. The first five of which were spent in the 1st Line, after which the volunteer transferred to the 2nd Line. The 2nd Line was open to men not over forty-five years of age who were physically fit. This Line could be regarded as a Volunteer Force reserve to be used in an emergency to bring active units up to strength. The 3rd Line consisted of men aged between forty-five and fifty-five with specialist qualifications to be used in grave national emergency. In practice only the 1st Line was available for service and constituted most of the Volunteer Force.

When properly trained and organised the Volunteer Force would form the major portion of the Irish Army. The government expected to have twelve thousand Volunteers by the end of the financial year 1935, and a full twenty thousand by the end of the following year. The Force was to be fully integrated, with its own artillery, infantry, medical, transport and signal units capable of functioning without any aid from the regular army. It was proposed to raise three reinforced brigades composed of volunteer force units, one each in the east, south and west of Ireland.

The perceived military role of these brigades would be to defend Ireland from an invading force. The reality however was that in the 1930s there were not enough funds to supply the regular army with enough equipment and material necessary for fighting a modern war, let alone to arm the three volunteer brigades. The primacy of the political role over the military becomes further evident from the fact that beyond giving each volunteer a rifle and a uniform and preparing for guerrilla warfare there was no serious consideration of military strategy.

31 DD, vol. 50, 7 February 1934, col. 1131.

Training was also limited. In order to establish a skills base all volunteer recruits had to attend an intensive basic training course held by the regular army lasting between fourteen and twenty days immediately upon joining. This initial course was to be reinforced by attendance at a two-week training camp each year and by test mobilisations topped up by a few training sessions taking place in the evenings and at the weekends. Volunteers did not receive pay or bounty in respect of local training but when called up for annual training and test mobilisations volunteers received the regular army's rate of pay and allowance.

The Volunteer Force was being created from the bottom up. Like the FCA today all members of the Force began as volunteers and could, by attending a series of military courses, be promoted through the ranks. Immediately upon its establishment training depots in nine army barracks were opened and regular army non-commissioned officers (NCO's) and commissioned officers trained the volunteers. Selected volunteers were permitted to enter the regular army for a further period of three months to undergo a NCO's course, which was done on a large scale. The appropriate corps[32] also ran specialist courses. For example the artillery corps ran a course for four months covering musketry and physical training. As the artillery batteries were still using horses, components on stable management and team driving were also included.

With the formation of the Volunteer Force the Fianna Fáil Government had to make a decision on the reserves formed under the previous Cumann na nGaedheal administrations. Only the Class A Reserve of army veterans was to last long enough to see service during the 'Emergency' (1939-45). The Class B Reserve was disbanded in 1935 due to the general poor quality of the recruits. The disbandment of the separate Volunteer Reserve, based in Dublin and Cork, and the possible transfer of its members to the new Force was continuously delayed because of internal opposition. In November 1934 the Chief of Staff finally announced a compromise:

> The Minister has decided that in order to avoid further serious difficulties in the matter, all officers of the Volunteer Battery and Battalion are to be posted to the General Reserve. This cancels the ruling that some of them would transfer to the Volunteers. In addition, all N.C.O.'s of these units are to be posted to the General Reserve of the Infantry and Artillery Corps. Only fourteen days annual training will be compulsory.[33]

The term General Reserve probably refers to the Class A Reserve. No explanation of the 'serious difficulties' was given but this decision meant the loss to

---

**32** Each department of the Irish Army is known as a corps, e.g. Artillery Corp, Supply and Transport Corps etc. **33** Memorandum to the Adjutant-General from the Chief of Staff, 26 November 1934, MA, 2/37481. The Military Archives has a small collection files relating to the Volunteer force which mainly cover the period 1934-6.

the new Volunteer Force of 231 trained volunteers, who would now be discharged from the army, and of the twenty-three officers and thirty-seven NCO's, who went to the Class A Reserve. The Volunteers Reserve was officially disbanded on 24 March 1935.

The failure of the Fianna Fáil government to integrate the battalion size Volunteers Reserve into the Volunteer Force did not follow international practice where former units or regiments are subsumed into one another over time. Of course there is the implication that this may be due to the fact that the Volunteer Reserve was established under the Cumann na nGaedheal government. However, the correspondence in the file relating to the disbandment of the Volunteer Reserve is more concerned with the fact that they would receive less pay than with any political considerations. Contrary to the difficulties with the Volunteer Reserve, the Officers Training Corps based in the universities was quietly merged with the Volunteer Force on 11 August 1935. It retained a separate identity as the new Regiment of Pearse.


OPERATION

The first time the new force paraded in public was at the 1935 St Patrick's Day Parade in Dublin. The parade took twenty-three minutes in all to pass the saluting base in College Green. The salute, being taken by Frank Aiken, was marred by chants from a small hostile crowd, probably republican. A test mobilisation was held from 11 to 14 April 1935 in the Eastern, Western and Southern Commands. In total 4,287 volunteers reported from 4,500 called (967, 1,370 and 1,950 respectively). The mobilisation was regarded as an outstanding success and was believed to vindicate the decision to set up the new reserve. Two months later the first military tattoo was held in the Royal Dublin Society involving volunteers from the Regiment of Dublin.

The initial response to the call for recruits was encouraging. Within a year of its creation the Volunteer Force had 11,594 members, the First Line had 9,819 Volunteers, 729 NCO's and 90 Potential Officers in Training, while the Second and Third Line consisted of 1,049 men in total.[34] When introducing the army estimates on 3 April 1935, Frank Aiken stated: 'The outstanding fact of importance in the life of the army during the year has been the development of the Volunteer Force. Applications for enrolment have exceeded all expectations.'[35] In 1936 it was hoped to gain an additional eight thousand volunteers. The estimates of the army vote for the financial year 1935-36 was based on the establishment of twenty-two thousand in all ranks and provided for the pay of three thousand five hundred non-commissioned and one hundred commissioned officers. At this stage there were 223 Sluaighte and hundred and

34 At this stage there were 912 2nd Line recruits and 137 3rd Line, making a total of 11,594.
35 DD, vol. 55, col. 1798.

twenty of them had various kinds of hired training halls. At eighty-four centres throughout the country arrangements had been made with the Gardai for the storage of demonstration purpose Lewis machine-guns and rifles for weekly drills. While the government did advertise through posters and radio broadcasts, Volunteer officers asserted that 'the most successful method of recruiting suitable patriotic young men to the Force was by personal contact and persuasion'.[36]

When the Volunteer Force was established the training and commissioning of officers in the force got under way immediately. The NCO training course was up-and-running in the summer of 1934 and on 1 September 1934 the first volunteers were promoted to the rank of corporal. A year later 1,525 volunteers had undertaken the course and 1,048 were successfully promoted. Volunteers who had reached the rank of sergeant and the standard of efficiency necessary went before an interview board headed by the Adjutant General of the Army, Colonel L. Archer for possible promotion to commissioned rank. Those who came through had the option of attending a commissioned officer course completed in six or eight months at the Military College or alternatively obtaining commissioned rank through nightly drills and weekend parades. On 28 August 1935 the first seventy-nine volunteers received their commissions in the Curragh's Pearse Barracks from President de Valera. The President addressed the new officers after the ceremony: 'what this force is to become depends on your devotion to work.'[37] On 6 March 1936 the second batch of seventy-four NCO's were commissioned including de Valera's son Vivion. This number of officers however was still well below what was needed for the projected force of twenty thousand men to operate successfully, which would require 651 officers and 2,450 NCO's.

PROBLEMS WITHIN THE VOLUNTEER FORCE

Despite its apparent success, the Force encountered serious problems from the start, including the inability of the regular army to provide training courses, the poor standard of recruits, and insufficient administrative resources. The General Staff identified various inadequacies in the scheme in a series of meetings in April and May 1934, just four months after the creation of the Force, stating that the early expectations for the Volunteer Force had proven premature.

The General Staff had initially given its full support to the scheme even though the army was not ready for such a reserve. It was between 10 per cent and 16 per cent below established strength and was consequently largely committed to garrison and routine duties. The Director of Infantry stated that to

**36** Feehan, 'Personal reminiscence of the Volunteers'. **37** A Volunteer Force appointment to commissioned rank, NA, S8051.

train the nine Volunteer Force first line battalions, ten depots with staff were needed. In addition there would have to be a pool of eight officers and eighty NCO's who could act as instructors to provide training at local parades, specialist courses and refresher courses. The Assistant Chief of Staff, Major General McNeill, claimed that the army was unable to provide these facilities: 'Experience with the Volunteer Force to date went to show that the present organisation of the Regular Army was utterly unsuitable to enable it to fulfil its new function in connection with the volunteers.'[38] As the army's new role was to act as a huge training and administration cadre for the Volunteer Force he felt reforms would have to be made but not before a little more experience with the scheme was gained. Some of the problems were subsequently rectified during 1935, but the regular army was limited to five hundred NCO's so the number of instructors that could be provided was limited.

The poor standard of education of most recruits was particularly detrimental among the first batch as they were to provide the future officers. Before recruiting had begun the Chief of Staff and the Minister had agreed that only volunteers suitable for training as officers and NCO's should be sent for initial training. However, by 26 April 1934 McNeill wrote: 'reports to hand from various depots go to show that a large proportion of the recruits sent forward for training do not conform to the requirements'.[39] At a subsequent meeting attended by the Directors of the various army corps, the District Executive Officers and the Area Administration Officers a memorandum entitled 'NCO's and Officers for Volunteers and local training' was discussed which stated: 'Too great a majority of the men sent forward for initial training are unemployed and the education of many of those selected for further courses is not good enough for the standard required of future NCO's or officers.'[40]

McNeill asserted that Sluagh Committees: 'finding themselves unable to get suitable potential leaders for various reasons are filling up their quotas as best they can'.[41] The acting commander of the Western Command later stated: 'I am aware that in the early days of the organisation of the Force in some instances men were appointed on NCO's courses and allowed to pass them because of strong recommendations made by AAO as to the influence it would have upon the organisation of the Force.'[42] It was clear that the local Area Administration Officers did not always have military efficiency in mind when recommending volunteers for promotion. On 24 January 1935, the AAO for the Leinster Regiment recommended six volunteer corporals for the first potential officer's course describing them as having a 'good national outlook'.[43] With other words being a republican was considered more important than suitabil-

38 Assistant Chief of Staff's Conference, 26 May 1934, MA, G2/0044. 39 Chief of Staff Meeting, 6 April 1934, MA, A.C.S. 2/46. 40 Agenda for the Chief of Staff's Conference, 26 May 1934, MA, G2/0044. 41 Chief of Staff Meeting, 6 April 1934, MA, A.C.S. 2/46. 42 Vickers Machine Gun Course, MA, D/Res. 2/46169. 43 Training V. F. Leinster Regiment 1934, MA, 2/37506.

ity for the position of officer. The memorandum quoted above argued that they should continue to select NCO's from volunteers and officers from the NCO's and 'that AAO's make a special search for fairly well educated, decent, responsible men who command a certain amount of local respect'.[44] However, things did not improve. Later that year the AAO of the Thomond Regiment wrote: 'the educational standard has been steadily on the decline since the training of the first draft in April.'[45]

The Volunteer Force indeed attracted mainly the un- or underemployed, especially labourers whose employment depended on the seasons. As a consequence the standard of education was low. In an article on the history of the 8th Field Battery[46] Lt Peter Durnin lists the employment status on attestations of all volunteers of the unit from 1934 to 1939. 68 per cent were labourers, while civil servants accounted for 4 per cent and clerks for 2 per cent. This would have been representative of the whole of the Volunteer Force.

Apart from difficulties with training and poor recruits, the heavy demands on the twenty-one AAO's and nine DEO's, which included administrative duties, recruitment and establishment of local training halls, also proved to be a major problem. The ultimate success of the force largely depended on these officers and their small staffs. As early as February 1934 at a Chief of Staff Meeting Colonel Costello had expressed the opinion: 'that rather too much work had been allocated to AAO's and there might be a consequent danger of their not being able to cope with it.'[47] This was confirmed in a letter from the DEO in Cork, Waterford District: 'In trying to visualise the scheme in about three or six months hence I do not think that I can cope with the duties laid down in the Draft Regulations.'[48] Within his district alone there were fifty-seven Sluaighte to be administered, the DEO continued: 'we should take steps to control this scheme instead of it controlling us'.[49] The problems which confronted the force were exacerbated by the Minister of Defence's desire to get going quickly. He believed it 'was very important that home training should start as soon as possible and that what we want is to get established in the minds of the people is that this force is being run among the people'.[50]

Recruiting of volunteers began to tail off in the summer of 1934, dropping to twenty-four in August. This was largely due to the harvest season in September, because when more labourers became available during the winter months recruiting picked up again increasing to 354 in December. However, it soon became clear that the Force was unlikely to reach its projected strength of twenty thousand. At the Chief of Staff Conference on 11 March 1935 it was

**44** Agenda for the Chief of Staff's Conference 26 May 1934, MA, G2/0044. **45** Training Volunteer Force Thomond Reg. 1934, MA, 2/37509. **46** Lt Peter Durnin, 'A history of the 8th Field Battery', *An Cosantóir*, August 1985. **47** Chief of Staff Meeting, 6 April 1934, MA, A.C.S. 2/46. **48** Ibid. Covering letter from officer commanding Cork District to director No. 1 Bureau. **49** Ibid. **50** Agenda for the Chief of Staff's Conference, 25 May 1934, MA, G2/0044.

admitted that initial training quotas were not being filled. The reasons given for the 'present slackness in recruiting' were insufficient propaganda, absence of some form of annual grant and the loss of unemployment benefit through volunteer training. Some Sluaighte Committees also appeared to be at fault, 'particularly in the Eastern Command, where they only accept one in six of those presenting themselves for admission to the Volunteer Force'.[51] Nonetheless, the scheme continued unchanged.

The dedication of those who had enlisted was also questionable. One of the more serious problems was the refusal of many volunteers to attend the annual camp. This was mainly caused by the loss of unemployment assistance to those attending overnight camps and test mobilisations. A further complaint was the delay in the resumption of assistance after initial training. The Department of Defence calculated that 50 per cent of Volunteers were normally unemployed and the loss of unemployment benefit was having: 'unfavourable repercussions on the Volunteer Force.'[52] The Department of Industry and Commerce, however, opposed any change of the 1933 Unemployment Act to remedy this problem, rather dismissively it asserted that 'the loss of one day's Unemployment Assistance twice a year is rather trifling' and that such amendments did not take account of volunteers who were employed and lost pay on those days.[53]

The failure to resolve these financial disincentives led to a significant drop off in turnouts for 1935. The first test mobilisation of the force during Easter had seen a 94 per cent response. However, after unemployment assistance had been revoked for the Easter 1935 mobilisation the turnout for annual training for the summer of 1935 went down to 44 per cent of those called,[54] only 2,799 1st Line volunteers out of a total of 6,325 had reported. Due to this poor response and representations made as to the unsuitability of training periods, it was decided to give non-reporting volunteers a second opportunity, but only another 681 reported this time, thus making a total of 3,480 or 55 per cent. The fact that volunteers from outside garrison towns and Dublin had to travel long distances to attend ordinary training on weeknights and weekends, and rarely saw rifles except at the annual camp reduced attendance there.

The hostility displayed by the IRA towards the Volunteer Force further diminished its attractiveness. From its inception in 1934 attacks on volunteers were reported. These were particularly aggressive and frequent in Kerry. In the beginning of the year a grenade was thrown into the military barracks in Tralee while volunteers trained there. On 11 October the Volunteer Force hall in Listowel was fired upon and local volunteers were attacked. At the 1935 St Patrick's Parade in Tralee the Volunteer Force units were shouted at by some sections of the crowd. The following year the situation was even more tense, forcing the Garda Inspector in Tralee to advise that no Easter Parade should be held by the Volunteer Force 'in view of the recent rather disturbed state of Kerry'. He felt that 'The holding of the Volunteer Force parades will only give the IRA an opportunity of showing activity and activity is the life of organisations of this type.'[55]

## THE 1936 REORGANISATION OF THE VOLUNTEER FORCE

After the poor attendance at the first annual Training Camps in the summer of 1935 the Chief of Staff ordered an inquiry into the Volunteer Force performance. The General Staff presented their report in October outlining their assessment of the force: 'in general, the progress of the Scheme cannot be regarded as satisfactory'. They expressed particular concern about the commitment and suitability of the recruits. All volunteers could resign from the force by giving seven days' notice and this escape clause had been widely used during the summer of 1935 so that discharges actually outweighed recruitment, and the strength of the Force fell from 10,578 in May to 9,597 by September. From the outset, attendance at local drills had been poor, the average being 30 per cent. The Sluagh Committees for the most part served their purpose, but 'many never functioned in the practical sense and latterly there had been a general decline in activities and enthusiasm'.[56] The report believed that this situation would not change until the committees were composed entirely of volunteers. On the issue of annual training it was clear that: 'over forty per cent of those called are not prepared to fulfil their obligations'.[57]

In an effort to redress these deficiencies a Cabinet Committee of Enquiry was established in August 1935. The committee submitted a five-page proposal on the re-organisation of the Volunteer Force in January 1936. It was suggested to reduce initial training to seven days so as to encourage enlistment: 'among the better class of employed in city areas, whose employments only permit of limited holidays.' However, those who could afford the time were required to serve a preliminary period of fourteen days with the regular army with the option of serving twenty-eight days. Annual training was to remain fourteen days but in exceptional cases attendance could be reduced to seven days: 'The elasticity thus provided will, it is confidently hoped, result in an increased percentage attendance at annual training.' Local drills were to be replaced by voluntary drills and overnight camps were reduced from twelve to eight a year. The report also recommended that army barracks, which it stated were unpopular due to their forbidding atmosphere, should be replaced with designated Volunteer Force halls. It was hoped this would lead to 'a considerable increase in strength and a more virile and popular organisation'.[58]

---

55 Ceremonial Parade Easter Sunday 1936, MA, 2/45765. 56 Irish Army Report on the Volunteer Force, 3, MA, A.C.S. G2/0044. 57 Ibid., 4. 58 Reorganisation of the Volunteer

Finally the Committee report 'revealed that some improvement in the rates of remuneration would be the most, if not the only effective, means of achieving the desired purpose'.[59]

Following on from its recommendations, a well-publicised programme of building Sluagh Halls was started on a limited scale in 1937. Within two years halls were built in Castleblayney, Drogheda, Swords, Midleton, Listowel and Lahinch. The major reform, however, was the introduction of grants in addition to normal pay from 1937: Officers would receive £10 per annum, NCO's £3, and other ranks £2. These payments were made in spite of the Department of Finance's assertion that 'the present value to the State of only imperfectly trained volunteers can scarcely justify the payment of grants'.[60] These measures led to a slight improvement in attendance in 1937 after the huge decline in the summer of 1935 which had continued in 1936. The figures for Easter Sunday Parades outside Dublin were:

|      | Called | Reported | Turnout |
|------|--------|----------|---------|
| 1936 | 8,231  | 3,074    | 37.3%   |
| 1937 | 4,722  | 1,948    | 41.3%   |

Attendance figures for St Patrick's Day Parades in Dublin were somewhat better:

|      | Called | Reported | Turnout |
|------|--------|----------|---------|
| 1936 | 1,735  | 817      | 47.1%   |
| 1937 | 1,874  | 980      | 52.3%   |

### CONTINUING PROBLEMS

The new system of grants caused further financial and organisational hiccups. Under Section 13 of the Unemployment Assistance Act 1933 all grants paid to volunteers were regarded as means. Money vouchers exchangeable for beef were issued only to those without means and the selection of men for employment on public works went to those in receipt of the highest scale of assistance. With the grant being considered means, volunteers were disqualified from receiving any of these public entitlements.

The volunteers themselves tried to force the issue by setting up their own representative organisation. On 5 January 1937 a meeting was held at 33 Gard-

Force January 1936, NA, S8596.   **59** Department of Finance Volunteer Force, NA, S4/1/34. **60** NA, So64/oo1/34.

iner Place, Dublin. Over two hundred reservists attended and it was decided to establish the National Army Reservists Cultural and Social Club. The club was open to all employed and unemployed members of the Volunteer Force and Class A Reserve and was to be strictly non-political. Its main aims were to promote the 'general welfare of all members including sport in all its branches, recreation, various social entertainments, the influencing of employment'[61] and more importantly the 'eliminating of existing victimisation.'[62]

This move by the volunteers was strictly illegal. Since the Army Mutiny of 1924 politicians and civil servants regarded any organisation of soldiers from the regular army or reserve with suspicion and establishing one needed the sanction of the Minister for Defence. In a letter to the club the minister, Frank Aiken, stated that as a matter of policy he could not sanction the club, but promised 'to consider favourably any representations made by individual members of the Reserve and of the Volunteer Force with a view to ameliorating their conditions as far as practicable'.[63] A month later General Mulcahy questioned the minister on the reservists' grievances in the Dáil: 'A new airport is being embarked on at Collinstown and the position of the army reservists in the City of Dublin is that under present circumstances they have no hope of getting a day's work up there.'[64] However, the Minister was unwilling to address the issue in public: 'The question of soldier's grievances and the method by which they can be redressed is laid down in regulations, and I do not propose to depart from that.'[65] Despite all this, the issue remained unresolved and the Volunteer Force grants continued to be regarded as means under the Unemployment Assistance Act.

Among the 149 Volunteer Force officers there were also signs of unrest. During July 1938 the army authorities intercepted a letter between two lieutenants of the Volunteer Force which they believed was calculated 'to cause disaffection among the officers of the Volunteer Force'.[66] The letter, which was badly written and misspelled, stated: 'We are just to remain weekend soldiers and it is up to us to disillusion the powers that be. With that object in view I wish you would get the addresses of all the fellows on the course, and their co-operation in organising all the Officers and have a showdown.'[67] However the writer did not expect too much from his initiative as he believed that the other officers 'are a lousy bunch, who would leave us in the lurch – holding the baby, if we put too much on paper' and warned the recipient to 'keep all this under your hat, and destroy this letter, which is treason'.[68] The letter while not detailing what they were proposing to do, resulted in the dismissal of one of the lieutenants from the Volunteer Force.

**61** The National Army Reservists Cultural and Social Club. Letter to the Minister for Defence from the club signed by the Secretary, Corporal S. Last, 6 January 1937, NA, S9499. **62** Ibid. **63** The National Army Reservists Cultural and Social Club, NA, S9499. **64** DD, vol. 65, 171 **65** DD, vol. 65, 173 **66** Dismissal of Lieutenant McKenna, 8 September 1938, NA, S10826. **67** Letter dated 27 July 1938, NA, S10826. **68** Ibid.

Considering these difficulties it is not surprising that recruitment and attendance continued to decline in 1938. By April there were just 9,525 volunteers
compared to its peak number of 11,594 in April 1935. Attendance at local training for the Volunteer Force had decreased to an average of 29 per cent, and as
a result thirty hired halls were surrendered. At the same time new halls were
being built in various other towns. On examination of forty-six halls in 1939,
the Committee of Public Accounts found that twenty-six showed little or no
use and a further nine 'could not justify their retention'.[69] In response to the
low morale the Minister for Defence Frank Aiken proposed another reorganisation of the Volunteer Force to the Cabinet on 23 September 1938, the second
in three years!

## THE 1939 REORGANISATION

However, the reorganisation plans were shelved due to the approach of the
Second World War. In November, de Valera requested that the army submit
plans for the defence of Ireland in the event of a European war. The scheme
they proposed was for the establishment of two reinforced brigades with a combined strength of 37,560 consisting of the permanent army, the Reserve and
the Volunteer Force. This plan was 'not based on the military requirements for
defence but on the personnel and equipment available or likely to be available'.[70] In a rather defeatist and typical manner the Minister for Finance dismissed the need for any expense on defence: 'The possibility of land invasion
is remote having regard to the value of British naval protection' and 'if Britain
became powerless, resistance to her conquerors would probably be futile on
our part.'[71] However, his cabinet colleagues disagreed and ordered a reorganisation of the regular army and the Volunteer Force along the lines proposed.
To fund an increase of one thousand men in the regular army and of nine thousand in the volunteers they sanctioned a growth in defence expenditure from
£1.6m to £2m. On complete mobilisation they optimistically hoped to provide thirty thousand soldiers: 'a striking force highly trained and equipped'.[72]

This reorganisation of the force at last tackled the key reasons for its failure. Heretofore volunteers had enlisted for twelve years but could resign upon
giving seven days notice except when mobilised. Between March 1934 and
March 1939, 16,146 men had joined the force but 8,270 of these had resigned
or been discharged from the army for poor attendance. From 1939 volunteers
joined for five years and discharge could only be obtained on the same terms
as in the regular army. The age limit was lowered from eighteen to seventeen

**69** Volunteer Force Halls Comptroller and Auditor General on appropriation accounts 1937-
38, 20 April 1939, NA, S7/9/37.  **70** Comdt. P. Young, 'The Way we Were', *An Cosantoir*,
September 1989.  **71** UCDA, Sean MacEntee Papers, P67/195 (2).  **72** DD, vol. 74, 520-
531.

years and raised from twenty-five to thirty and in the case of specialists to forty. By reducing the age limit it was hoped to attract boys 'who while having completed their education have not taken up employment and are in a position to undergo the full period of initial training'. Initial training was extended from twenty-eight days to ninety days but volunteers also had the option of ninety days training through local drills. Annual training was reduced to nine from twenty days. The lowering of the age limit and the reduction of the annual training would allow volunteers of the 1st Line to carry out their initial and annual training with the least possible interruption to their civilian occupations. Grants were increased for volunteers to £6 but of this £2 was conditional on attending annual training, £3 upon attending local drills and £1 upon the general efficiency of the local Sluagh. The three Lines of the force were still maintained but there was no direct recruitment to the 2nd Line, which was to consist solely of volunteers who had served in the 1st Line. The personnel of the 3rd Line was to be recruited directly and would consist of specialist people only. The territorial regiment organisation of 1934 was disbanded and replaced with five infantry battalions.

The existing volunteers were all discharged but given the option of re-enlisting. On 1 March 1939 there had been 7,278 volunteers left, of these 3,731 re-enlisted and the remainder resigned. After the reorganisation of the force and with World War Two seeming inevitable, recruitment began to increase. At the time of the declaration of neutrality on 2 September 1939, 237 officers, 557 NCO's and 6,429 volunteers reported for duty. This was largely due to the large number of schoolboys, availing of the new entry age of seventeen, who were undergoing training at the time.

### CONCLUSION

Considering its poor record in the 1930s there are two questions to be asked about the force. Was the Volunteer Force a viable military reserve and what was its real purpose? From its inception the Volunteer Force suffered from the fact that the Regular Army was under resourced and unable to provide the equipment or personnel to run the force properly. The kind of recruits it attracted never met the expectations of its organisers, and as a part-time militia it depended upon volunteers giving up their free time, but without adequate monetary compensation their enthusiasm was bound to fall off. The ulterior motives of the Fianna Fáil government in setting up the force were apparent from the start. Placing the force outside direct military control but within the structure of the army showed its distrust of the existing army and their desire to create a force with strong republican credentials. The key to this was the twenty-one AAO officers who ran the force and their civilian support the Sluagh. Nevertheless, the AAO's had to work within the structure of the regular army and most importantly their commanding officers were regular army officers.

The Volunteer Force's evolution, between 1932 and 1939, reflected both the Army's desire to enhance its defensive role and public standing and Fianna Fáil's need to placate hard-line republicans. It is evident from this article, that during this decade, negative perceptions and financial disincentives dogged the success of the Force. The military problems of the Volunteer Force at one level are no different from those of the Local Defence Force of the Emergency period and the modern day Foras Cosanta Aituil, in that it is poorly financed, that there is a high turnover in recruits and the standard in training varies all over the country. The difference lies in the fact that the government closely watched the Volunteer Force, that two cabinet committees were established between 1934 and 1938 and that a number of changes and reorganisations were initiated in attempts to make it more successful. While an ambitious scheme on paper, political objectives superseded military ones in its implementation and it therefore never became a viable military reserve.

# Notes on the contributors

LABHRAS JOYE completed an MA in Modern Irish History at University College, Dublin, and has recently obtained an MA in Museum Studies at Leicester University. He was curator in the Art & Industrial Division in the National Museum of Ireland from 1996 to 1998, and is currently Head of the Irish Film Archive in Temple Bar, Dublin.

ADRIAN KELLY is a parliamentary reporter in the Houses of the Oireachtas. He researched his doctoral thesis at the National University of Ireland, Maynooth, and the University of Helsinki, Finland. His MA thesis, which concerned the Irish language and the education system, is the basis of a book forthcoming from Irish Academic Press.

FEARGHAL McGARRY is a lecturer in modern history at TCD. He graduated from UCD in 1992, and obtained a PhD from Trinity College in 1998. His doctoral thesis forms the basis of his book 'Irish Politics and the Spanish Civil War', forthcoming from Cork University Press. He is currently researching a biography of Eoin O'Duffy.

GILLIAN McINTOSH completed an MA at UCC in 1992 and a PhD at the Queen's University of Belfast in 1996. Her doctoral thesis is the basis of a book to be published by Cork University Press entitled *The force of culture: Unionist identities in twentieth century Ireland*. She is currently a researcher at the Institute of Irish Studies at Queen's.

KIEREN MULLARKEY obtained a BA in St Patrick's College, Maynooth. He worked on an MA in UCD and has a diploma in Higher Education and one in Legal Studies from the Dublin Institute of Technology. He is a qualified secondary school teacher and currently works in a primary school.

MARGARET Ó hÓGARTAIGH has an MA in history from University College, Galway. She has completed a PhD thesis for the National University of Ireland, Dublin entitled: 'Far from few. Professional women in Ireland between 1880 and 1930'. Currently, she is a tutor in history at St Patrick's College, Drumcondra, and honorary membership secretary of the Irish Economic and Social History Society.

ELIZABETH RUSSELL obtained an MA from University College, Dublin in 1995. She has worked as a press officer in the publishing industry as well as being a regular contributor to a book trade magazine. In 1996 she graduated from the National University of Ireland, Maynooth, with a Higher Diploma in Education and in 1997 from the Dublin Institute of Technology with a Post-Graduate Diploma in Media Studies. She now teaches in Gorey Community School, Co. Wexford and writes for a local newspaper.

ANNE-MARIE WALSH has an MA in Modern Irish History from University College, Dublin (1993) and an MA in Journalism from Dublin City University (1998). She has tutored and lectured at UCD and currently works as a journalist in Dublin.

# Index